SCENES FROM THE MARRIAGE OF LOUIS XIV

Scenes from the Marriage of Louis XIV

NUPTIAL FICTIONS AND
THE MAKING OF ABSOLUTIST POWER

ABBY E. ZANGER

STANFORD UNIVERSITY PRESS

STANFORD, CALIFORNIA

1997

Stanford University Press
Stanford, California

© 1997 by the Board of Trustees of the
Leland Stanford Junior University

Published with the assistance of Harvard University

Printed in the United States of America

CIP data are at the end of the book

Last number below indicates date of this printing:
05 04 03 02 01 00 99 98 97

To Roy, who married me in Truro, the tenth of Sivan, 5747

Acknowledgments

It is quite ironic that my generation of scholars continues to place proper names on the title pages of books. Formed by Foucault's and Barthes' deconstruction of the notion of authorship, how can we continue asserting our scholarly work is written by one person? This project was not. Many friends and colleagues helped it along. So, while I take complete responsibility for all the errors in these pages, I share credit for what is worthwhile in it with those who have been my witting, and sometimes unwitting, collaborators.

Most particularly I thank Alexandra Halasz for reading multiple drafts of the various chapters, often on very short notice, familiarizing me with new language and critical models when necessary, and keeping me attuned to the real issues. I thank Steve Ungar and Nelly Furman for providing me with important intellectual insight at crucial junctures, and Roger Chartier for patiently answering my endless questions about print culture and seventeenth-century history. Without the friendship and unfailing support of these four I could never have completed this project. I also thank many other friends and colleagues for their input. The list of those who have read sections of the book at various phases, or listened to my obsessions include Dudley Andrew, Nadine Berenguier, Natalie Davis, Maud Ellmann, Robin Flemming, Caroline Ford, Lisa Gasbaronne, Mary Gaylord, Elizabeth Goldsmith, Sarah Hanley, Erica Harth, Cheryl Herr, Carla Hesse, Nancy Hirschman, Alice Jardine, Christian Jouhaud, Florence Ladd, Debra Laycock, Jacqueline Letzter, Christie McDonald, Anne Menke, Debra Minkoff, Hélène Merlin, Per Nykrog, Lorna Olson, Jeff Ravel, Kathleen Ross, Jay Semel, Susan Suleiman, and Alain Viala. This book also benefitted from the insights of my students in courses at Harvard and at the University of Iowa and from audience response in talks given at Cornell, Brown, Harvard, Iowa, and at conferences too numerous to reiterate. And it could never have been brought to fruition without the unfailing aid and excellent archival assistance of my research assistant, Elizabeth Hyde. Finally, I thank Helen Tartar, John Zeimer, and Peter Kahn at Stanford University Press and my copy editor, Peter Smith, for their work on bringing this volume to the public.

Numerous institutions also played a crucial role in this project. I first found material on the marriage in the summer of 1985 while a junior fellow at the Folger Shakespeare Library in Washington, D.C. The University of Iowa funded research trips to the Bibliothèque Nationale in 1988 and 1989 and underwrote the purchase of microfilms and photocopies of source materials. The Harvard University Mellon Fellowship Program supported the completion of my research at the Houghton Library during the 1989–90 academic year. Most recently Harvard University and the George Lurcy Foundation funded a leave in 1993–94. During that year the Bunting Institute at Radcliffe College provided space and inspiration to complete revisions of the manuscript.

An early version of Chapter 2 appeared as "Fashioning the Body Politic: Imagining the Queen in the Marriage of Louis XIV" in Louise Fraedenburg, ed., *Women and Sovereignty* (Edinburgh: Edinburgh University Press, 1992). Portions of Chapter 2 also appeared as "Making Sweat: Sex and the Gender of National Reproduction in the Marriage of Louis XIII" in *Yale French Studies*, 86 (Fall 1994), pp. 187–205.

Last but not least, in a category by himself, I thank Roy Tishler, who lived this project with me from its inception during a steamy Baltimore summer to its closure on the banks of the Charles River. I dedicate this book to his unfailing belief in me and in the importance of my work.

A.E.Z.
Cambridge, 1997

Contents

Twelve pages of illustrations follow p. 20.

List of Illustrations

All illustrations are in a section following p. 20. Nos. 1–3, 5, 6, and 8–12 appear by permission of the Bibliothèque Nationale de France, Paris. Nos. 4 and 7 appear by permission of the Musée du Louvre, Paris. No. 13 appears by permission of the Houghton Library, Harvard University.

A Note on Translations

All materials from the marriage written in prose are translated into English in this study. Unless otherwise indicated, all the translations are mine. Titles and citations from early modern texts retain the original spelling, capitalization, and punctuation whenever possible. The only exception to this practice is the modernization of *i*, *v*, and *f* to *j*, *u*, and *s* when applicable. English translations reflect this early modern French orthography as much as possible. I follow this practice in the text as well as in the bibliography.

SCENES FROM THE MARRIAGE OF LOUIS XIV

Nuptial Fictions

In early June 1660, the courts of Louis XIV and Philip IV met on the banks of the Bidassoa River, the frontier between their two countries. Despite generations of mutual hostility and an apparently unbridgeable cultural chasm, the two groups mingled on the border for ten days. The occasion was the signing of a peace accord, the Treaty of the Pyrenees, a pact meant to end long-standing territorial and political enmity between two early superpowers. The treaty was one of the year's major political stories.[1] Its clauses worked out the disposition of land recently won by the French in Spanish-occupied Flanders, clarified issues of French allegiance to allies such as Portugal and Catalonia, arranged France's repatriation of the last Fronde rebel (the Prince of Condé, who had been fighting for Spain in Flanders), and set the terms for Louis XIV's marriage to the Spanish infanta.

Details of the treaty and its signing were reported across France. The story of the marriage between the young French king and the daughter of his former enemy riveted attention to the reports. It provided a titillating story line for the accounts of otherwise prosaic diplomatic ceremonies. Indeed, the narratives of the treaty and marriage were inextricably related. For Mazarin had negotiated a treaty in which an apparent concession, the infanta's renunciation of her right to accede to her father's throne, was conditional on the payment of a very large sum. Noncompliance by the Spaniards would allow the French queen to claim rights to her father's throne for herself and her offspring. The clause requiring the infanta to renounce her claim on the Spanish throne was nothing new. The 1660 marriage contract was almost identical to that of the previous Bourbon–Hapsburg alliance between Louis XIII and Anne of Austria, Louis XIV's parents. But making the infanta's renunciation conditional on the payment put a new twist on the treaty. Although not apparent from a cursory reading, the terms were clearly in France's favor since they opened the possibility of invoking the princess's prerogatives in the case of default.[2] Unlike the Hapsburg–Bourbon treaty marriage of a generation earlier, the 1660 treaty would reconfigure the balance of power in Europe. With its signing, the political preeminence of Hapsburg Spain would wane, making France the hegemonic power in Europe and laying the groundwork for the Bourbon accession to the Spanish throne in 1701. Reports of the marriage and details about the new queen in particular served this project well by constructing a set of fictions aimed at political consolidation in a period of rebuilding.

These fictions of marriage—what will be referred to in this study as nuptial fictions—differ from those that would later promote Louis XIV's absolute power. Despite a large body of texts describing and celebrating the marriage and its rituals, images of the monarchy fabricated around the June 1660 marriage treaty have received no critical attention.[3] In his 1992 study of the fabrication of Louis XIV's image, for example, historian Peter Burke touches on the treaty only in passing, noting that there "are relatively few visual images of Louis between the early 1650s and the year 1660, when he suddenly appeared as a young adult with an incipient moustache and short wig."[4] That Burke undervalues the copious iconography of the marriage is not surprising. Despite its contemporary and far-reaching impact, the peace with Spain was eclipsed by the events that preceded and followed it, most particularly the civil uprisings of the late 1640s and early 1650s known as the Fronde, and the dazzling trajectory of the Sun King's reign that began in early 1661, upon the death of the minister Mazarin.[5] Blinded by the richness of these events from Louis XIV's childhood and maturity, scholars of early modern French history, literature, and culture have reduced 1660 to a mere dividing line, a year without cultural or historical import preceding the more remarkable beginning of the classical era, which is also the beginning of Louis XIV's personal rule.[6]

Despite such erasure, the fictions of Louis XIV's marriage are crucial to the making of his power because they are the product of a liminal or transitional event. Liminal periods must be studied because, as the anthropologist Victor Turner has demonstrated, they are fundamental to social ordering. Marked by ambiguity, flux, and transition, liminal periods encourage the interrogation of fixed ideas and the perturbation of established structures. If such moments disorder structures and habits, they nonetheless tend to precede more stable, familiar periods. Allowing for the transformation and reformulation of familiar elements, liminal or transitional periods are intimately related to, even foundational of, ordered life.[7] The 1660 marriage may be seen as such a period of interrogation and reformulation, one that reorders what are considered today to be the prototypical fictions of Louis XIV's reign, representations of the king produced after 1660 that have been canonized by the seminal studies of Jean-Marie Apostolidès and Louis Marin.[8]

At the heart of this reordering is the marriage ritual. Its unique symbolic practices have attracted little attention because the anthropological, political, and symbolic properties of royal marriage arise from a process that involves not one, but at least two principal figures. Such a system is inconceivable within the paradigm of monarchical power that revolves around one figure, the king, whose only plurality is his own two bodies. Royal nuptials are characterized not just by the representation of the king, but also by the prominent role of the queen. Nonetheless, marriage ceremonies and their representations engage the same issues of dynastic continuity and succession at the heart of what are today taken to be the paradigmatic fictions of sovereign power.

That royal nuptials engage such issues and produce a symbolic apparatus for processing these concerns is in keeping with what the sociologist Norbert Elias has shown, that court society revolved around symbolic interactions.[9] In fact, the marriage ritual offers a particularly striking example of how social groups engage in symbolic activities for social ordering. Louis XIV's 1660 treaty marriage to the Spanish infanta offers a classic example of how groups come together in highly prescribed rituals with the goal of displacing enmity and violent competition from the battlefield to the civil or symbolic relations of social interaction. For it was what Lévi-Strauss characterized as a "cross-cousin alliance," a marriage of first cousins related on the matrilineal side; Louis XIII's sister was María Teresa's mother and Philip IV's sister was Louis XIV's mother. Closely related by mothers, but marked by antagonism among male in-laws, such an alliance is precisely the kind Lévi-Strauss singles out as most exemplary of how kinship exchange offers related (but antagonistic) groups an effective way of interacting socially.[10] The 1660 marriage between first cousins offers an intriguing illustration of how kinship practices establish (and advertise) the organizing fictions of political culture.

Despite its participation in the establishment of absolutist political culture, kinship exchange has never been considered one of the central rituals of monarchy. Rather it is the juridical fictions of monarchy and the funerary ceremony that have provided the principal lens for studying the symbols of monarchy.[11] Royal marriage has not been a central model for understanding fictions of sovereignty because it was not an official constitutional activity like the *sacré*, the *lit de justice*, or the state funeral.[12] It was, nonetheless, a ritual that helped establish and preserve dynastic power both because it often played a role in international relations by settling territorial disputes and because it provided a means of producing legitimate heirs. Because Salic law dictated that French queens have no right to property and thus no way to inherit the throne, the marriage ceremony did not appear formally linked to the building of the state (even if it often touched on issues of the transfer of territory and dynastic continuity at the heart of political power).

In the juridical texts that have served as the basis for understanding the fictions of sovereign power, there is little or no serious treatment of marriage. That is not to say that theorists such as Le Bret, Loyseau, Seyssel, or even Bodin do not talk about the nature of royal marriage. On the contrary, they do discuss it, but only to argue for the practical necessity of Salic law, which denies women property rights and thus political power. Bodin, for example, argues that if a queen could rule, her marriage would endanger the state by bringing in a second sovereign authority.[13] Seyssel likewise worries that female succession would invite foreign domination. He emphasizes the importance of Salic law in upholding masculine succession, because "by falling into feminine line it [the throne] can come into the power of a foreigner, a pernicious and dangerous thing, since a ruler from a foreign nation is of different rearing and condition, of different customs, different language, and a different way of life from the men of the lands he comes to rule" and would thus advance the customs and interests of his nation.[14] Thus, for jurists and theoreticians of monarchical law, marriage (and its rituals) must be considered unimportant in order to undercut a queen's power. The king does not share his power, nor designate his successor, since succession is legally determined by family genealogy. He cannot, furthermore, transfer or divide his estate, which is not his personal property. These are laws that protect the integrity of the state. While marriage provides certain supports for these laws by producing the legitimate heir who assures dynastic continuity, marriage does not (and cannot) play a role in the constitutional process of state building, which it actually threatens. Dead, the king's corpse is embalmed by juridical protocol and circumstantial pomp. Nuptial, the king's body *qua* body is not subject to legislation beyond its ceremonial presence.

It is therefore not surprising that in Kantorowicz's study of the medieval jurists' discussions of monarchical law, he focuses only on metaphorical marriage, the king's union with the state, an alliance between an idealized, divine body and an abstract political body.[15] Kantorowicz focuses on the duality of the king in prioritizing the dissonance between the king's biological person and his divine status. Semioticians examining images of the absolutist monarch have been profoundly influenced by Kantorowicz's findings. For

example, when Louis Marin and Claude Reichler analyze representations of Louis XIV's sexual body, they highlight the practices
and discourses that recuperate the dissolution and decay of the king's
biological body to reinvest the sacred and powerful body of sovereignty. Their understanding of the symbolics of the royal body
remains within the framework of the mortal-divine polarity that
founds the constitutional debates of the period they are examining.[16]
They cannot take into account issues raised by the participation of
other bodies in the reproduction of political culture.

Recent scholarship on the representation of queens has begun
to redress this imbalance, although it has not easily moved beyond
the two-body paradigm. For example, analyses by Lynn Hunt and
Sarah Maza have shown how the sexual body of Marie Antoinette
was portrayed as corrupting the body politic.[17] By highlighting how
a queen's sexuality is politically threatening, these extremely rich
and important analyses follow Kantorowicz' thesis that the mortal
dimension of the queen threatens monarchical authority because it
undermines the divine image of the sovereign. This study follows a
different direction when it analyzes the deep-seated discomfort over
a queen's prominent role in the marriage ceremony. In marriage,
the queen's sexual, mortal body is as fundamental to the fictions of
dynastic continuity as is the king's divine persona. For the nuptial
body of the queen is not just the ceremonial body that engages in
the rituals, but also the body that will be needed to engage in the
procreation that follows the rituals of heterosocial alliance. Indeed,
Webster's Dictionary defines nuptial as related to the marriage ceremony, and as characteristic of the breeding season.[18]

Of course, the importance of the queen's nuptial body as
procreator was problematic for the symbolic process of kinship
exchange. As French feminist theorist Luce Irigaray's critique of the
anthropological model of kinship exchange points out, in Lévi-
Strauss' framework, women become abstract signifiers (ceremonial
bodies) in a homosocial interaction.[19] Such an abstract status is
coherent with the fiction of kingship that gives precedence to the
divine royal body. But the fact that the infanta is necessary to
produce heirs suggests it is difficult to reduce her to an abstract body

in a system. Indeed part of the traditional symbolism of royal marriage involves suggesting the infanta's readiness for producing offspring. The shaping of this image by French reports on and celebrations of María Teresa's transformation from Spanish princess to French queen reveals her central position in the representation and construction of absolutist power, even if a queen's agency in state building is problematic for a symbolic economy based on notions of divine right and primogeniture. In analyzing the representations generated around a marriage treaty, this study thus often returns to images of the queen to show how her sexuality (her mortal body) could be one of the primary components of the fictions of dynastic continuity. While this role for the queen does not lessen the way a mortal body might threaten fictions of dynastic power, it does offers a new perspective on how images of women participated in constructing (and not just deconstructing) fictions of sovereignty.

It is not the intent of this study to refute the paradigm of the "King's 'Two Bodies,'" a model that has productively oriented discussions of sovereignty and the fictions of kingship in early modern Europe. Rather, its goal is to highlight fictions of monarchy that have slipped out of sight in privileging the symbolism of the royal funeral over that of other ceremonies. The marriage ceremony has been singled out for study here because it offers a particularly striking complement and contrast to the funereal *topos* of the "King's 'Two Bodies.'" On the one hand, there are important similarities between the two phenomena. Both are rituals of sanctification within the Catholic church. Both are highly choreographed occasions whose rites and discourses of self-legitimation are produced by the state apparatus with the goal of securing dynastic continuity through unperturbed succession. Nonetheless, although they function within the same sacred system and promote the same goals, they each engage a significantly different symbolic economy.[20]

Some basic differences in each economy are immediately evident. The funerary ceremony is a rite of transition that adjudicates tensions within one system, that of the state. It sets the protocol for passing on the power of one ruler to another. But the succeeding ruler is simply a replacement for the first. Thus, the funerary symbolism highlights the dichotomy between the mortal and divine dimensions of one body. The spotlight on duality functions only to uphold unity; it downplays the importance of the finitude of one dimension of the body to emphasize the eternal nature of another. The funeral is thus a ritual that marks an end and anticipates a beginning, merging those two moments together to preserve the integrity of *one* state. It is a process of substitution that reduces multiplicity to singularity.

The marriage ceremony, on the other hand, is a process of combination that adjudicates tensions between simultaneously existing systems, between two states. As such, it focuses on two individuals. It concerns the joining of two royal bodies and not the separation of one body from itself. The dichotomy between the mortal and the divine is transformed (and worked through) by the joining of the male and the female. Marriage, also a ritual of transition or passage, joins two bodies or two nation-states, absorbing difference, which it cannot erase. To do so would defeat the purpose of the symbolic event. Maintaining a trace of difference offers a reminder that there has been an exchange of kin, an interaction between two groups. Keeping that difference in sight also emphasizes the power of the group that triumphs in the exchange process. Marriage is a ritual that does not so much *preserve or maintain the constitution of the state as it works at state building or change.* It is an activity that underlines its processes of incorporation, although there is a price to pay for needing to incorporate foreign elements. The funerary ceremony, by contrast, rids itself of the problematic body by polarizing the relation between the mortal and the divine in the name of a particular genealogy aimed at producing absolute oneness. The marriage ceremony does just the opposite, keeping the foreign body as a central presence on the scene. Both ceremonies promote the dynasty. Yet marriage, as opposed to death, is always necessarily dialogical, even if there is a power struggle between single and dual perspectives within its symbolic field.

Despite its obvious interest for the semiotics of sovereignty and the political culture of absolutism, the royal marriage ceremony is uncharted territory. Liminal periods are difficult to study. As transitions, they leave artifacts as evanescent as the events themselves. Such is the case of the archive produced around the marriage. It is a large corpus. Unlike the corpus that portrayed and celebrated the mature Louis XIV, however, it does not comprise monumental works but ephemera: occasional pamphlets, programs [*livrets*] that accompany celebrations, memorial writing, diplomatic correspondence, almanac images, news accounts, and minor literary and dramatic works. These materials did not initiate literary or cultural trends. Rather, open in form and often contested in nature, these texts facilitated the rearrangement and adjustment of culture and its myths. Like the marriage treaty and its fictions, these materials were in process, genres in flux, forms and formats ranging from the pamphlet to the novel that were vying for visibility in the print universe taking shape around the young king in June 1660. But this corpus has never been studied in such a light. Rather, it has served historians of the marriage such as Edouard Ducéré in 1903, Madame Saint René Taillander in 1928, and Claude Dulong in 1986 as a mirror on reality, transparent sources that provide facts and details about historic events. The corpus has never been analyzed as a generator of fictions, "information" that might be slanted or even fabricated. Other materials studied here, a treatise on fireworks by Claude Menestrier, a machine play by Pierre Corneille, and the introduction of a novel by Madame de Scudéry, have never been considered as participating in construction of the king's portrait, let alone that of the marriage treaty's political fictions.

But in 1660, all these forms and media were drafted into the project of advertising and recording the activities of the king. They participated in what the historian Michèle Fogel has called the "ceremonies of information." As "ceremonies" they produced not only images of the marriage, but also produced and reproduced the larger symbolic process of the ritual activities. For nuptial fictions continue the work of symbolic adjudication begun by the kinship exchange of the marriage treaty; in telling the story of the marriage, its fabrications continue the adjudication of tensions between two regimes, tensions transposed by the fictions' images and the vehicles that construct and project the images. The best way to explore the nuptial fictions' images, their construction, and their reception is by engaging in the kind of close, contexualized readings Roger Chartier and Christian Jouhaud characterize as "pratiques historiennes des textes."[21] Such "historical readings" merge the most contemporary practices of literary and historical analysis, utilizing the tools of literary critics or semioticians without losing sight of the fact that "sense" is also produced out of history (or histories, of reading, print, culture, politics, etc.).

The five chapters in this book all examine the network of issues concerning gender, politics, and representation that characterize nuptial fictions. The first two, however, lay out the central images of the marriage, while the second two examine the technologies that produced those images. The last chapter offers a gloss on both the images and the vehicles that produced and disseminated them. More specifically, the first chapter studies almanac engravings that predate the marriage to illustrate how the representation of kingship during this period is dialogical, relying on multiple bodies and elements. In the almanacs, the image of the future queen as she was imagined before any marriage had been arranged epitomizes how such other bodies are necessary props for the glorification of the monarchy in the liminal moment between war and marriage. The position the future queen will occupy in the nuptial fiction is marked out in the engravings studied. How the necessary, albeit problematic, body of the queen is fashioned to fit the space allotted to its image is the topic of the second chapter, which examines sources ranging from diplomatic correspondence to news reports and memoirs. By uncovering the necessity of the queen's biological, mortal body to depictions of the king's power, this analysis challenges the wholesale application of the political fiction of the "King's 'Two Bodies.'" It shows that nuptial fictions are dialectical in nature, combining two bodies and not substituting one for another.

The third chapter examines the chief technology for constructing and disseminating the nuptial fiction, print. It offers a case study of the relation between writer, printer/publisher, and the apparatus of state control that exemplifies how print functions as purveyor of nuptial fictions. The chapter suggests that the pamphlet, another appendage to the king, functions in a manner homologous to the image of the queen (and the nuptial fictions more generally) that it disseminates. All three—pamphlet, nuptial fictions, images of the queen—are fashioned by the state and fashion the state. Dependence on such props (images and technologies of representation) contradicts the project of absolute power. It is thus not surprising that displaying mastery over the images and media of the wedding is a central aspect of its fictions. The fourth chapter examines how such mastery is rehearsed in two other media used to celebrate the marriage, specifically in fireworks and in a baroque machine play. These nonprint formats are technologies that exemplify how the absolutist monarchy dealt with the necessity of props for its representation by staging the threat they posed as a strategy for rehearsing the danger and containing its impact.

The final chapter concerns the last stage of the marriage, the royal entry into Paris. While the first four chapters deal mainly with material generated by the state, the last chapter analyzes another kind of discourse, that of a novelist writing outside the web of state interests constructing and disseminating nuptial fictions. The novelist, Madeleine de Scudéry, is particularly interested in curiosity about the event. Her remarks offer insight into the fate of nuptial fictions (their images and the archive out of which they are generated): they are relegated to the shelf of history, or the curiosity cabinets of the king. Scudéry explains how and why these fictions must be stored away on the eve of Louis XIV's taking of power. This shelving of nuptial fictions (or more precisely, of their chief image, the queen) seems to offer the king a new, less dependent relation to the fictions that prop up his image.

Taken together, these chapters do not constitute a history of the marriage. They provide detailed analyses of exemplary moments or scenes from the royal wedding. In particular, they uncover the dialectic at the heart of nuptial fictions. Like the kinship exchange out of which they emerge, fictions of marriage manipulate antagonistic forces into the service of promoting the political culture of absolutism during a period of transition. Dialogical, the nuptial image suggests a king who, while central, is not yet absolute, but

depends on other images and representational forms to become
visible. That reliance on appendages such as the queen and forms
such as print (or the machinery of fireworks, drama, or the queen's
body) is crucial, yet problematic. A calculus of addition, this
dependence cannot be perceived from within the models previously
used to explore the representation of sovereignty, models based on
such rituals of substitution as the funeral rite. While the fictions
generated during Louis XIV's marriage are not the central ones of
Louis XIV's rule, they do have an impact on the king's portrait and
provide insight into the making of an image scholars too frequently
take for granted. Studying nuptial fictions invites us to reexamine
what have become clichés about the representation of absolutist
power, generalizations drawn from the portrayal of Louis XIV
during his fabled reign, images that do not fully characterize the less
monumental (but equally crucial) periods of his kingship.

CHAPTER I

Liminal Images

Most studies of the representation of Louis XIV focus on the king at the height of his power. Such scholarship portrays a king depicted as largely autonomous.[1] Examining nuptial fictions deconstructs this formulaic vision of French absolutism and its representation by considering images of Louis XIV from an earlier, more tentative moment in his reign, before his "prise de pouvoir," or personal rule. The successful French military campaigns in Spanish-occupied Flanders in 1657 and 1658, a period of military victories during which the French gained territory in Flanders, turning the balance of power toward France and providing Mazarin with the leverage to negotiate the Treaty of the Pyrenees, are one such preliminary stage in the performance of French absolutism. At this early stage of his "reign," the king was still under the tutelage of Mazarin, and his portrayal reflects his connection both to the minister and to the players of the larger political arena. Indeed, portraits of the king associated with military triumph relied heavily on the depiction of other bodies: his ministers and generals, his family, French soldiers, and the allegories of vanquished disorder. As a marriage treaty was negotiated, and images of kingship moved toward what has been described as "the pastoral image of monarchy based upon love, harmony, and peace,"[2] Louis XIV's power was promoted by displaying his marital (and hence mortal *qua* sexual) body. In this shift, Louis XIV's political body was further framed and complemented by supporting characters and props.

Images of the monarchy produced during this transitional time differ significantly from the now canonical fictions of sovereignty elucidated by Ernst Kantorowicz and Ralph Giesey. Such fictions of the royal body, split between its mortal and divine dimensions, arose in response to a specific political crisis: the death of the monarch. It was the aim of these conceptions of sovereignty to attenuate that crisis by playing down the importance of the king's mortal body and by creating the conditions in which one ruler's body could be substituted for another. It was their aim to reduce multiplicity (multiple bodies or rulers) to divine unity.

Fictions of sovereignty produced during the period between war and marriage were not primarily a response to the threat of a monarch's death. They arose out of the activity of diplomatic interaction and emphasized how adjudication of territorial disputes and the exchange of kin could stabilize power in a period of change. Representations of the king during such flux depended on his interaction with other persons—courtiers, generals, the queen mother, the minister, a future queen—and with the props of sovereign performance—clothing, royal limbs, even the frames that surrounded and highlighted those performances or representations. Such images of sovereignty relied heavily on the perception that the king's mortal body was vigorous, not to counter fears of his death, but to counter questions about his virility. Born under the cloud of Louis XIII's impotence, Louis XIV would have had to demonstrate his own sexual potency to project the strength of his political body. Indeed, in the years before he took power, images of the king's virile, hence mortal, body did not undermine his sovereignty, but were fundamental to relaying the potential strength of his rule. It was thus that in the period before Louis XIV assumed the throne, the king's sexual body was not detrimental to displays of his power, but constitutive of it. The representation of other persons and things around him was necessary to drive home that potency.

It is important to note that such images of the young Louis XIV emerged from a period of transition and flux. Even though it is accepted today that the events in Flanders in 1657 and 1658 occasioned the marriage of Louis XIV and lay the groundwork for the political stability on which Louis XIV would begin his personal rule after the death of Mazarin, during the campaigns proper the outcome of the military engagements was unknown. Indeed, in early 1659, the treaty marriage and its political triumphs were only a goal coming into view, a fantasy of the fixed, socially and politically stable state to which the French aspired. This study begins by focusing on that fantasy of the fixed and stable, examining various representations of the flux that preceded the fixing of the king, albeit momentarily, in the state of royal matrimony. Examining images of those fantasies is the first step in comprehending fictions generated during the later stages of the treaty negotiation and marriage ceremonies. For as the goal of marriage came into view, props of the king's power also came into focus, or rather parts of them did, as they emerged onto the as yet unstabilized stage of Louis XIV's reign.

"Flying Sheets"

A means of exploring this phase of rule, its characters, and its props, is the examination of a series of almanac engravings from 1658 and 1659 depicting the king's military triumphs and suggesting the possibility of royal military and matrimonial success. Such images of war and marriage emerge from what the anthropologist Victor Turner referred to as the "betwixt and between": the liminal, the neither here nor there, the undefinable and uncontrollable, often chaotic moments of transition, becoming, or transformation.[3] According to Turner, such periods have "cultural properties" that are distinct from those that characterize definable states such as marriage; for Turner, liminal periods are transforming while states are confirmatory. As such, liminal periods are often marked by ambiguity and paradox, by a confusion of customary categories and divisions, and by the unknown, unbounded, and limitless.[4] In such liminal moments of flux, many fixed ideas are open to interrogation, oppositions (such as high–low, history–allegory, divine body–mortal body, male–female, and war–marriage) tend to dissolve and collapse, while liminal persons or phenomena tend toward structural invisibility. Despite this general tendency toward disorder and dissolution, it must be understood that liminality is an activity linked to reordering. Preceding or bordering stable, familiar states, liminal periods help transform and reformulate old elements into new patterns. As Victor Turner has noted, if "liminality may perhaps be regarded as the Nay to all positive structural assertions," it must also be seen as "in some sense, the source of them all, and more than that, as a realm of pure possibility whence novel configurations of ideas and relations may arise."[5]

It is the uneasy, yet productive, relation between the flux of liminality and the fixity of established, stable, recurrent states or conditions that is the focus of this first stage of analyzing nuptial fictions. For images of military triumph that point toward the dream of a stable state emerging out of military victory and out of the empire building of royal marriage were efforts on the part of the representational apparatus of the absolutist state under Mazarin to freeze the flux of historic events, to contain their unknowns and uncertainties and reestablish the fundamental oppositions and hierarchies upon which the performance of sovereign power rested. These images thus offer a unique glimpse into the struggle of representational forms to maintain fixity in a situation of liminality or flux, of betwixt and between. This struggle is especially evident in an iconography whose two most salient images are of legs and frames, most particularly, but not exclusively, of the king's legs and most particularly, but also not exclusively, of frames that contain cameo images of potential queens. It is the play between the visual role of the leg or limb as a space of demarcation, a limit (indeed, limb and liminal share a common etymology in the Latin *limes*, limit, and *limen*, threshold) and the nature of what is being demarcated, limited, encircled, and framed (i.e., ordered) that is of particular interest in the series of almanac images from before the marriage.

Limits and frames appear in these almanac images precisely where fixed boundaries (and the order they imply) are threatened, that is, at the meeting of the liminal and the fixed, what Turner characterized as "that realm of pure possibility." This realm is also, paradoxically, the place where boundaries and order may be established. It is precisely that play between fixing and unfixing shown on the microscopic level of iconography that reproduces the larger historic movement from war (before marriage) to peace (after marriage) that is pertinent to analyzing these almanac images. The properties of the representation of this "realm of pure possibility," a realm stirred up and constructed from this encounter, set the stage for the nuptial fictions created in June 1660.

Before examining the almanac images, it is important to note that the genre of almanac engravings itself engages in the mediation of flux and stability on two levels. For almanacs incarnate both the transitory nature of time and the attempt to foretell and fix the ephemeral. They encapsulate both recovery and anticipation insofar as their upper register recaptures and freezes images of a year recently completed, while their lower half lays out and projects the as yet unknown year ahead in a grid of numbers and lines. Often almanacs made elaborate observations about planets and such conditions as their eclipses.[6] The almanacs studied here simply list saints' days or predict the weather. The first set examined, produced to mark the year 1658, refer to events occurring during the summer of 1657: the battles between Turenne and Condé that resulted in French victories at St. Venant, Montmédy, and Mardyck, and the first rumors of a possible marriage for the king. The second set of images, produced to mark the year 1659, pertains to events from 1658: the French victories at Dunes, Dunkerque, Gravelines, and Ypres that culminated in the Peace of the Pyrenees. They also allude to the agreement of nonintervention negotiated with the Electors of the Austrian Hapsburg Empire, the king's recovery from a near fatal illness contracted while on a military campaign in July, and, again, much more specifically this time, to the possibility of a marriage match for the young monarch. Looking back, they also look toward (and claim to predict) the future.

This play between past and future (as well as the condensation of several events from throughout the year into one image) that

seems to freeze the flux of time may also be seen to function more
generally for the status of the almanac in the larger sphere of print
culture. These one-page broadsides covered with visual images and
numbers were a particularly potent form for fixing ideas in the public
imagination.[7] As almanac specialist Geneviève Bollème has noted,
the mission of historic almanacs in particular was not to give facts
to "readers," but to form readers.[8] Produced by engravers according
to a system of permissions or *privilèges* like that which organized the
print trade more generally, and sold in shops and by peddlers
(*colporteurs*) on the streets of Paris and in the provinces, such
broadsides widely and easily disseminated authorized (legitimized)
images to the largest public possible, both readers and nonreaders.
Bollème gives impressive figures for the numbers of almanacs published and their broad social reach, calling them "the books of people
who hardly read [*lisent peu*]."[9] In this light, one may say almanacs
participated in the flux of events that they could also anchor in the
French field of vision, serving the machinery of symbolic power as
they moved the stage of the king's out-of-sight battlefield activities
onto the streets and into the households of the kingdom. The term
"stage" is used literally here because the almanacs' images are often
depicted on an Italian proscenium arch stage. Richelieu had promoted this design in a rationalization of the space of illusion that is
now understood as founding the performance of absolutist power by
organizing and controlling the gaze of the spectator. With their
combination of iconography, information, prognostication, and political allegory, these 50-by-80-centimeter sheets cut a broad swath
across a large audience of viewers and readers. It is perhaps for this
reason that the French historian of publishing, Henri-Jean Martin
picks up the seventeenth-century language found in Antoine
Furetière's *Dictionnaire Universel* in referring to these almanacs as
"feuilles volantes," loose sheets—more exactly, flying sheets—because they were able to literally fly in and out of the public eye, fixing
images, and then disappearing when they were no longer timely.[10]
Furetière actually characterized the form in a somewhat derogatory
manner, noting "[O]ne also calls *loose sheets, sheets* of paper that were
not bound together, like those of school children where they write

their glosses. This certificate that was brought forth does not induce confidence, it is only a *loose sheet*."[11] But if this supposedly insignificant format provides the entryway into scenes from the marriage of Louis XIV, it is because the almanac should not be underestimated. It offers an exemplary case of how the ephemera of print culture reproduced and reworked larger political concerns in effectively delivering the regime's "message" to the public.

1658: *Lim(b)inal Images*

The first almanac image, "THE MAGNIFICENT TRIUMPH" (Figure 1), does not broach the issue of an upcoming marriage, but refers only to the king's military victories. It presents a *topos* common to military triumph, a monarch in his chariot crushing what is out of control or disorderly, here represented by the allegorical images of Rage, Envy, and Sedition.[12] The engraving's depiction of these passions is traditional. It is based on widely accepted images from the manuals of iconology.[13] Barely visible, Rage, Envy, and Sedition are reduced largely to sinewy limbs (arms and legs) wrapped with equally powerful serpents emerging from under the wheels of the chariot crushing them, as well as from under the hooves of the horses pulling that chariot. These limbs and snakes suggest the powerful and predatory nature of these passions. They are sexualized images of potency and penetration, the kind that had been linked to personal disorder and state lawlessness in the political pamphlets of the Fronde.[14] It is not surprising that the king is figured above these problematic passions. He is placed on a higher plane, surrounded by higher-order images, the historical figures of the court situated behind him to the right and the other trophies of his victories off to the left. These trophies are to be contrasted with Rage, Sedition, and Envy; they are not invidious limbs being crushed, but whole cities, controlled not by dismemberment, but by containment. Put into relief, they are miniaturized, immobilized, and placed on a portable surface carried high above the heads of the soldiers in the fashion of a Roman triumph. If disorder and movement mark the limbs of Rage, Envy, and Sedition, the cities are the model of containment, as are the neatly covered limbs of the soldiers who carry them.

The prose text at the top center of the engraving offers further indices for reading the figures below. Interestingly, the prose does not open with a reference to the moral victory over the disorderly allegorical limbs, nor does it refer to the military victory over the now ordered, contained cities. Instead the text turns its attention to another kind of triumph, one not figured visually in the engraving, the celebration of the king's own self-mastery, his triumph over *his* (disorderly) passion, as it announces:

THE MAGNIFICENT TRIUMPH

Where our August Monarch is seen mastering himself and his enemies because he places his passions among his war trophies.[15]

Invoking a king's self-mastery is not an unusual rhetorical move in this sort of material.[16] Such stoic self-control was a desirable trait in a king, and the implication of the statement in the almanac is that the king's visible mastery over others is causally related to his unseen and perhaps unrepresentable mastery over himself. It seems a bit paradoxical, however, to draw attention to an invisible kind of mastery in the heading over an image meant to make a king's authority visible. It also seems paradoxical to attempt to make authority visible by drawing attention to the king's mastery over passions he should not have. Suggesting the king may have had uncontrollable urges would tend to emphasize his humanness. As the work of Ernst Kantorowicz has demonstrated, an early modern European king's constitutional entitlement rested largely on his ability to repress the fact of his humanness via elaborately ritualized fictions of his divine status. It would seem that underlining a dimension of the king such as his passions, a dimension he is not supposed to have, might serve not simply to fit the king into a traditional stoic framework, but also to arouse the viewer's curiosity by drawing him or her outside the fixed moral and military boundaries to reflect on the passions and personal disorder edging those boundaries, in particular a king's own potentially disordering passions: the unspoken, liminal, disorderly, invisible side of monarchy.

1. *The Magnificent Triumph* [B.N. Dép. des Estampes, Hennin, 3886]

2. *The Legitimate Wishes of France for the Marriage of the King*
[B.N. Dép. des Estampes, Qb^1 M92062]

3. *The Gifts Offered to the Very Christian King Louis XIV by all the Virtues* [B.N. Dép. des Estampes, Qb⁵ P68486]

4. Peter Paul Rubens, *Henry IV Deliberating on His Future Marriage* [Louvre]

5. *The Celebrated Assembly of the Court upon the Convalescence of His Majesty and upon the Successful Outcome of His Arms*
[B.N. Dép. des Estampes, Qb¹ M92093]

6. FRANCE RESUSCITATED *by the Remedy Sent from the Heavens to the Greatest Monarch in the World for the Peace of His People and the Confusion of His Enemies* [B.N. Dép. des Estampes, Qb⁵ P8487]

7. Hyacinthe Rigaud, *Louis XIV en habit de sacré* [Louvre]

8.   *Flanders Being Stripped of Her Spanish Clothing and Being Re-clothed in the French Style* [B.N. Dép. des Estampes, Col. Hennin, 3908]

9. (*Top*) *The Royal Interview*, Engraving from Lebrun [B.N. Dép. des Estampes, Qb^1 M92166]

10. (*Bottom*) *Non LÆtior Alter* [B.N. Dép. des Estampes, Qb^1 M92250]

NOVVELLE RELATION

CONTENANT

L'ENTREVEVE

ET SERMENTS

DES ROYS,

POVR

L'ENTIERE EXECVTION

DE LA PAIX

ENSEMBLE TOVTES LES
Particularitez & Ceremonies qui se font
faites au Mariage du Roy, & de
l'Infante d'Espagne.

*Auec tout ce qui s'est passé de plus remarquable
entre ces deux puissants Monarques
jusqu'à leur depart.*

❊❊❊❊❊❊❊
❊❊❊❊❊❊❊❊
❊❊❊❊❊

A PARIS,

Chez IEAN BAPTISTE LOYSON, ruë Saint Iacques,
prés la Poste, à la Croix Royalle.
_____

M. DC. LX.

AVEC PRIVILEGE DV ROY.

---

11. Title Page: *Nouvelle Relation contenant l'entrevue* [B.N. Imprimées Lb[37] 3395c]

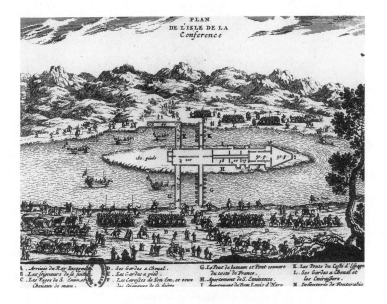

12. *Plan of the Isle of the Conference* [B.N. Imprimées, Lb^{37}3316]

13.   *L'Arc de la Place Dauphine* (detail)
[Houghton Library, Harvard University]

The prose text thus invites the viewer to comb the image for residues of such disarray emerging from the vision of domination and reordering. And indeed, if the dismembered limbs of Rage, Envy, and Sedition suggest a world of such lawlessness, the curious viewer can also find traces of the potentially unfixed passions of the king by easily matching the limbs of defeated passions first to those of the horses, and then, moving higher, to those of the king, as muscled and sinewy as the legs of the animals.

Of course, all limbs in the picture are always lower-order members. One goal of the image seems to be to reprocess lower-order, lim(b)inal images into containable trophies. The diorama as trophy epitomizes this movement, since, as the text noted, the king placed his passions "among his war trophies." Reading these images after the age of Freud, it is easy to recognize the repression and condensation at work in the image. The work of Michel Foucault has made critics aware, furthermore, that exclusion and policing, framing sexuality out of the picture (which is what often happens in the representation of a monarch's body), are methods for dealing with the sticky issues of sexuality.[17] But Foucault also characterized such an exclusion as a manner of keeping *"jouissance"*—gratuitous, ephemeral, nonutilitarian pleasure—and the power that contains it, in the picture.[18] This play between exclusion and exhibition is evident in the treatment of Rage, Sedition, and Envy. Although in pieces, these lim(b)inal figures, objects to be crushed by military and visual mastery, are nonetheless always hovering at the edge of the image, as if it is their energy that keeps the wheels of the king's machinery of domination moving forward.

If the engraving of "The Magnificent Triumph" leaves the viewer more interested in the king's disorderly and uncontrolled ephemeral passions than in the parading of his permanent military control, other almanac images from the same year bring these passions into relief, containing them in a manner that makes them more visually available (although perhaps less powerful and interesting). Consider, for example, another 1658 almanac, "THE LEGITIMATE WISHES OF FRANCE FOR THE MARRIAGE OF THE KING" (Figure 2). This image more overtly organizes the relationship between

disorderly affairs of passion and the (ideally) more stable affairs of
state, legitimizing the king's passions which had been, so to speak,
rolled under the bed or the triumphal chariot in the previous image.
Indeed, "legitimation" is the first modifier in the description heading the image:

> THE LEGITIMATE WISHES OF FRANCE FOR THE MARRIAGE OF THE KING.
> Dedicated and presented by the love of virtue and by that of France
> itself to our invincible MONARCH Louis XIIII followed by the Joy of
> the people[,] the desires for peace[,] and the wishes of Renown, one
> in the hope of one day seeing a dauphin born[,] the other of soon
> seeing the christian princes in perfect harmony[,] and the third the
> empire united to the crown of France[;] and below[,] the conquests
> of Monmedie[,] Mardic[,] St Venant[,] the shameful flight of the
> Spaniards from Ardres with the representation of abundance and
> victory[,] firm and solid support of the French monarchy.

As the prose text states, the legitimized wishes or hopes for (the
legitimate passion of) marriage are placed center-stage in this engraving, displayed in the middle of the image in a framed picture of the
king holding out his hand to a woman dressed in the French queen's
traditional wedding garb. A banner inside this interior image reads
"Great King place yourself henceforth under Hymen/Upon this sacred
bond [noeud] depends the holy bond of peace." Note as well that the
interior picture is being presented to the king by the allegorical figure
France, and that each of the two central figures, France and the king,
is surrounded by similar characters: grouped around France on the left
are the three (actually four) allegorical female figures, the Joy of the
People, the Desires for Peace, and the Wishes of Renown (the fourth
figure, barely seen, is not named); grouped around the king on the right
are five historical persons, the king's brother, his mother Anne of
Austria, the minister Mazarin, and two other figures, perhaps Le Tellier
and Le Marechal de Créqui.[19]

   This combination of right and left imagery (allegorical and
historical) echoes the visual play seen in the "Magnificent Triumph"
(Figure 1) between the domain of unregulated allegory as passion
and that of regulating military victory. Here, however, the allegorical emerges not as dismembered Rage, Sedition, and Envy, but as

full-bodied Peace, Joy, and Renown, legitimate passions carrying legitimate wishes for a Bourbon heir, for reconciliation between Philip IV and Louis XIV, and for an agreement with the Electors not to interfere in the events in Flanders. As such, these allegorical figures and their passions can be revealed and advertised. Particularly important is how this meeting of now-legitimated allegorical figures and historical personages allows the entry of the king's passion into the scenario—or rather, it allows the emergence of a legitimated and civilized form of the king's passion, the royal and regulated (productive, heterosocial) marriage represented within the framed image as if in an equation:

Wishes (Allegory) + Royal Family (History) = The Scene of Marriage

To understand more fully how this equation factors passion (albeit now a stable and contained passion because set apart, legitimized, and sanitized) into the scenario, it is necessary to find a way to re-bisect this image, shifting from the grid set out to frame our gaze—that is, the division between left (allegory) and right (history)—to a different split between top and bottom (high and low). To do so, one must resist the temptations of the framing scene and look at details or limits, in this case, limbs. In adopting this perspective, it is evident that even legitimized sexuality (i.e., the framed image) is a lower-order member, occupying the domain of the king's own lower-order member, his iconic leg.[20] Visually positioned at the same level as the picture, the leg seems to counterbalance or suggest the limit of the interior image's framed, legitimized sexuality. A similar tension can be seen between the king's regal upper body, draped in, or framed by, formal robes, and the lower, more functional part of himself that is involved in the less regal but equally important (and tempting) aspects of kingship, not just walking, but coming together in a "holy bond" [*saint noeud*] to make babies (indeed, one definition of the word *noeud* is erect phallus). The idea that procreation, and therefore sexual bodies (erect penises or women), are a necessary, if knotty (or naughty) aspect of monarchy is also reinforced by the fact that the king's limb is situated opposite the medallion held by the Wishes of the people:

an iconic scene of Anne of Austria invoking God's help to become pregnant after nearly two decades of childlessness. The restrained, legitimized, framed scenario of heterosociality France offers the king thus plays off the less restrained sexuality of the leg. Both elements work together, however, to reinforce what is announced in the last line of the heading, that "abundance and victory" (in bed and on the battlefield) are "the firm and solid support of the French monarchy." This description, actually of two caryatids in the bottom, missing half of the engraving, suggests once again that the monarchical body rests on the lower-order, either in its lim(b)inal (unstable and ephemeral) or in its framed (fixed and monumental) form . . . or as the two work together.

The status of framed images as a basis or limb of the monarch's power can be more fully examined in another almanac image in which the king is being shown a collection of portraits of potential queens (Figure 3). In this image, where the issue of marriage takes center stage, the passion eliminated from (or crushed in) the "Magnificent Triumph" and allowed, framed, into the "Legitimate Wishes" as a necessary component, has exploded and multiplied to assert its presence more fully in the king's scenario. The history–allegory division has now shifted to line up with that between upper and lower: historical figures (the king, his family, and his advisors) situated on the top of the image, and allegorical ones (Virtues holding portraits of potential candidates for queen) situated below.[21] The occasion of this display is given in the title of the almanac, "The Gifts offered to the very Christian King Louis XIV by all the Virtues." The gifts [*estrennes*] are probably those given on the New Year, a theme in keeping with the almanac, although a second possibility might be that these are gifts offered at the beginning of a new undertaking, a foretaste of things to come. As such, they would mark the king's maturity and potential entry into matrimony upon the successful completion of the military campaigns. The latter, figured in the top corners of the graphic, recede into the margins or frame of the almanac, acting as pendants to the cameos below depicting the king's new field of action. The banner above focuses exclusively on the field of the portraits, the scene within the proscenium arch:

The Gifts offered to the very Christian King Louis XIV by all the Virtues. The Virtues, charmed by the merit of our great Monarch, after having chosen from all the Provinces in Europe, those they found the most perfect and accomplished come to present to he whom they consider their protector, expecting this happy choice which will raise to the height of the highest grandeur and the most charming fidelity, she whom his Majesty will wish to honor with this love.

The text emphasizes that the king will make a choice from among the offered gifts. His choice will be a happy one, "which will raise to the height of the highest grandeur . . . she whom his Majesty will wish to honor with his love." The accent placed on choice here is important and can be understood in terms of the framework provided by Marcel Mauss's observations about the activity of gift exchange as one in which relations of submission transform the physical violence of the battlefield into symbolic interaction.[22] In gift exchange, it is the recipient and not the giver of the gift who ultimately finds himself in a position of submission since he is the one who will have to reciprocate. One possible action, albeit a dangerous one, is for the recipient to choose not to respond with a gift. According to Mauss, such behavior is the strongest possible response to the gift, for it is a display of independence (and this is the sovereign position). Here the king adopts a version of that posture by not accepting just any gift, but by choosing among gifts in a kind of fairy-tale fantasy of the king choosing from the fairest in the land. Thus, if there is a veritable explosion of choice in this image, that multiplicity does not privilege the possibility of royal disorder either because of submission, sexual excess, or polygamy. Rather, it offers the king the possibility of displaying his power over his passions and over the allegorical women who present him gifts in showing him exercising his power to make "a happy choice."

Looking at the image, one cannot help but recognize that a choice has already been made. Only one of the five cameos is completely visible, the one suggestively situated to the right of the king's leg, as if ready to slide up along the limb or limit separating the allegorical and historical registers to join the royal family. Even if the king does not look directly at his chosen princess, she is the choice displayed for the viewer of the almanac. Situated diagonally opposite an unframed female, her predecessor, Anne of Austria, the cameo is the only image that might garner as much interest as that of the king. Note, as well, that all the other portraits have little pieces of them obscured by the plants that frame them, as well as by the bodies of the Virtues holding them. Of course, something is also missing from the portrait of the chosen princess: her body. Indeed, the dissonance between the king's full body and the framed, cameo image of the queen is striking. Her body seems to replay the truncation of the historical figures surrounding the king, although in the case of the queen, the framing echoes the tension of the gift-exchange paradigm. Just as gift-exchange reprocesses potential social violence into a containable, symbolic activity, so too the cameo polices, frames, and contains the potentially disruptive parts of the woman. If an unmarried woman has been allowed to enter into the picture, it is only insofar as she is framed and contained in a form that is as easily distributed among the courts of Europe as the almanac engraving could have been among the households and streets of the realm. There is no danger of this female image walking around: she has been crippled, desexualized, cut in pieces like the disorderly Rage, Envy, and Sedition seen in the "Magnificent Triumph."[23] But there is no denying that her excluded parts (breasts, womb, etc.) will be the origin of the dynastic continuity, just as the gift-exchange dynamic is the foundation of social interaction, or as, on another level, kinship exchange (the paradigmatic model of gift exchange for Lévi-Strauss) serves as a basis for civil accord. In both cases (gift and kinship exchange), tension over the unseen (social aggression) does not disappear, but is simply policed by the structure. So, too, the almanac engraving has found a way to circumscribe the necessity of the limbs (sexual body parts) supporting the sovereign performance by making them at once visible and invisible.

1659: Framing the Body's Politics

The iconographic *topoi* of "The Gifts" are not new to the marriage of Louis XIV, but actually repeat and popularize an image predicated on many of the same dynamics between war and marriage, framing and curiosity, politics and sexuality seen in the almanac images that preceded it: Rubens' painting of Henri IV receiving the portrait of his intended bride (Figure 4), produced approximately thirty-five years earlier in a series depicting the life of Marie de Médicis. In the Rubens image, Henri IV has discarded the trappings of war at the sight of his intended wife. In "The Gifts" of 1659 (Figure 3), while there are wishes for peace, the process of marriage is one not of playful relaxation, but of Herculean labor. Is it possible that "The Gifts" makes a subtle pun on Rubens' painting by placing at its base, not cheerful cherubs, but two figures straining to support the proscenium arch?[24] The lion's skin between them underlines their Herculean labor, reminding the viewer of at least two forms of labor behind the royal alliance: that of skinning the Spaniards in Flanders (the lion being the symbol of Flanders) and that of holding up (and together) the stage of the king's passions.[25] There are also cherubs in the almanac engraving, but they are located at the top, not at the bottom of the visual field. And they are not playing with the trappings of war, but seriously displaying them, exhibiting the lion's head-helmet on the right and tail-helmet on the left along with the medallions of the battlefield. Rubens' image also includes the battlefield in the distance, evaporating in a wisp of smoke.[26] Finally, in Rubens' painting, the allegorical and the historical figures are intermingled and not separated. Indeed, in Rubens' canvas it seems as if there is no need for any boundary between allegorical and historical registers. Likewise, there seems to be no need to place the object of desire (the framed image) on a lower register than the king in Rubens' painting.

Of course, Rubens' work and the almanac engraving are different genres with different formats. The first is a large oil painting 3.94 x 2.95 meters, meant to be hung in the palace, while the second is an almanac engraving approximately 80 x 50 centimeters in size, meant for popular circulation. They are also the product of two distinct historical moments: Rubens' piece was painted in the 1620s to describe earlier events, and the almanacs were printed in the late 1650s contemporaneous with the events they depict. One might, nonetheless, pause over the way sexuality seems less fraught, more elevated, in the portrayal of Henry IV looking at Marie de Medicis. Perhaps that is because the image was painted after the king's death and his establishment as the lusty "Roi vert galant." Another reason for the elevation of the queen might be that Rubens' painting was not underwritten by the king but by the subject of the elevated portrait, Marie de Medicis, who utilized the king to present herself and not the other way around as in the almanac.

This difference is clarified when Rubens' painting is juxtaposed with another almanac from the year 1659. In it, Rubens' iconographic *topoi* are once again reworked (Figure 5). The engraving puts in relief the similarities with and differences from Rubens' image, most particularly in the position of the cameo portrait as it is being shown to the king, but also in the relation between the registers of history and allegory, and in the juxtaposition of the images of war and passion, all of which affect the presentation of the potentially disorderly roles of political bodies in the (hopefully) more ordered affairs of the body politic. Once again, it is the banner over the image that guides its reading: "THE CELEBRATED ASSEMBLY OF THE COURT UPON THE CONVALESCENCE OF HIS MAJESTY AND UPON THE SUCCESSFUL OUTCOME OF HIS ARMS." A new element in the *mise-en-scène* of the period between war and marriage appears in this heading: the acknowledgement (after the fact, of course) of the king's near-fatal illness in late June 1658, just after the surrender of Spain at Dunes that turned the tide of the war irrevocably toward the French triumph and occasioned the marriage. At that time, the king fell victim to what his own physician Vallot characterized as a "hidden venom," caused by "the corruption of the Air, the infection of waters, and the large number of ill people, of several dead bodies, and many other circumstances."[27] If the king is portrayed in the almanac as convalescing, it is because his illness had been so serious that even if it had occurred in Calais, outside the French field of vision, it had surely occupied the French imaginary. During the course of the illness the king almost died: his physicians recorded that the king's body was purple and swollen, he was feverish and convulsive, and, at one moment of crisis, the king was unable to breathe.[28] According to Madame de Montpensier, Louis XIV was even given the last rites in the expectation of his death.[29] It is not surprising, therefore, that in announcing the king's convalescence, the *Gazette* acknowledged that the illness "appeared to threaten France with the most painful and distressing loss possible."[30] Of course, in recording the progression of the ailment, the king's physician, Vallot, was understandably reluctant to suggest that the king's illness was in any way connected to the monarch being a weak physical specimen. Indeed, Vallot's notes underline that it was not any bodily weakness, but the king's own courage, the "too great impatience and keenness that he had to be present at opportunities, without sparing his life or health" that caused his malady.[31] Despite this caveat, however, Vallot's journal, Montpensier's memoirs, the *Gazette*, and even popular almanac engravings leave no doubt that the illness that threatened the king's body in the summer of 1658 also threatened the body politic.[32]

Concern expressed for the young king during the crisis and convalescence was thus also concern expressed for the health of the Bourbon dynasty. Less than a decade after the crises of the Fronde, and in the midst of victories against the longtime enemy Hapsburg Spain, the tide seemed to be turning in favor of the Bourbon dynasty, which could at last look forward to the assumption of power by a young and virile king. Were Louis XIV to have succumbed to his illness in July 1658, the vigor of the body politic would have been far less certain, since the crown would have passed to his younger brother. The Duke of Anjou would have been a less compelling figure in the French imaginary since there were already grave reservations about his ability to procreate, let alone rule. It was apparently no secret that the Duke of Anjou took after his father, Louis XIII, a king more interested in the bodies of other men than in the more manly affairs of the body politic or state.[33] Indeed, Louis XIII's lack of interest in women had left his marriage barren for many years, underlining the dynasty's dependence on mortal urges for its continuity by raising the specter of having to move laterally to a monarch's brother for succession in the case of his having sired no heirs to the throne. In this context it seems likely that Louis XIV's "scandalous" romance with Marie Mancini, begun during the king's convalescence and ending only with his marriage in 1660, may have been utilized or even staged by Mazarin in order to demonstrate to the country that the king's body was once again in good working order after his brush with death.[34] With broadside almanacs widely circulating grim images in late 1658 and early 1659, such as "FRANCE RESUSCITATED by the remedy sent from the heavens to the greatest monarch in the world for the peace of his people and the confusion of his enemies" (Figure 6), the idea of a young king giving in to passion—that is, lusting after a politically inappropriate or even potentially threatening consort—may have offered an indication of the king's (and France's) ability to erect himself (itself) from the sickbed (or the turmoil of civil war) and escape the shadow or frame of Thanatos to move into the full, fertile field of Eros. Note how in this almanac, the king himself has been relegated to a cameo image, framed by the bed in a representation resembling the kind of portrait within a portrait noted earlier as a form of containment. Such usage is not surprising in a genre of interior portraits popular in this period, not only as a way to introduce potential queens, but also as a manner in which to memorialize dead persons. Note here that the ill king's image is enclosed by a square frame and not the round ones in which the living queen candidates had been portrayed. This difference is also part of the convention of such commemorative portraits.[35]

In the face of such dire images, it is not surprising that the king's mortal body, missing or framed in "FRANCE RESUSCITATED," is the first focus of "THE CELEBRATED ASSEMBLY," in the descriptive banner that tells the reader or viewer:

> Our August MONARCH is admired on his Throne, Adorned only by his healthy appearance [*bonne mine*] because the brilliance of it is so beautiful that it takes away the luster of the Richest clothing that he wears. The Queen his Mother, the Duke of Anjou his Brother, the Duke of Orleans, and the Prince of Conty, are regarded with the respect owed to the Majesty of one and the conditions of the others. His Eminence the Chancellor, Messieurs Turraine, La Ferté, Grammont, Villeroi, augment by their Presence the Pomp of this Assembly, Where France is seen Presenting the King with the portrait of a Princess who is unnamed, As a certain omen of his future Marriage.

Flanders, Reduced to his mercy, Expresses simultaneously by her Silence, both her admiration and Astonishment, not being able to comprehend the Wonders that this Great Monarch performed in his last Campaign, and by the sound of his Renown and by the force of his Arms, the four Elements Represented at the four corners, the four successful Battles, the Great Victories of this young conqueror and the taking of the cities, with the ceremonies of the Alliance of France with the Elector Princes of the Empire, as well as the Actions of thanks rendered by his Majesty upon his Convalescence in order to move his people to follow his Example.

This image and its prose heading underscore the relationship between the health of the king's body and that of the state. In so doing, it also legitimizes curiosity about the king's mortal body. Indeed, it is the mortal body that is the center of focus here, as the heading insists that the king is adorned only by his healthy appearance [*bonne mine*]. But if the viewer perceives the king's power or health by looking at his body, there are still a large number of accoutrements that establish his power qua health in the picture. In fact, one perceives the king's *bonne mine* (meaning not just face, but countenance or bearing) only from what drapes it, since most of the healthy body is obliterated by clothing. Only a small part of the face, the hands, and the leg, are visible. The last item, the leg, is actually covered by a silk stocking, although its contour is emphasized, not effaced, by that clinging material. It seems odd that the viewer is supposed to perceive that the king's appearance outshines his garments since the garments encase a body whose appearance can only be imagined. And yet, one is drawn to the royal body not just because of the words over the image but because of what one is supposed to admire. The real object of our interest, while covered over, is also exposed, or signified by a leg and the scepter rising from it that is now clearly identified with power, both sexual and political. The phallic dimension of that martial-marital power is underscored by a new addition to the iconography, the fashionably wide petticoat breeches (wide enough to contain the master's absolutist genitalia) and even the *fleurs-de-lys* motif strewn over the royal robes (the *fleurs-de-lys* being not only the royal emblem of France, but also of male genitalia and semen).[36]

The healthy appearance that indicates the victory over the disorder of disease is thus a celebration of successful arms (or legs)—or rather, tools—the most successful of all being the king's sexual potency (his ability to stay erect) on the battlefield, in his sickbed, and in the marital chamber. In it, the king's mortal-sexual body is an asset to state building and not the liability it has been too often categorically assigned when evaluated within the framework of constitutional fictions of monarchy generated around the funerary symbolism. It may not be the king's sexuality that could be a problem in this image, but rather the fact that displaying sexuality requires other images and props (stockings, women, etc.). Indeed, the king's sexual power would be one of his icons in later representations of Louis XIV, as, for example, in Hyacinthe Rigaud's 1701 *Louis XIV en habit de sacré* (Figure 7), which displays the sixty-two-year-old king as virile. Louis Marin and Claude Reichler both note tension in this painting between the sexuality of Louis XIV's leg and the aging face, a tension they read as undermining the projection of the king's power.[37] One might also note that in Rigaud's painting, the king is the only human figure on the canvas. Portrayed alone, it is as if his potency were innate and eternal, rising like the phoenix out of its own ashes in a vision of absolute, onanistic masculinity. As Marin and Reichler suggest, this image is ultimately about decay. The king alone is sterile. In "The Illustrious Assembly," however, as well as in the other almanac engravings considered here, the young virile king is posed (or framed) not just by his royal robes or by the architectural backdrop stage, but by the group setting that includes those with whom he still shares the spotlight: in the upper register, his mother, his brother, and the duke, and in the lower register, the now legitimate allegorical female supporters, conquered and awed Flanders and France, seen offering what the prose text refers to as "the portrait of an unnamed princess as a sure omen of his marriage," an object also labeled in the actual image as "the picture of his desires."

Elements and *topoi* such as the opposition between high and low, the dichotomy between allegorical figures paying tribute to historical ones, the suggestion of gift-exchange, the equation be-

tween submissive cities and submissive women, the framed, unnamed princess, the leg leading to her portrait as libido or drive to
its object, and Mazarin's hand pointing out and legitimizing his
protégé's leg can now be read as familiar elements of the iconography from between war and marriage. Here, however, the potential
threats to the king's power—ill health, sexuality, military insubor-
dination, etc.—are contained by the various enclosures (frames and
clothing, for example). The display of the king's healthy body as
evidence of his military and sexual prowess is always dependent on
these framing images. As such, the process of celebrating the king
is that of celebrating the assembly around him as well as the
assembled images and objects. This process plays out the etymological meaning of allegory: from *allos*, meaning other, and *agorein*, to
speak publicly, as well as *agora*, assembly, which can be combined,
meaning to speak of the other in public assembly. Here the figurative
other is not just the king's masculine power or his prospective bride,
but also his dependence on other *limen* or on the limbs of the royal
entourage (the celebrated assembly of the court, an assemblage of
family, courtiers, a cameo female, conquered territories, an implied
viewing public, frames, and so forth). Without these elements,
would the king's power be so evident? Such dependence is virtually
banished from Rigaud's image of the mature, well-ensconced Sun
King.

Indeed, returning to Figure 5, it is the other assembled "bodies,"
those liminal to the king's centering image, that finally attract the
viewer's attention in a picture where passion has been enrobed,
conquered, framed, and stabilized for display. These other bodies
highlight this passion and offer an acceptable field on which to
display or stand the king's desires. Just as his clothing serves to drape
and thus enhance interest in the real site of his male power, so too,
modestly dressed and submissive allegorical figures and cameo
images with missing bodies (Rage, Envy, and Sedition's limbs
amputated and framed into submission) also safely pique viewer
interest in the king's own well-wrapped limb and then in the process
of peace. But this process of allegoresis, or speaking of the (unspeakable) other in a manner suitable to public assembly, is more complex.

For if the liminality is wrapped up, might it nonetheless reemerge in the engraving to disrupt the happy family picture of the successful, virile, and healthy king on his throne with his appropriate political and sexual fantasies? Indeed, could not some alternative, competitive urges lurk in the hearts of those happily assembled family members and courtiers? Could alternative and disordering fantasies or bodies transgress this scene of family romance?

Answers to both these questions may be found by considering the figure on the far left edge of the engraving, the king's younger brother, the Duke of Anjou, next in line for the throne should Louis XIV die or should his projected marriage prove sterile. It is interesting that this potential pretender is the only member of the assembly whose full body is portrayed in the upright position. Of course, the frame around the image cuts off the duke's right leg, the very member so prominently displayed by the king on his throne. Does the duke's walking stick, an object longer than the king's scepter, compensate for the elim(b)ination of his leg? Note as well that if it totters at the edge of the focal field, the body of the Duke of Anjou nonetheless occupies a unique position or site: he straddles the two registers of the engraving, the upper zone of mimetic portrayal of historical characters and the lower, allegorical field of women. Is it perhaps because of the brother's own liminal position that he, like the potential queen, stands in the register of the king's limb as her pendant? For in 1658, he is the least significant (smallest and youngest) in the royal family, while also being the most crucial member because he is the next in line for the throne, a point driven home by Louis XIV's near death before his marriage and the birth of a dauphin. Or might his position be, rather, a function of his well-known effeminacy, a predilection apparently encouraged in order to further enhance the power of Louis XIV, and yet also elided when the duke was married off twice to assure heirs in the event of a threat to Bourbon succession.

The duke's position is parallel to that of the "imagined" queen who is also necessary yet liminal, central yet peripheral, hopefully fertile yet visually castrated. In the engraving, Louis XIV seems to cast his glance more in his brother's direction than in that of the "picture of his desires," suggesting that in this scenario of precarious health, the duke may offer a source of anxiety about the virility and power of members or limbs supporting the Bourbon family and thus about the permanence of the titular monarch. As the king recovers his health and the marriage treaty is negotiated and signed, the new queen will replace the prince as the object of such anxiety, being seen in contemporary terms as the vessel necessary for the Bourbon dynastic procreation and for the memory of the enemy line of Philip IV, her father. It is at this point that she will become the central propping (and anxiety-provoking) image of the nuptial fictions.

In 1659, however, it is another female figure who visually mediates such unspeakable fantasies, again in the form of a disembodied female head. The head belongs to another former Spanish infanta who became a French queen, Louis XIV's mother, Anne of Austria, a woman intimately acquainted with all sorts of disorders or liminal phenomena: the vagaries of Bourbon homosexuality from her years of marriage to Louis XIII, the nature of competition among the blood princes from her experiences during the Fronde uprisings in the late 1640s and early 1650s, and the significance of the female liminal position for the representation of sovereign masculinity during such moments.[38] Positioned unframed between her two sons, she is a reminder that liminal issues are always lurking at the edge of the absolutist state, since they are, so to speak, the limbs on which the monarchy rests, or the female body that breeds and bears those limbs. As a still-present trace of such liminality, however, she is also the visual proof that if disorderly, ephemeral passions or lim(b)inality (propping liminality) cannot be fully contained by representational frames, they can be utilized and fashioned, shaped, to fit into the larger image of, or frame for, a stable, absolutist, body politic.

In recognizing the role of such images in state building, one begins to recognize how such liminality has been groomed out of the picture by scholars who have forced all the images of monarchy into the Kantorowicz–Giesey framework of the fiction of the king's two bodies. That paradigm, rooted in the discourses and rituals of death, can account better for the decay of the king's mortal body than for its life (or sexuality). The almanac images from 1658 and

1659 were not generated from the funereal model, but were created from the fictions of war looking toward the fictions of peace and marriage. In such a context, highlighting the king's humanness would not be detrimental, but fundamental to making the ruler (and his rule) seem strong. In the almanac images considered here, the king's mortal body as healthy and virile plays a crucial role in state building, as do all the props and players—persons, limbs, frames, etc.—that work with him to project his (state's) vitality. Of course, as the king moves beyond the liminal period between war and marriage, such props and bodies may no longer profitably serve to structure his image, becoming distractions, *divertissements*, in a symbolic logic predicated on promoting his divine autonomy and authority. The representations of this later period have been productively accounted for from the Kantorowiczian perspective precisely because these images do not contain and display liminal passions. Rather, they suppress them in producing a portrait of the king alone on his stage, staving off death (real or political) in a struggle to obliterate the many frames and limbs supporting him and move beyond the liminal moment toward the (fantasy of) absolute unity and stability. Portraits of the king between war and marriage, however, are fictions that require supporting props. They organize Louis' image, disordering and reordering it, much in the manner of the liminal moment out of which they are produced. How these fictions evolve during the actual marriage is the subject of the following chapters.

CHAPTER 2

Fashioning the Body Politic

As predicted by the almanacs, the military battles of 1657 and 1658 did indeed result in the marriage of Louis XIV. In the late fall of 1658, after the king's convalescence, the French court went to Lyon to negotiate a marriage between Louis and the Princess of Savoy, one of the choices offered in the almanac engraving "The Gifts" (Figure 3). The meeting accomplished its purpose, not an alliance with the house of Savoy, but rather a response from the Spaniards, who sent their envoy, Pimentel, to Lyon in the middle of the night with an offer of marriage to the infanta (and thus a treaty). Negotiations followed that summer between the French minister, Mazarin, and his Spanish counterpart, Don Luis of Haro, the two meeting on the Island of the Conference in the middle of the Bidassoa River, which would be the site of the treaty signing and handing over of the infanta in June. A diplomatic mission went to Madrid in November of 1659 with a formal request for the infanta's hand. The marriage itself took place in June 1660, when the Spanish and French courts assembled on the border to engage in a series of ceremonies: the marriage by procuration in Spain on June 2, the reunion of Anne of Austria with her brother Philip IV on the Island of the Conference on June 4, the meeting of the two kings and the oath of peace on that same island two days later, the handing over of the new queen to the French on June 7, and celebration of the Marriage Mass in France on June 9.

Liminal issues played a central, albeit potentially disruptive role in organizing the fictions of absolutist state building throughout this period. In the betwixt and between of war and treaty, it was the iconography of passion and the frames containing that instability that laid out the precarious dialectic of figuring absolutist power. As the transition shifted from treaty to marriage, curiosity about the soon-to-be queen of France grew. With the negotiations of the treaty progressing and the accord with Spain solidifying, images of the new queen came more clearly into focus as the central limb of the nuptial fictions' dialectic. Descriptions of the new queen gave form to the narrative of the treaty negotiation and most particularly to reports of the June 1660 events. But, as in the case of the liminal passions, accounts did not focus directly on María Teresa. Rather, they would continue to frame her, skirting the unsettling issues of the role of passion (and the queen) in enabling the activity of the body politic.

As she came more and more to epitomize the precarious dialectic between passion and political control found in the imagery of absolutist state building in the period between war and marriage, María Teresa was both taken out of her frame and contained by new frames. More precisely, her image was not shaped by offering direct details about her looks, but by focusing on her attire as what attracted the gaze of diplomats and onlookers alike. Indeed, the topos of clothing, like that of legs and frames, is pervasive in materials ranging from correspondence produced during the treaty negotiations to pamphlet accounts of the infanta's arrival in France. On the eve of the marriage and during the treaty signing, fashion (particularly that of the queen) became the limb that carried the display of Bourbon power and framed the regime's anxiety about its future.

The role of fashion first appeared in a letter Mazarin wrote to his war minister, Le Tellier, from the border in August 1659. In the letter, Mazarin stressed the importance of keeping the French and Spaniards apart during the treaty negotiations in order to avoid a replay of Spanish interactions dating back to Louis XI and Henry

IV of Castile, in which the difference in clothing was a subject of mockery. Underlining contemporary differences in French and Spanish clothing styles, Mazarin also expressed his exasperation at the course of the 1659 treaty negotiations in writing: "I do not expect, given the differences between these two nations, that whatever agreement we may come to, we shall be able to meet each other dressed in the same manner." In so doing, he also cautioned Le Tellier not to read the letter in public since the topic of clothing would seem ridiculous and could have "bad effects" on the course of the negotiations.[1]

A few months later, a member of the French diplomatic mission to Madrid, providing the public with the first eyewitness description of the Spanish infanta who would soon be the new queen of France, characterized her as *una bona roba*, literally "a good dress," what one would call today "a good skirt." His comments, reproduced in an occasional pamphlet, are evocative of the 1940s' hard-boiled detective's metonymic elision between the moll's tight skirt and the body it wrapped. The diplomat wrote: "if it is permitted to speak of our future Queen in these terms, I would say that there is every indication that she will be *una bona Roba*, and that our King will not have any reason to complain of the necessity that the greatness of Kings imposes on them to marry crowned royalty."[2] If the diplomat worried that his characterization might skirt the limits of acceptable discourse about royal bodies, it was because the language he used came from popular, albeit risque, texts such as Rabelais' *Quart livre*, Marguerite de Navarre's *L'Heptaméron*, and Brantôme's *Dames galantes*, where the expression "bona roba" was used to suggest sexually appealing women.

Another allusion to fashion can be found in the Mareschal de Grammont's report to Mazarin on the same mission to Madrid. In his account, Grammont assured the minister about "the qualities of the body" of the infanta. But while he offered a positive assessment, Grammont underscored his lack of concrete physical details, noting he was unable to judge the stature of the future queen because of the "the height of her shoes and the large size of her farthingale [hoop skirt]."[3] Spanish clothing impeded Grammont's clear view.

Finally, the memoirs of Daniel Cosnac, Archbishop of Aix,
relate an anecdote concerning the wife of the minister, Hughes de
Lyonnes. Having accompanied her husband on the 1659 mission to
Madrid, she was also among the first to see the infanta. While in
Madrid, and because she was the same size as the future bride, the
minister's wife had a dress made in the style of the one she saw on
the infanta. Upon her return to the court, she modeled the outfit
for the king to give him a living portrait of his future wife. Cosnac
reported that the vision shocked the king who, viewing the tiny
figure, wondered if his bride was a dwarf. This incident created a
rift between the wife of the minister and Anne of Austria.[4]

The Body as Booty

The above comments were found in correspondence, in memoirs of diplomatic figures, and in occasional pamphlets. They were
not private narratives, but stories circulated among the French and
Spanish courts by word of mouth, in manuscript copy, and in
printed texts produced to provide timely news coverage.[5] The first
example focuses on the clothing of the Spaniard in general. The rest
concern the dress of the Spanish infanta, clothing that relates to and
reflects on her body. No other figure is the object of such scrutiny.
Indeed, no one else involved in the marriage has his or her wardrobe
criticized or even commented upon beyond the traditional description of the sumptuous clothing worn by the French during the
wedding ceremonies. One can begin to comprehend what is occurring in this *topos* by focusing on the second example, the reference
to the infanta as *una bona roba*. While the comparison was risqué,
the metonymic elision between the woman and her apparel may
have highlighted the political reality of the marriage treaty. In France
in the seventeenth century, according to Furetière, *robe* meant first
and foremost the "apparel that covers the whole body."[6] But the
word *robe* had also connected clothing with war booty since the late
Middle Ages.[7] Furetière offers this association in his etymology for
robe, *raupa* or *rauba*, "which means in Latin *clothing* [*habit*], as well
as *to make off with* [*desrober*], meaning *to steal* [*voler*]." More interesting

is Furetière's list of colloquial uses of *roba*, in which he includes the expression *una bona roba*, defining it as a "beautiful woman, or any other thing that is valued, because it is a good *robbe* [bonne *robbe*], after an Italian phrase, *bona roba*; because in that language *roba* means all sorts of property and objects."[8] Whatever its national origin, the expression clearly offered a double message. On the one hand, it suggested that even if the king's marriage was an obligation to the body politic, Louis XIV would not be marrying just any political body, but a beautiful woman. On the other hand, the expression underlined that the king's good fortune emanated not only from the appeal of the body's beauty, but also from the appeal of the booty it brought France (the second meaning of *roba*) in a description that drew attention to the relation between the infanta as a body and the larger interests of the body politic in acquiring not just pleasure for the king, but riches for the nation.

It is thus that the writer, displacing his gaze from the infanta's body to her skirt, did not actually focus on the infanta at all, but on what she represented: material value. In so doing, the diplomat did not overstep the bounds of propriety. On the contrary, he was able to remind his readers delicately that the future queen was property or booty acquired by the French from the Spaniards. He was able to address the underlying (unspeakable) issues of the marriage, that a new queen (and, indeed, the treaty more generally) offered enrichment or pleasure not just for the king's mortal body, but also for the larger political corporation he was building.

Indeed, one of the pamphlet writer's agendas seemed to be to size up the Spanish booty in general. This evaluation occurs on many levels, ranging from a discussion of the Spanish nobility's dress (and their awe of the French courtiers' attire), and a description of the dinners the Spaniards provided, to comments on the furnishings of the various places visited. Many of these remarks can be seen as symptomatic of the ongoing evaluation (and suspicion) of Spanish cultural differences in texts describing the initial contacts made with Spaniards after generations of enmity. Other comments seem to size up the Spanish booty more overtly as, for example, an observation that immediately follows the citation about the infanta being a "una bona roba." In it, the writer describes the lodgings of the retinue: "All the tapestries of the [Spanish] Crown are hung there. I will not tell you that they are beautiful, that is evident enough, Brussels belonging to the King of Spain, I have never seen more superb ones in my life."[9] In gazing around his room and insisting on the evidence of the richness of the tapestries lining the walls, the writer links their acquisition to territory formerly controlled by the Hapsburgs, territory (and riches) that could well have been retained by the French in their 1658 sweep of the Low Countries, had political accord not been reached.

Of course, such enrichment was the goal of royal marriages in early modern Europe. The alliance between Hapsburg Spain and Bourbon France was no exception. The Treaty of the Pyrenees was meant to settle generations of territorial and political enmity. Working out the disposition of conquered territory, clarifying issues of allegiance, repatriating the last Fronde rebel, the Prince of Condé, and setting the terms for Louis XIV's marriage, the negotiations concretely and symbolically repositioned the Bourbon monarchy in the international and domestic arena. Such repositioning was a logical consequence of the marriage treaty. As noted in Chapter One, the treaty set in motion a process of kinship exchange that, like gift exchange, masked political aggression. To consider the marriage treaty in this light is to see it in terms of Lévi-Strauss' theory that the exchange of goods or kin allow social groups to organize their interactions, moving from violent relations to civil accord, displacing enmity with the carefully choreographed rules of reciprocity.[10] Understood within such an anthropological model, the marriage of María Teresa and Louis XIV can be seen to have allowed the displacement of the animosity of the battlefield and the ensuing territorial negotiations onto the clauses of the accord which exchanged concessions, territories, citizens, alliances, and an infanta. The diplomat's evaluation of the infanta as booty may have been inspired by one such concession: the infanta's renunciation of her right to inherit both her own lands in the Low Countries and, in the event there would be no male heir to succeed him, her father's throne. In exchange for this double renunciation, the Bourbons would get two kinds of goods: the infanta and 500,000 gold crowns. The second commodity would increase the infanta's value as a good skirt in the event of a default, since the treaty contained a proviso guaranteeing that the renunciation was conditional upon the payment of the sum on a specified schedule. Should the Spaniards prove unable to meet the deadlines, the French would not only have their queen, but the goods she would potentially produce for them: heirs to both the Bourbon and Hapsburg thrones. When the member of the 1659 French diplomatic mission to Madrid noted that the infanta was a good skirt, he thus focused on something associated with her body to point out its value to the French body politic as cloth and cash exchanged or wrested from the enemy: her body was a good prize, one that represented all the others, and whose worth could grow. He also displaced the animosity of the battlefield and treaty to a discussion of clothing, wrapping enmity in a whimsical side issue.

The anecdotes cited above shift the negotiation of affairs of state and questions of territorial negotiation onto affairs of fashion. The latter, clothing and the arena of fashion, offered a safe sphere on which to play out the larger anxieties of the treaty being negotiated. The clothing of the infanta apparently offered the safest sphere of all for such displacement. Indeed, the surreptitious analogy between her body and the political body of Spain allowed the French to discuss the long-term goals of the Bourbon political culture coming into view without insulting the group with whom they were negotiating. On the eve of Louis XIV's formal ascension to the throne, during his liminal rite of passage from youth to manhood, such an analogy between the body and the state also allowed the French to imagine their own as yet uncertain political prospects.[11]

The work of anthropologist Mary Douglas has shown how symbols of the body function to work out otherwise unmentionable boundary issues raised in transitional rites of purification, such as the marriage ceremonial. According to Douglas:

> The body is a model which can stand for any bounded system. Its boundaries can represent any boundaries which are threatened or precarious. The body is a complex structure. The functions of its

different parts and their relation afford a source of symbols for other complex structures. We cannot possibly interpret rituals concerning excreta, breast milk, saliva, and the rest unless we are prepared to see in the body a symbol of society, and to see the powers and dangers credited to social structure reproduced in small on the human body.[12]

Of course, in seventeenth-century France it would be unlikely for political propaganda about monarchy to focus on the body of the king (or queen) and its excreta. As explained in Chapter One, while there could be advantages in stressing the vitality of the king's mortal body, such emphasis is liminal or disordering to a system where continuity depended on a fiction of the monarch as divine and eternal. It may be for this reason that, on the eve of a treaty that would forever change the face of Europe, fantasies about the body politic were transposed onto the queen's body, or rather her clothing. Substituting an item of clothing for its wearer moved the various diplomats' gazes even further from the hard facts of the political goals of the marriage (and the mortal body of the king) to the apparently softer sphere of the material goods wrapping a foreign princess and future queen. In so doing, it processed anxiety about the sovereign body, Bourbon and Hapsburg, and the body politic both crowns represented. Extending Douglas' model from a parallel between the boundaries of the body and those of the state to issues of clothing and political culture therefore clarifies how political issues are transposed onto the infanta. It also clarifies what issues are processed in this sphere and whether such a symbolic arena (clothing and a queen's body) is actually a safe domain on which to play out political relations between two early superpowers.

Fashion and the Body Politic

An examination of how the French discussion of their new queen's clothing played a major role in symbolizing and fashioning discussions of the Bourbon body politic is best served by looking at descriptions of the infanta's arrival in her new country as reported in the occasional pamphlet, the genre that made up the largest portion of the marriage archive. There are several reasons for the occasional pamphlet's dominant role in formulating and disseminating nuptial fictions. First, like the almanacs studied in the previous chapter, pamphlets were easy and inexpensive to distribute. Printed by royal privilege and sold by their publishers or by closely monitored peddlers [*colporteurs*], these 10- to 16-page texts were easily regulated. Unlike almanacs based on elaborate engravings, occasional pamphlets could be produced very quickly, allowing a contemporaneity with the events they described. One particular pamphlet, *La Pompe et Magnificence faite au mariage du Roy et de L'Infante D'Espagne, Ensemble les entretiens qui ont esté faits entre les deux Roys, & les deux Reynes, dans l'Isle de la Conference et Relation de ce qui s'est passé mesmes apres la Consommation,*[13] exemplifies such qualities. The pamphlet underscores its simultaneity with the events it reports by its form: a dated chronicle of the court's activities recounted by a first-person narrator who adds forgotten details and inscribes in the narrative the conditions of its transmission as an eyewitness account. This style is typical of the pamphlets describing the events on the border. *La Pompe* was likely a model for all the occasional reports from the border since it was the first printed report of the meeting between the two courts, having been set in installments by the nearest authorized printer, the king's printers [*Imprimeurs ordinaires du Roy*] in Toulouse, as each event took place. A copy was then forwarded to Paris for an edition published there, probably with no more delay than it would have taken to travel from one city to the other.[14] It is not surprising that such a text was vetted by the authorities and printed by publishers the king supported. Speed was crucial to keep the king's (and Mazarin's) activities in view while other journalists and publishers prepared their reports in Paris from accounts they received. Those reports will be discussed in detail in the next chapter in the context of an analysis of the occasional pamphlet's participation in (and emulation of) the economy producing nuptial fictions. Of interest here are the images that are highlighted in this first pamphlet, most particularly its extensive description of one of the most dramatic moments of the marriage narrative, the new queen's arrival at the border and her transformation from Spanish princess to French queen.

Organized chronologically, *La Pompe* is divided into two parts. Section one, dated June 8, begins with an account of the meeting held two days earlier in which the king was first formally introduced to his new bride on the Island of the Conference. That same section also recounts the June 7 encounter in which the infanta was actually handed over to the French. Section two, dated June 11, details the infanta's first days in France, the French Marriage Mass, and the activities around that ceremony, including allusions to the consummation. In sum, the narrative describes one of the most highly charged and formalized moments of the marriage treaty: the signing of the accord and the transfer (and consumption) of the goods. What was recounted may thus be seen as a liminal or transitional moment in which the two courts, former adversaries, are face to face, literally and figuratively on the threshold of a new political and familial coexistence. No figure better embodies that transition than the infanta: married to Louis XIV by procuration in Spain before being handed over, as was traditional in such alliances, the infanta, in the moments described, was no longer Spanish and not yet truly French.

Put in simple terms, the very first pamphlet reporting the marriage narrates the story of a princess's transformation from *infanta* María Teresa, to *reine* Marie-Thérèse. It recounts her rite of passage as she moves from one culture or symbolic system (Spanish) to another (French). This transformation is suggested early in the text when the narrator recounts a conversation between Louis XIV and his mother prior to their departure for the island where they would finally take custody of the infanta:

> His Majesty, leaving to go there, said that he intended that very night to consummate the Marriage that he believed to be otherwise well accomplished, and he showed much ardor for this: But the Queen Mother who wished to dress the Queen in the French style before-hand, and thus make her even more pleasing [*aymable*], said to the King that there remained some Church ceremony that could take place only today. (*La Pompe*, 7).

In the queen mother's estimation, for Louis XIV to consummate his marriage it was necessary to make the infanta look French, to make her fit the French notion of desirability. It was as if, dressed in her native garb, she could not speak the language of Bourbon taste; she was true to the etymology of her title, *infans*, without language.[15] She would be desirable only if she were able to communicate within her new cultural context. That communication, however, was to be largely passive; the queen mother's goal was simply to make the infanta readable as object of desire, that is as wearer of the clothing or signs of the French court.[16]

Exactly what message those signs, that clothing, were meant to transmit merits further consideration in order to understand what language the infanta was to be made to speak to or for her husband. One available image (Figure 8) suggests the message could well have been that of the Bourbon triumph over the Spanish Hapsburgs. For the act of reclothing was, quite literally, a territorialization of the Hapsburg body by the Bourbon family. This image of appropriation or colonization is from an almanac produced to mark the year 1659 by celebrating the 1658 French conquest of Spanish-occupied Flanders, the victory that ultimately led to the larger Spanish defeat. In it, Flanders is having her Spanish garments removed and is being reclothed in French fashion by the allegorical female figure of France. The top center medallion contains just such a description, which clarifies any doubt as to what is occurring in the tableau. The French garb that Flanders is to put on is clearly identified by its *fleurs-de-lys* motif and its prominent position in the center of the picture where it is held high by one of the soldiers. A cape, also covered with *fleurs-de-lys*, is held by a second allegorical female figure located behind and to the right of France. This is not a private event. The audience is large and includes soldiers with their swords drawn; figures viewing from below glimpsed in the spaces between the central characters' lower bodies; the king carried by cupids in a medallion above; and the reader or viewer for whom the act is staged, or more precisely framed by the miniatures of the various cities conquered by Louis XIV (these cities being epitomized by the figure of Flanders). In short, the almanac offers a scenario of Flander's disrobing that depicts the triumph of the French Bourbons over the Spanish Hapsburgs being reenacted on the body via the reclothing of the allegorical princess, Flanders. As discussed in

Chapter One, an almanac broadside, a visual tableau, would have been accessible to a large cross-section of buyers and viewers from all social classes. It would have been even more widely encountered than the information in an occasional pamphlet.[17]

The engraving would also have been clearly understood by a wide public as part of the tradition in which rape is a founding gesture of the nation-state—as, for example, in the myth of the Sabine women who were raped by the Romans and then taken as their wives. That myth exemplifies the anthropological paradigm in which the establishment of family bonds between former enemies, even by the violent territorialization of women's bodies, facilitates political reconciliation by means of the exchange or appropriation of *una bona roba*. The myth, furthermore, had a visual tradition within the French absolutist context, as Margaret Carroll has shown in her analysis of Rubens' *Rape of the Daughters of Leucippus*. Carroll argues that the canvas was produced to commemorate the previous Hapsburg–Bourbon alliance between Louis XIII and Anne of Austria and links it to "a tradition that emerged among princely patrons at the time, of incorporating large-scale mythological rape scenes into their palace decorations." She argues that "With fundamental shifts in political thinking and experience in early sixteenth-century Europe, princes came to appreciate the particular luster rape scenes could give to their own claims of absolutist sovereignty."[18] The connections Carroll makes also seem to apply to the case analyzed here. Carroll's conclusion that Rubens' "*Rape of the Daughters of Leucippus* succeeds at once in making manifest the latent function of royal marriages and in glamorizing them at the same time" might also be applied to the case of Louis XIV and María Teresa, not only in the light of the anthropological reading Carroll gives such alliances, but also in relation to the fact that the Bourbon marriages, by and large, repeat the same rituals with each generation to show, as Carroll suggests, "the sacred importance of these nuptials" to the powers of the divine monarch.[19]

It thus seems clear that the infanta María Teresa, as she was described in the pamphlet, was meant to occupy the same position in the scenario of her marriage that previous queens had occupied and that Flanders occupied in the engraving considered above: she was the object of ritual rape that would allow not only the adjudication of violence between men, but that would, from that violence, (re)produce the nation-state. Just as the reclothing in the engraving figures the rape, the reclothing in the pamphlet would seem to replay the founding rape scenario, albeit in a more civil manner, since even the queen mother participated in it.[20] In the pamphlet, the infanta is thus slipped into a symbolic matrix that was already available, that is, into the service of the machinery of royal symbolism building political culture. Or rather, she would have been had she been an allegorical symbol like Flanders or a mythical character like the Sabine women. But as the pamphlet describes her, the new queen has a material reality that is capable, even in an officially sanctioned prose narrative, of placing that symbolic scenario in question.

In this sense, the infanta transcends the position that Irigaray identifies for women in kinship exchange. She is not simply material on the market that tends toward abstraction. Her very materiality resists abstraction and offers her some agency.[21] In this context, it is striking that the infanta's problematic materiality confronted the French within or via the sphere of fashion. For even if one thinks of clothing as only a cultural signifier, something abstract or symbolic, it is immediately apparent in reading the pamphlet description that what the infanta wore caused very concrete problems for the French. Consider, for example, La Pompe's description of the mechanics of the infanta's definitive departure for France: "She was then put into her beautiful carriage where she took up the whole front because of her *gard'Infant* [farthingale] that she did not wish to remove. The King and Queen Mother were in back. . . ."[22] In taking possession of their new queen, the pamphlet tells us, the French were obliged to give her the entire front of the carriage because of an item of clothing, her *gard'Infant*, that she *chose* not to remove. One surmises from the explanation that something was amiss in the carriage. Indeed, a contemporary Spanish description of the event also noted the placement and went out of its way to explain the infanta's position: "They got into the coach, seating the bride on the horse's side [in front], which in France is the best place."[23] When the writer underlined that the infanta was in front, near the horses, the best place in France ("que es en Francia el mayor lugar"), he subtly suggested, by needing to explain the placement, that she may indeed not have been in what the Spanish reader would consider the appropriate spot.

In the delicate matters of diplomatic relations, such a cultural faux-pas would not have been insignificant. It might have needed qualification, if only to save face, to indicate that the Spaniards were not being insulted. Although it would be difficult to ascertain exactly what the issues were, it seems likely that it was not so much the exact position in the carriage that was abnormal, but rather that the infanta was not next to her husband. She sat alone in what might have been her mother-in-law's seat. What had apparently occurred was that the expected shift in position between the former queen, now a queen mother, and the former infanta, now a queen, had not taken place. The Oedipal implications of this triangulation are evident. Indeed, there are hints in this text and in others of the queen mother's resistance to stepping aside for another woman. What should be emphasized for this discussion, however, is that the infanta was not yet a queen and the queen had yet to become a queen mother, even though the already married new French queen had set foot on French soil. This deviation was portrayed as of the infanta's choosing. The text underlines that it was she who had chosen not to remove her *gard'Infant*. Since the Spanish clothing had not been removed, the *roba* had not been appropriated. The founding rape had yet to take place, delaying the (re)birth of the nation expected to result from it.

Skirting the Issue

To understand why this item of wearing apparel (in English, the farthingale; in seventeenth-century French, the *garde-infant*, *vertugadin*, or *vertugale*) was so imposing that it caused (or allowed) the French to displace the infanta from her rightful place as queen (and lay the blame for that displacement on the princess's choice), one must look beyond the journalistic accounts to other contemporary references to the item in question. One source, the memoirs of Madame de Motteville, is particularly helpful. As an aide to Anne of Austria, Motteville's comments may perhaps represent the sentiments of the queen mother, the figure who first raised the issue of clothing in the pamphlet. Indeed, in the preface to her biography of Anne of Austria, Ruth Kleinman states that Motteville "worshiped Anne and, with the queen's permission, kept notes on the queen's remarks." Kleinman uses this fact to argue that Motteville can be "reasonably trusted to have reported accurately whatever Anne actually said to her."[24] While one should be skeptical of any assertion of "true" reporting, there probably was some overlap in the interests of the two women. Motteville's comments on Spanish fashion in general, and on the *garde-infant* in particular, seem to echo (and justify) the queen mother's desire "to dress the queen in the French style" when she writes:

> It pained me to see the clothing and coiffure of the Spanish women . . . their *Gard-Infante* was a machine half round and monstrous, because it seemed that it was several wooden hoops sewn into their skirts, except that hoops are round and their *Gard-Infante* was flattened a bit in the front and the back, and swelled out on the sides. When they walked, this machine moved up and down, and made for a very ugly appearance.[25]

Motteville referred disdainfully to Spanish women's skirts as monstrous, invoking a traditional link between women and monstrosity.[26] She also articulated a more contemporary attitude toward the outmoded or baroque. The *garde-infant*, the huge hoop-skirt style popular across France, Spain, and Italy in the late sixteenth and early seventeenth centuries, had ceded to a less bulky, more natural cut in France by 1660.[27] This shift in style was coherent with the larger aesthetic shift from baroque to classical, from the ostentation that characterized the exaggerated Spanish skirt to the less excessive and more discreet style that was coherent with the classical exigencies of hidden art.[28] The skirt may, furthermore, have seemed monstrous to Motteville because in framing and positioning the Spanish body as outmoded (baroque), it made that body more noticeable than the

French classical body. Indeed, by its very size the farthingale overpowered the French body, both male and female, as we can see in tapestry depictions of the events made from sketches by Lebrun (Figure 9).

It is interesting that Motteville uses the term "machine" to describe this monstrous item. Derived from the Latin *machina* and from the Greek for expedient or means, the term machine suggests something that enables or empowers its user.[29] The "fort laide figure" of the Spanish woman as she walks, her machine-like skirt bobbing up and down, may well be more than simply ridiculous, it may do more than just mark the Spanish difference. The metal and wire infrastructure (actually the farthingale, not the skirt), the very material of torture when taken within the Spanish context, can become that of liberation when moved to another milieu, one with a different order of symbolic relations and signs and one in which the Spanish woman plays a different role than she does on her home turf. Indeed, the "machinery" of the large skirt, which provides distance and cover, may also raise the specter of a threat to the French order as it suggests the operation and protection (the enabling of) some power (real or symbolic) hidden beneath it. That idea dovetails with the meaning of *machine* offered by Furetière, who focuses on how machines enable their users to do things "above their power." According to Furetière's many definitions of the term, personal force can be enhanced, for example, by the machinery of war, of theater, or of any artifice or ruse (even moral ones).[30] Motteville would have added machines of fashion to Furetière's list.

Furetière's two dictionary entries on the farthingale provide further insight into the enabling machinery of this particular fashion. The first definition is found under the entry *garde-infant*: "A large *vertugadin* [farthingale] that the Spanish Women wear just above their hips, and that used to be worn some time ago in France, which serves to stop them from being disturbed in a crowd: it is a kind of belt, stuffed, or held up by thick wire, which is very useful to pregnant women." The second is located under the term *vertugadin*: "An item of women's clothing, that they used to put on their belt to raise up their skirts four or five inches. It was made of heavy linen stretched over thick wires. It protected them from a crowd and was quite favorable to girls who had let their figures be spoiled."[31] Like Motteville, Furetière characterized the *garde-infant* or *vertugadin* as an unwieldy, uncomfortable, and outmoded fashion, something that "used to be worn some time ago" in France, but that Spanish women still "wear." Interestingly, he also pointed out certain advantages of the skirt, namely that it could protect women from being crushed in a crowd just as it "protected" the infanta from being crowded in the carriage. The farthingale could also conceal bodily defects, figures spoiled, even by pregnancy. What should be obvious about the farthingale from both Furetière and Motteville is that this object functioned on two levels: its very size and construction actually protected the woman from a crowd, but at the expense of reconceptualizing or refashioning her figure, making her appear misshapen or monstrous. The abnormality may have helped shelter the infanta, making her psychologically inaccessible, providing her refuge from the role the French construed for her as queen in much the same manner as the skirt guarded her concretely from "the crowd," in this case, from the Bourbon royal family. It may have thus been perceived as offering some nefarious or secret agency.

Such protection and secret agency is signaled by one aspect of the *garde-infant* noted explicitly in the dictionary and implicitly in Motteville's memoir. The item was "very useful to pregnant women" because it concealed their misshapen (pregnant) bodies and thus allowed them to continue appearing in public.[32] That is why it was called a *gard'Infant* in the pamphlet and a *garde-infant* in the dictionary. Both spellings translate the Spanish term *guardainfante*, guard of the *infante*, the latter term meaning "child" or "fetus" in Spanish. In French, the term for "Spanish prince" was *infant*. Interestingly, however, Madame de Motteville referred to the apparatus as a *gard-Infante*, adding an "e" and making the term feminine in French. She thus transformed the prince to a princess (or infanta), subtly suggesting the truth about the item: it actually protected the woman or *infanta* by concealing her unborn child (or bodily secret); indeed, it did not protect the child/ prince at all, but more likely threatened it (with miscarriage), given the weight and construction of the apparatus.

Of course, it is possible that this spelling was a printer's error and not the writer's intended orthography.[33] Indeed, the first edition of Motteville's memoirs was printed after her death. But even if the slippage between the fate of the woman and that of the fetus was a printer's error, it was also a telling (and even repeated) Freudian slip. Not only do dictionaries make the connection between the skirt and the protection of its wearer, but so does the anecdotal story of the style's origin: Queen Juana of Portugal was supposed to have invented the fashion to hide a pregnancy that apparently could not have been caused by her invalid husband. This same association crops up in John Webster's 1623 play, *The Duchess of Malfi*: when Bosolo suspects that the Duchess is concealing a pregnancy and bemoans "these bawd farthingales" that impede his view.[34] The spelling in Motteville's memoirs thus reflected an established perception, subtly shifting the protected position from fetus to woman, eliding the two identities since, in fact, the *garde-infant* protected the woman by making her childlike, *infans* or silent, in its covering or concealing the "pregnant" or adult female body. This silencing allowed the wearer of the farthingale to participate in court events by providing a social or symbolic contour at a moment when her own shape would have been considered decidedly unappealing or transgressive, even disruptive, of the categories of sociability or desirability. Is it not possible that what might appear to be a linguistic slip on the part of Madame de Motteville (if not a printer's error) might actually not have been a faux-pas at all, but subtle pun made by a woman who, as the daughter of a Spanish mother and French father, was fully bilingual and bicultural?[35] As such, Madame de Motteville would have had a unique perspective on the boundaries of clothing and body, as well as on the experience of crossing cultures, a perspective gained from contact with her mother and her queen.

As an aide to the queen, Motteville may also have been uniquely positioned to point out what might be troubling or anxiety-provoking within this political scenario of the treaty marriage: the female as site of concealment.[36] Although characterized as a *bona roba*, material of value, the infanta's actual worth would have been a large question mark under her voluminous skirt. It is interesting in this light that in Grammont's report to Mazarin on the mission to Madrid mentioned above, the Mareschal underscored his inability to describe the infanta's figure because "the height of her shoes and her farthingale, two ells in size" concealed it. If the new queen was *una bona roba*, the signifier of her worth, her clothing, blocked a view of the goods. Or, it raised the issue of the correspondence between the visible material of the skirt and the invisible material of the body. The obfuscation highlighted the body under the goods.

Indeed, the goods for the French would not be the infanta's shape [*taille*] or sex appeal, or at least only insofar it affected her ability to bear the royal seed and produce heirs to the Bourbon and, the French hoped, Hapsburg thrones.[37] Such virtual fecundity had to be suggested in presenting the new queen to her country, even if it threatened the image of her virginity, the purity necessary for symbolic reasons. The dilemma facing the Bourbon imagination in this case, therefore, was how to suggest the infanta's virginity—that she was a blank screen upon which the French could play out or write their scenario of conquest—without negating her fecundity, something necessary, but potentially menacing because virtual (being in essence or effect, but not in fact). The Spanish skirt, with its connotations of pregnancy, may have aided in projecting that contradictory message. It is interesting in this case that the very aspect of being virtual is suggested by one of the French terms for the farthingale, *vertugadin*. Although the term would seem to imply that it is an item that guards virtue, the word's etymology actually points to a more subtle issue. *Vertugadin* comes from the Middle French and Old Spanish for verdant, green, as well as for the young shoot of a tree.[38] Thus, the skirt does not actually guard virtue, but suggests instead a presence that is incipient (and unpredictable) because not yet ripe or mature. That incipience suggested by the skirt was what made the infanta *una bona roba*, a good value for the Bourbon dynasty. It also made her problematic, since the foreign barrier suggested the Bourbon body politic's inability to penetrate Spain. This political anxiety was grounded by the possible suggestion of Bourbon sexual impotency or effeminacy. While Louis

XIV's escapades with Mazarin's niece displayed his own virility as
well as his full recovery from a near-fatal illness while on campaign
in Flanders in 1658, it was no secret that Louis' father, Louis XIII,
had almost failed to impregnate his own infanta.

Finding the Queen's Body

The *guardainfante* thus encircles the *infanta*, suggesting the
embryonic, potential dauphins and infantas, while also making her
inaccessible for Louis XIV's sexual conquest, as the queen mother
had maintained. For the *infante*, or baby, had to be brought out by
the French in their display of the body of the infanta to the whole
world. Her potential as breeder had to be highlighted in order for
the Spanish princess to become a French queen. To do so illustrated
that the infanta was available for their political appropriation or
encoding (insemination), and demonstrated that the French were
symbolically and sexually potent. But if the infanta had to be
disrobed to show she was *una bona roba*, she also had to be reclothed
in order to make her readable or attractive, as the queen had also
made clear. The French did not actually want to display the infanta's
body, but they had to indicate that it existed and functioned for
them.[39] Anxieties about the treaty with Spain were thus figured via
the reclothing of the infanta; anything her clothing concealed,
revealed, or suggested had to be quickly eliminated. She therefore
had to be transformed or reclothed before the marriage was con-
summated in a rite of passage that skirted the human body in
working out social and political uncertainties.[40]

That such rerobing occurred was underlined by *La Pompe* in its
description of the ensuing ceremonies. According to the pamphlet,
the infanta appeared at Mass the next day "in Spanish clothing,
coiffed half in the French style," which made her "more beautiful
and more attractive than she had looked to that point."[41] The
process was completed a day later when the infanta appeared at the
French Marriage Mass "clothed in the French style in a dress of
white brocade, still coiffed a bit in the Spanish manner, the crown
on her head enriched with many gems, & the Cape of the Queen

which was of blue velour strewn with gold fleurs-de-lys and lined with ermine."[42] At the Wedding Mass, María Teresa was finally purged of protective Spanish clothing, her body rewrapped to produce the perfect symbol of French queenship. Without her Spanish skirt, the new French queen retained only a pleasing and safely positioned hint of that which had been erased since she was "still coiffed a bit in the Spanish manner." Covered in *fleurs-de-lys* like her allegorical sisters Flanders and France from the 1659 almanac engraving, the infanta had been appropriated as an allegory of French triumph and potency.

Or, rather, she would have been had the pamphlet ended its discussion of the infanta's transformation there and moved on to more formulaic topics such as naming the nobility in attendance, recounting what was said at the Mass, or chronicling what occurred the next day. Instead, the pamphlet followed the royal family back to its quarters from church: "The Royal party arrived at the Queen Mother's quarters at around 2:30: The queen was dripping with sweat [*toute en eau*] because of the weight of her clothing, of her gems and of her large cape, she was undressed and put to bed where she dined alone."[43] Shifting focus from the now rectified clothing of María Teresa to her body, the pamphlet focuses on the reaction of the infanta, now a queen, to the weight of her new heritage. In so doing, the narrative seems to underscore the difficulty of making queens into symbols. For, if wrapping an infanta in ermine in June in the Pyrenees was meant to produce a French queen, it also produced a sweaty one! It produced a queen who did not slide easily into her role as symbol when the Spanish body was un-wrapped to verify the nature of the French queen's (biological) body. Indeed it seems, at least upon a first reading, that unwrapping and rewrapping the Spanish infanta did not integrate her into the new French family. Rather it served, once again, to separate the infanta from her new family when "she was undressed and put in bed where she dined alone," removed from her new family who remained in the larger public sphere of the court activities follow-ing the Mass.

It is tempting at this point to argue that the sweat of the infanta is a sign of her resistance to the French program. For in seventeenth-century France, a society that defined status and position by style and that was in the process of redefining notions of bodily cleanliness, sweat did not result in bathing the body, but required the cleansing or changing of clothing.[44] Thus, one might conjecture that while such interrupting detail may have denigrated the infanta, it may also have allowed her some resistance to the French symbolic matrix, or at least its clothing. The removal of the infanta's French garb did not reveal her purity (or lack thereof) as much as it underlined that there was an uncontrollable body present under the signs of Frenchness imposed on it. In so doing it sullied the symbolic display of power by interrupting the more formal and formulaic language of royal ceremonial and by underlining the dissonance between the idealized image of the queen and the reality of the infanta.

The description of the queen's sweating might thus be seen as suggesting the new queen's body engaged in a habitus of the abject: her bodily fluids corrupted the rules or boundaries of the French symbolic system from within, more precisely from the dampened space between the Spanish body and the French fashion system. One might think here in terms of the Kristevian notion of abjection in which the sweating infanta would be characterized as being outside, and thus disruptive to acceptable categories. In Kristeva's schema, "[I]t is thus not the lack of cleanliness or health that causes abjection but what disturbs identity, system, order." According to Kristeva, the abject is "[w]hat does not respect borders, positions, rules. The in-between, the ambiguous, the composite."[45] In the case of the infanta, even if the processes of abjection as theorized by Kristeva are capable of producing meaning, the abject is that which has no position within the system, or whose position is neither inside nor outside. The abject is always liminal, just as is the infanta. She is both the organizing center of attention who produces the meaning for nuptial fictions, and she is the displaced or decentered artifact of the marriage ritual since she is no longer Spanish, but not really French. She is betwixt and between, the abject (and uncomfortable) producer of (at times unsettling) meanings.

It is important to note that the description of a queen sweating during her Marriage Mass is not unique to the marriage of Louis XIV. While significantly absent from correspondence, memoirs, and other pamphlets, this incident seems to have been a traditional element of the French Bourbon–Hapsburg marriage ritual, part of the choreography of the event, or at least of its reporting. A similar incident can be found in the official account of Louis XIII's wedding written by the Jesuit François Garasse: *La Royalle Reception de leurs Maiestez tres-chrestiennes en la ville de Bourdeaux, ou le Siecle d'or ramené par les alliances de France et d'Espagne, recueilli par le commandement du Roy.*[46] Although much longer and detailed than *La Pompe*, this official account of the 1615 Bourbon–Hapsburg wedding does not discuss details of the new queen's sartorial transformation, perhaps because French and Spanish fashion for women was similar in 1615. It does, however, offer a description of the new queen during the Marriage Mass that may be a precedent for the one examined here. In the account, Anne of Austria is described as wearing the traditional cape covered with *fleurs-de-lys*, "dressed majestically, the Crown of gold on her head, the royal dress of purple velour and innumerable *fleurs-de-lys*, the cape of the same with a long train and lined in ermine, carried by three Princesses." Her body also reacts to this attire: "The King looked at her often laughing: she [the queen], although burdened by the weight of the robes and gems and sweating large drops [suant à grosses gouttes], could not contain herself from smiling back at him, & at the Duc de Monte Leone, the ambassador from Spain, with a marvelous grace and majesty."[47] Despite the fact that this detail appears in both seventeenth-century Bourbon–Hapsburg marriages, historians have attributed it simply to the enormous weight of the ceremonial clothing worn by the new queens.[48] Their interpretation is not inappropriate. The texts themselves certainly suggest a link between the richness of the French clothing and the sweating of the formerly Spanish (now French) bodies. Nonetheless, one should read these passages less literally since the king also wears heavy clothing and gems during the ceremonial but he is never described in the literature as *tout en eau*. On the contrary, no such physiological reaction on the part of

the king is depicted in the texts in question. Clearly, sweat in these
marriages (and perhaps physical affect in general) lies in the domain
of the symbolic apparatus of representing queens.

The sweating queen signifies something important and necessary about Spanish–Hapsburg princesses who would be French
queens, something that demonstrates a Hapsburg infanta's worth to
the Bourbon dynasty, while also making her interesting to the eager
readers of these texts. In that sense, Anne of Austria's large, almost
luscious drops of sweat (*grosses gouttes*, not droplets or *gouttelettes*)
might be likened to another item adorning her face: her amorous
smile. Since smiles (along with gazes) were an important *topos* in
courtly romance, a link can be made between adorning sweat and
sexual desire. Indeed, this connection was available in seventeenth-
century erotica. For example, the 1610 best seller, *Erotomania or A
Treatise Discoursing of the Essence, Causes, Symptomes, Prognosticks, and
Cure of Love or Erotic Melancholy*, by Jacques Ferrand, recounts the
effects on a man of seeing the woman he loved: "for so soon as she
ever but entered into the Chamber, his colour changed, his speech
was stopped, his lookes were smiling, and pleasant, or else . . . his
face burned, and hee was all in a sweat, his Pulse beat very disorderly,
and lastly his heart failed him: he grew pale, amazed, astonished
often with such like symptomes which (as *Sapho* affirmed) are wont
to appear in Melancholy Lovers."[49] When Ferrand remarks that
the symptoms his melancholy lover exhibits are like those described
by Sappho in her *Sonnet 31*,[50] it becomes apparent that although he
takes the example of the male lover, the libido that sweat indicates
is not limited to the male, but might also be a characteristic of the
female. That fact, too, was a commonality of contemporary erotic
literature. In his *Conjugal Love; or Pleasures of the Marriage Bed
Considered*, Nicolas Venette devotes an entire chapter to the subject
of the libidinous woman. In this chapter ("The Signs of a Woman
who is of hot Constitution, and naturally prone to the Act of
Copulation"), Venette argues that one can identify ardent women
by their sweet-smelling sweat.[51] This olfactory libidinality echoes
Ferrand's original French which read not simply sweat, but *sueurs
acres*, or pungent sweat.[52]

In light of these texts, it is clear Anne of Austria was not just described as adorned by French ceremonial clothing during the Mass in Bordeaux in October 1615, but also by her sweet, sweaty, libidinous desire for her new husband.[53] Such adornment was not gratuitous titillation. In underlining the new queen's libido and her ripeness for the picking, the description not only piqued reader interest, but also underlined the availability of the new queen for what would be her major role in state building: procreation, reproducing, and thus ensuring the continuation of the Bourbon lineage. Indeed, writers on sexuality (in both scientific and pseudo-scientific texts) generally attributed generative powers to wet heat in both men and women.[54] Adorned by her swe(a)et desire, Anne of Austria was thus set into a familiar system for understanding human biology, one that linked affect with the physical fluxes of the body. Since the understanding of physiology in early modern Europe was no less culturally constructed than was fashion, humor theory can also be seen as a manner in which to symbolize and work out anxieties about how the body functions in the biological, gendered, or politicized world. As Thomas Laqueur has noted, "the history of anatomy during the Renaissance suggests that the anatomical representation of male and female is dependent on the cultural politics of representation and illusion, not on evidence about organs, ducts, or blood vessels."[55] One might say along with Laqueur that if "anatomy is representational strategy,"[56] so is sweat. As such, the depiction of the infanta's sweat can be seen as similar to remarks about her unwieldy Spanish skirt. Both *topoi* offer a way to symbolize and work out anxieties about the queen's body and its readiness for reproducing the body politic.

If the readiness of the new queen for reproduction is an issue fraught with anxiety for the Bourbon dynasty, that is because the reality that a queen's body (and not simply her clothing or the sweat that also enrobes it) could be constitutive of the display of monarchical power unsettles established notions of the body politic—normally figured by a divine (disembodied) monarchical figure. Indeed, a sovereign's mortal body was normally considered a threat to the body politic, as, for example, in the case of the monarch's dead body, which Ralph Giesey has shown unsettled rites of succession in the Renaissance, or that of Marie-Antoinette's sexual body, which Lynn Hunt has demonstrated played a role in the state unbuilding of the Revolutionary tribunal.[57] The new queen's "grosses gouttes" of libidinous desire, on the other hand, are produced in the service of buttressing political culture. In underlining what Foucault would term the productive heterosociality of royal marriage, they legitimatize a (shaky) political alliance between two adversarial nations.[58]

By stressing the practical (procreative, heterosocial) dimensions of lawful alliance, the former Spanish infanta's sweat serves less to figure her resistance to being transformed into a French queen than to drive home the permanent (reproducing) nature of the Bourbon dynasty. As such, making sweat in royal marriage was a necessary part of making the state. That may be why its description had a place in official texts.[59] Nonetheless, such a representational strategy also had its dangers. For if the accounts of María Teresa's sartorial transformation adjudicated tensions between Bourbon France and Hapsburg Spain, details about her sweat may have allowed the emergence of tensions over the importance of the mortal body to the French state. This possibility seems especially evident in a symbolic process that relies on metonymy. In metonymy, something that is part of the queen, sweat or the skirt, is used to represent her. This representational strategy should be contrasted to metaphor, a figure in which a word or image denotes something else by being used *in the place of it* as an analogy—as, for example, referring to the king to represent the state. With its close relationship between signifier and signified, however, metonymy underlines the connection between the procreating body and the state and not its separation.

It is not surprising that nuptial fictions utilize metonymic images since they are based on combination, while metaphor, about replacement, is more akin to the substitutional algebra of absolutism seen in the funeral ritual. Invoked by metonymy, the queen's sweat is not an arbitrary signifier, but one that reproduces the adjudicatory process occurring within an algebra that combines depictions of the body and images of the body politic. In this context, sweat is the result of the labor of that difficult process. For taking a foreign princess and making her into symbolic capital, especially where her importance to the treasury is intimately dependent on the performance of her body, is a laborious process in a symbolic economy rooted in substitutional metaphors of the body politic. Such labor produces anxiety, particularly in a tradition where sovereignty is not supposed to construct itself. Monarchs are not made, but are born into divine entitlement. If they are constructed, the reigning notions of classical aesthetics dictate that the effort of such artistry is always to be hidden. This was certainly the case by 1660, and the image of the absolutist monarch honed by both Richelieu and Mazarin, soon to be perfected by Louis XIV, was no exception to the model.[60] In 1660, therefore, any labor of constructing the monarch (especially in relation to his bride) was certain to produce something sticky.

In the slippage from the round skirt to the round drops, the slippery issue of constructing symbols threatens to emerge. If such displacement occurs in the early representations of the queen, that may be because she is being depicted in a moment of passage (from Spain to France, from infanta to queen, and from body to image or symbol). Anthropologists have shown how rituals adjudicate tensions around liminal or ambiguous moments such as marriage and childbirth. At such times, changes of status threaten to unsettle social order. In this case, marriage may be seen as a liminal phenomenon, a ceremony of combination marked by the infanta's passage from Spain to France, a linking of two countries. While this combinatory process is necessary to the ongoing representation of a stable Bourbon body politic, it is also one that may alter it. Interestingly, anthropologists have noted that rituals of transition or passage often utilize water, a protean and changeable entity to suggest fertility.[61] But water is inherently unstable and the turbulent waters of the treaty marriage are complicated territory for the French to navigate. Nonetheless, like the river they cross to obtain their infanta, María Teresa is a body they need to cross over and put behind them.

(Re)Casting the Body Politic

When Anne of Austria and María Teresa sweat, they might be said to be reacting to the labor of their symbolic processing. The treatment they receive in their presentation reflects the press's effort to ward off chaos, reorganize ideas about the state, and rearrange the royal family (or dynasty). But such a representation has trouble freeing itself from the queen's body and clings to areas contiguous to the body (sex, tight skirts, libidinous sweat) in order to capture reader interest. In this slippage from the body to the round skirt or round drops, the stickiest issue emerges as that of the necessity of the queen's body for reproducing the state (both symbolically and biologically). If, as Mary Douglas has argued, "rituals concerning excreta, breast milk, saliva, and the rest" are symbols for the complex structures of the state,"[62] these figures are metonymic ones in which fungible fluids, like sweat, do not stand in for or simply reflect the state, as Douglas suggests, but offer up a constitutive piece of it.

The description of the infanta thus disrobes or lays bare at least one long-skirted scenario of the portrayal of sovereignty: the participation of the female body in the workings of the body politic. It also raises the issue of whether there can be clear distinctions between symbols and what they portray, or if the boundaries may be less clear. It should not be surprising that such a problem arises around a marriage treaty in which the new queen not only stands in for the former enemy, but *is* the former enemy. It also suggests that the French narrative attempts to maintain boundaries (between France and Spain, male and female, divine and mortal) that may not be so easily defended.

La Pompe concludes by attempting to reassert such boundaries when it describes what occurs after the Mass (and the sweating): the new queen dresses herself and joins the royal family and the minister to "throw a large quantity of gold and silver medals to the crowds of people and soldiers."[63] In moving from a description of the sweaty, ripe body to one of throwing of medals, the pamphlet seems to take distance from the momentary lapse into metonymy. Since the nuptial fiction is ultimately about raising the stock of the monarchy, it is not surprising that a description of throwing medals should follow such a lapse. For with it, the regime returns from the watery milieu of sweat (or the impermanence of fashion), to more solid and permanent ground, the image of the king and queen forged in the hard material of the medal, a form more easily appraised and distributed.[64] Instead of describing bodily processes centering on the unknown, here the focus is on a symbol detachable from the king's mortal body, one meant to immortalize the king's divine power. Attention is thus shifted from the couple, to images of them embossed on material that is so solid and valuable it can stand in for the royal body.

It is noteworthy that comments about the new queen's clothing disappear at this point in the narrative, which simply states that "The queen dresses." Commentary on clothing is replaced with details about the medals embossed with "the figure of the King & of the Queen on one side, with their names and titles, & on the other a beautiful day, with a golden rain, the device: no greater joy [*non laetior alter*]" (Figure 10).[65] It is also significant that what is embossed on the medals does not stray far from the themes of the pamphlet discussed here. For not only does the emblem glorify the monumental body, but it returns to the watery milieu. If the device announces that "there is no greater joy," that is because of the golden rain described in the pamphlet. It fertilizes the barren land figured on the medal below the motto about joy. The rain is significant because it is a reference to the myth of Jupiter and the Danaë. In the legend, Danaë, the daughter of the king of Argos, is imprisoned by her father, who has been warned by an oracle that she will bear a child who will kill him. But the ever-protean and amorous Jupiter nonetheless reaches Danaë by descending to her as a shower of gold. In his list of the figurative uses of the word rain, Furetière makes reference to this myth: "Jupiter changed himself into a golden *rain* in order to possess [*jouïr de*] Danaë."[66] On the medal for the marriage, the arid earth would be the personification of Danaë, being fertilized by Jupiter, who is the golden rain.

Louis' medals reenact the golden rain of the myth. They are thrown or sent out to fertilize, not Danaë, but the crowd present and the readers of the description, offering both groups solid images of fluids. If Jupiter/Louis' gold ejaculation reminds us of the sweaty infanta enveloped by the cape of gold *fleurs-de-lys*, his fertility is figured metaphorically and not metonymically. The separation of the signifier and its signified is underscored by the very act of the throwing. Medals are neither skirts nor drops of sweat gliding down the body. They are objects thrown off and separated from the body. Note, as well, that the theme developed for the queen is now transferred to the king. The water and its metonymic relation have become totally allegorized, placed onto the mythic realm to serve as a safe metaphor for impregnation, moving the decidedly sticky issue of the role of the queen in the body politic onto firmer and drier ground in symbols forged to be easily grasped.[67] These symbols or coins, unlike the queen, do not soil the royal raiment of power with the stickier substances of the construction of sovereignty.

This chapter began by suggesting that the political agenda of the Treaty of the Pyrenees was transposed onto the queen's body (via fashion), which served as a model or microcosm of society. Seen as such, however, the body seemed to be a rather static model, the passive receptor or mirror of another scenario. After reading an official pamphlet in which issues of Bourbon hegemony are replayed on the body of the Hapsburg princess at the moment of her passage into France, one may question if the equation between body and society is simply one-sided. The sweat on the body of the infanta actually seems to add a dynamic to the analogy, speaking for or producing a new queen, albeit in a somewhat unexpected manner, via a bodily process that unsettled the categories organizing the scenario of the Bourbon conquest of the Spanish Hapsburg (woman). One might characterize the bodily process of sweat as a habitus of the abject that corrupts the rules or boundaries of the French symbolic system from within, more precisely from the dampened space between the Spanish body and the French fashion system. This transgressive refashioning of the body politic within the highly choreographed and ritualized atmosphere of the court society offers a more complex notion of the relation between body and state, one that supersedes Mary Douglas' idea that the first is a model for the second.

In her model, Douglas set up a metaphoric relationship between the body and society. A more accurate means of describing the representation of the infanta's body may be to read it in terms proposed by Luce Irigaray, for whom the feminine is the fluid and its force is comparable to the complex dynamics of slippery matter:

> It is already getting around—at what rate? in what context? in spite of what resistances?—that women diffuse themselves according to the modalities scarcely compatible with the framework of the ruling symbolics. Which doesn't happen without causing some turbulence, we might even say some whirlwinds, that ought to be reconfined within solid walls of principle, to keep from spreading to infinity. Otherwise they might even go so far as to disturb the third agency designated as the real—a transgression and confusion of boundaries that is important to restore to their proper order.[68]

While Irigaray's association of women with water is admittedly essentialist, such a connection between the potentially transgressive nature of turbulent fluid mechanics and the similarly disruptive metonymy of the infanta's sweaty body allows us to revise Douglas' equation of society with the body. For after reading *La Pompe*, it becomes evident that the relation between body and society is more dynamic, that the body can actually exert force on society and its representations. In this sense, the infanta's body with its excreta can no longer be understood simply as a model or mirror for the prince (and his absolutist scenario), but as energy or force necessary to the momentum of that sovereign body that may *also exert force on it*. The turbulent eddies such energy gives off produce the dialectic at the center of nuptial fictions. How this energy is channeled to serve the regime is the subject of the next two chapters, which examine the practices of creating and disseminating the images that are simultaneously tradable signs and dynamic forces.

CHAPTER 3

Views from the Border

After the June 1660 publication of *La Pompe*, the apparatus for constructing and disseminating nuptial fictions began functioning at top speed as a myriad of pamphlets appeared describing the activities at the border. Other media would also reproduce images from the border: almanac engravings for the year 1661 commemorated scenes from the marriage and panels from Lebrun's tapestry history of Louis XIV produced in 1670 refashioned images of the ceremonies.[1] But the ongoing and immediate nature of the June 1660 events necessitated a form that could portray the seriality of the activities in a timely manner. Quickly written, cheaply and easily produced and distributed, occasional pamphlets could best disseminate the detailed reports that kept the treaty marriage in public view while its events unfolded far from the centers of population. As a body performing in the service of state building, however, the occasional pamphlet was no more a static format for figuring the body politic than was the image of the new queen.

Like the Spanish princess, the pamphlet was a body fashioned by the state. It could not appear without official "clothing," the royal *privilège* accorded to the publisher (or to the author and ceded to the publisher). *La Pompe*, for example, was produced directly by the king's printers. In Paris, texts fewer than twelve pages could be printed with permission from the local police.[2] Longer works required a formal *privilège* from government officials. By law, the *privilège* had to be entered into the registers of the Book Syndic and an abstract of its official text had to be printed in the front of the volume.[3] The regime thus regulated print through appointment of official printers, surveillance of independent publishers and book vendors, and by pressing the institutions of print culture into the service of the regime in exchange for economic assurances to the industry. But if the regime fashioned the print industry, it was also fashioned by print. Mazarin depended on print for the description and dissemination of his and the king's activities. To see the king and his minister on the border of France and Spain, it was necessary to read about them. Pamphlets were one more body propping up the king. Similar to the queen's body, they were dynamic, exerting force on the images they reproduced, giving them shape and momentum.

Like the relationship between the queen and the body politic described in the previous chapter, the alliance between the culture of absolutism and that of print (both the corporations organizing print culture and the individuals working within that corporate structure) was a complex collaboration. On the one hand, the pamphlet supported the regime by producing positive images of it. On the other hand, in 1660, the pamphlet was strongly identified with threats to moral and political stability. It was still thought of as the purveyor of stories about sensational crimes that it had often been during the Renaissance. It was also associated with the subversion it had promoted more recently during the Fronde.[4] Indeed, the enormous corpus of pamphlets engaging in satirical attacks on the monarchy published during that period brought the English word "pamphlet" to France in 1653 with the connotation of libel.[5] Not surprisingly, a large number of decrees and ordinances regulating the distribution and publication of printed works were issued in the ten years between the Fronde and the marriage. In February 1658, for example, the composition and distribution of *gazettes à la main*, handwritten pamphlets, a close relative of occasional pamphlets, were prohibited under pain of corporal punishment.[6] In June 1659, general *privilèges* accorded to authors for series of books to be published over a number of years were revoked, obligating book-sellers and printers to obtain separate authorization for every volume published.[7] Such prohibitions established tight control over what circulated in the streets of the realm and made it less risky for the absolutist regime to rely heavily on print for advertising its diplo-matic triumphs. To that end, the government monitored, or, in Foucauldian terms, "policed" the *privilèges* its agents awarded to report on the marriage. The awarding of such permissions by the government thus encouraged the production of pamphlets favorable to the king if only because they afforded him visibility. Wrapping the regime's diplomatic activities in the kind of sensational stories for which it was best known, the pamphlet could be expected to draw in a wide and eager readership.

The absolutist state thus entered into a wary compact with a formerly antagonistic form in which nuptial fictions were con-structed (and deconstructed) by a network of complementary and competing interests determined by Mazarin, the king, journalists, and booksellers. Theirs was a symbiotic relationship in which everyone would gain: the king and Mazarin had images of their prowess reported and distributed by journalists, booksellers, and printers, who likewise profited from their collaboration. All these groups utilized nuptial fictions to increase their visibility and estab-lish their importance. Working together, they attempted to tran-scend their shaky pasts, the Bourbon regime reestablishing its authority, and the pamphlet form and its producers rehabilitating themselves after the Fronde.

The discussion of the infanta's fashioning has already pointed toward this collaboration. The pamphlet analyzed extensively in Chapter Two was produced in Toulouse by "The King's printers" [*Imprimeurs ordinaires du Roy*], who were assured government pa-tronage for jobs such as printing edicts and other official materials. Indeed, they were also called upon to publish a copy of the marriage contract.[8] The report from the border was apparently official work. The printer in Toulouse also benefited from being able to have his text reprinted and sold in Paris by a prominent producer of pamphlet literature, Jean Promé.[9] But beyond these details, the publication history of *La Pompe* sheds little light on the network of connecting forces that forged the nuptial images.[10] More can be learned by examining the work of Jean Baptiste Loyson, the Parisian book-seller who published the largest number of pamphlets about the treaty marriage. Loyson was the only one to publish descriptions of the treaty negotiations. He also produced the majority of pamphlets concerning events on the border, the voyage back to Paris, and the Paris entry of the king and queen.[11] In all, Loyson published at least thirty-four titles on the marriage. Unlike others who published on this topic, many of Loyson's texts appeared in multiple editions. The summary of the *privilège* printed in the front of each pamphlet explains why Loyson's texts are so pervasive in the marriage archive. On December 5, 1659, he had been awarded official permission to print and sell *The Summary of the History containing the true Relation of the Voyage of the King, and of his Eminence for the compact of the marriage of his Majesty and of the General Peace. Composed by Mr. F.C.* [emphasis in text].[12] Note that despite laws requiring that publishers print an abstract of their *privilège* in their texts, most pamphlets concerning the marriage did not include such information. Perhaps Loyson followed the law because he was one of the few publishers of pamphlets about the marriage to have applied to the Syndic for an official *privilège*. He may have done so because he intended to publish pamphlets longer than twelve pages. Pamphlets less than that length could receive permission directly from the police.[13] Loyson may also have followed the rules because his was essentially a blanket permission, the kind no longer officially awarded authors as of June 1659.

Such an authorization that allowed publication of a series of texts without repeated request to publish indicates great confidence in the publisher-bookseller and in F.C., the author of the texts, also mentioned explicitly in the extract. F.C. was François Colletet, son of the noted poet and theorist Guillaume Colletet. Along with Pierre Corneille and his brother Thomas, Guillaume Colletet was one of five authors Louis XIII's minister Richelieu called upon to

collaborate in writing dramatic works.[14] That collaboration served
to anchor the alliance between art and political power so central to
the evolution of French absolutism. When Guillaume died earlier
in 1659, François continued the family tradition of service to the
monarchy and its ministry.[15] While never to become an important
author in his own right, François did compose and publish poetry
before he turned to such activities as writing pamphlets, putting out
his own newspaper, and, when that failed, writing guides to Paris.
It is not without significance, furthermore, that the younger Colletet
was imprisoned for three years by the Spaniards in Luxembourg,
having been arrested in 1651 while on his way to offer his services
to Mazarin, who had been driven into exile, at least in part, by a
pamphlet war. Mazarin had, of course, returned to power by the
time Loyson (and Colletet) were granted the exclusive right to
report on the marriage.[16]

Loyson took advantage of the privilege soon after receiving it,
publishing four twelve-page pamphlets describing the ongoing
negotiations of the treaty: *Journal Contenant La Relation Veritable et
Fidelle du Voyage du Roy, & de Son Eminence, Pour le Traitté du Mariage
de Sa Majesté, & de la Paix Generale* (1659); *Suitte du Journal Historique
Contenant la Relation Veritable et Fidele du Voyage du Roy, & de son
Eminence* . . . (1659); *Journal Historique, Contenant la Relation Veritable
et Fidele Du Voyage du Roy* . . . *Journal Troisiesme* (1659); *Quatriesme
Journal Historique, Contenant La Relation Veritable et Fidele* . . .
(1660).[17] The series was later revised, renumbered, and reissued in
one volume.[18] By the time the pamphlets were reissued, the peace
treaty had been negotiated, the Duke of Grammont had traveled to
Madrid to formally request the infanta's hand in marriage, and the
French and Spanish courts had assembled on the Pyrenees border.
When Loyson and Colletet began producing pamphlets again in late
June 1660, they turned their attention to the encounter on the
border for the marriage. Descriptions of this meeting must have
provided Loyson his greatest profit, there evidently being sufficient
interest in (or governmental underwriting of) the material to assure
multiple editions of these texts, even after the appearance of *La
Pompe*. These reports include such titles as: *La Nouvelle Relation*

Contenant L'Entreveue et Serments des Roys, pour L'Entiere Execution de la Paix. Ensemble Toutes les Particularitez & Ceremonies qui se sont faites au Mariage du Roy, & de L'Infante d'Espagne. Avec tout ce qui s'est passé de plus remarquable entre ces deux puissants Monarques jusqu'à leur depart (four editions), and *La Suitte de la Nouvelle Relation Contenant la Marche de Leurs Majestez pour leur Retour en leur bonne Ville de Paris: Avec toutes les particularitez de ce qui s'est fait et passé en leur Reception aux magnifiques Entrées des Villes de leur passage jusqu'à present. Ensemble les Presens que sa Majesté, la Reyne Mere, Monsieur, & Son Eminence ont faits à nostre Incomparable Reyne* (two editions).[19] The marketability of these pamphlets indicates that the nuptial fictions' scenes from the border were of great interest to readers, to the regime, or more probably, to both.

Glimpses of Narrative Interest

La Nouvelle Relation Contenant L'Entreveue et Serments des Roys pour L'Entiere Execution de la Paix, the first pamphlet Loyson put out describing the events at the border, seems to have been the most popular one in the marriage archive. Produced in Paris early in the summer of 1660, soon after the publication of *La Pompe* in Toulouse, it appeared in four different editions, making it the single most reprinted of all the pamphlets on the treaty marriage. It was the "best-seller" of the marriage archive.[20] Even without opening *La Nouvelle Relation*, one can glean information as to how it organized its nuptial fictions. Its title page (Figure 11) announces what can be found inside—a new (not previously told) relation of the meetings of the two kings, their signing of the treaty, and all the (remarkable and particular) events of the ceremonies of the marriage up to the court's departure. Upon closer inspection, however, three elements take precedence: **Entreveue**, **Roys**, **Paix**. Printed in bold and produced in a larger typeface, the meeting between the kings about the peace is advertised as the central topic, the one meant to attract readers. But after reading the sixteen-page pamphlet, it becomes evident that the words in bold are misleading. The description of the meeting to sign the peace is not found at the center, but at the end of the text. It seems unlikely that such placement was meant to pique reader interest by deferring information, since the meeting is treated summarily, almost as an afterthought. In fact, images of such historical import as meetings between monarchs for peace are presented in the pamphlet only in terms of the particulars or details discussed. Such details include remarks about Philip IV's sadness upon leaving his daughter when he hands her over definitively, a description of the reunion between brother (Philip IV) and sister (Anne of Austria), and a detailed account of Louis XIV's first view of the new bride. These intimate accounts offer glimpses into domestic moments that seem to prop up the topics in bold print, formal subjects, the two kings, their meeting, and the peace. These formal topics take second place in the narrative tension of the text.

The presentation—wherein glimpses into private details carry along the public topic and offer it indirectly, the play between a direct presentation and a circuitous or mediated one—is similar to the strategy seen in the almanac engravings. Here the method is suggested in the notion proposed by the first large-print word, ENTREVEUE. The contemporary definition for this term given in Furetière's *Dictionnaire universel* is "a visit or meeting of two persons to see each other or speak to each other." Furetière's illustrative example for this term, "There was an interview [*entreveüe*] of the Kings of France and Spain on the frontier," is the event announced in bold in the title and which will be referred to here as an "interview." But there is also another possible meaning for the verb form *entrevoir*, from which *entreveue* is derived. Furetière defines this term as "To see imperfectly or in passing," and illustrates it by the following examples of indirect and at times illicit or obscured viewing: "The witness could not have recognized this murderer because he had only glimpsed him [*il ne le fait qu'entrevoir*]; I glimpse [*j'entrevoy*] something that shines through the thickness of this wood; this man is almost blind, he only glimpses [*il ne fait qu'entrevoir*], he does not distinguish objects well."[21] While the first definition of *entreveüe*—face-to-face encounter—is proposed in the title of the pamphlet as of legitimate interest to the reader, it is actually the second definition—glimpsed viewing—that takes precedence in the text. Indeed, it is the *entreveüe* in the second sense of the term, a glimpse that occurs in the liminal space of the border, the site of negotiation, political and familial rearrangement, clandestine views, and expectations, that offers a model for the dynamic economy of the occasional pamphlet. This activity will be referred here to as an "inter-view."

This second kind of glimpse or "inter-view" serves as the center of the *Nouvelle Relation* in a description of the king's first glimpse of his new bride. This scenario is not described in *La Pompe*. But its appearance in the marriage corpus is not surprising, since the generic scene of the first look between lovers is, as literary critic Jean Rousset has demonstrated, an exemplary episode for prose fiction, a narrative moment that engenders and organizes stories. According to Rousset, the scene's "quasi-ritualistic character" and its "ceremonies" and "protocols" offer narratives "a beginning and determine the choices that will reverberate throughout the future of the story and that of its characters."[22] Interestingly, the fiction of the first look is also a traditional element of French royal wedding rituals and protocols, providing narrative logic to the choreography of the event, or at least to descriptions of it, in official reports of the marriages of Louis's predecessors.[23]

Perhaps that is why François Colletet placed the scene at the center of *La Nouvelle Relation*. In the four pamphlets describing the treaty negotiation, Colletet relied heavily on poetry and allegory, including in his reports verses comparing each diplomatic figure to some mythic hero. Describing the events of June 1660, Colletet changed his narrative style, adopting "novelistic" overtones that look forward to the psychological novels of Lafayette and not back to the allegory of the pastoral form popular earlier in the century. For Colletet, scenes from the marriage lent themselves more readily to story-telling than allegorizing. Rather than constructing nuptial fictions using allegorical characters, as had the almanacs, the pamphlet writer took advantage of the sentimental dimension of the love story. Whereas the almanac had opposed history and allegory, the pamphlet and its producers organized the nuptial fictions by hybridizing fiction and history. Foreshadowing the popularity of the

historical novel a decade later, this interplay between history and
fiction offered the pamphlet and its producers an effective and
profitable strategy for organizing nuptial fictions. Examining the
pamphlets of Loyson and Colletet thus offers a case study of how
print culture (and its complex collaboration between printer, writer,
and state patronage) utilized the various gazes of history and fiction
(nuptial and otherwise) to promote its political culture.

Scenes from a Marriage

The scene of "the first look" in royal marriage most often occurs
in liminal spaces such as borders or provincial towns. In the marriage
of Louis XIV, it occurs on the Isle of the Conference in the middle
of the Bidassoa River, the frontier on which the French and the
Spanish met for the negotiations and signing of the marriage treaty.
The site, like the viewing that took place on it, marks the complex
relationship between the two dynasties. It was a carefully bisected
space, largely taken up by a building constructed especially for the
treaty negotiations to assure each side identical space (Figure 12).
Even the common meeting room was scrupulously divided between
France and Spain. Exactly equivalent, clearly demarcated areas for
each side were meant to aid an activity of joining. The symmetry
also highlights the fragility and liminality of the treaty marriage. Such
careful demarcation of boundaries, even on no-man's land, suggests
that the détente between the two longtime enemies might easily
break down without the concrete architectural supports and the
rules of protocol fashioning every step of the encounter. It is on this
highly circumscribed site that Louis XIV is described seeing his bride
for the first time.

Traditionally, such viewing is presented as unofficial and private. In this case, the viewing is slipped into a more formal
"interview," the reunion of Anne of Austria with the brother she
had not seen in 40 years, when the narrative indicates: "The Queen
Mother left at noon to go to the Isle of the Conference, where the
King of Spain had also come; and it was there that the long wished
for Meeting [*Entreueuë*—sic] would take place."[24] It is not without

reason that the text draws attention to when the queen mother leaves for the island. This piece of information highlights the separate departure of Louis XIV two hours later:

> At two o'clock the King got on his horse, followed by only ten or twelve Lords that he had named, the rest of the court by express order remained here . . . and with this little troupe the King, incognito [*incogneu*], approaching the isle of the Conference and following the project that had been laid out. He promptly alit at the end of the bridge, & followed only by his Captain of the Guards, crossed the bridge and entered into a small room where he found the Cardinal with Dom Louis of Haro and in order to content his Majesty, he saw through a jalousie, which looked out on the Room of the Conference, all that he had a passion to see and without being seen, but without being entirely satisfied; he made his way to another part of the Room, where the King of Spain & the Infanta with the Queen Mother and the King's brother were, and with the help of the Cardinal and Dom Louis of Haro who placed themselves in the outside of the open door of this room, the King behind them, which also covered up his scheme [*dessin*], saw the Queen, his spouse for a long time.[25]

The scene described is not spontaneous, but part of a series of planned events. Like the site on which it takes place, it is highly organized, "following the project that had been laid out." In this *mise-en-scène*, the king does not go to see his new bride openly. He is "*incogneu*." The term does not suggest to the seventeenth-century reader that the king was incognito, unrecognizable. Rather, as Furetière defines the term, it underlines that he traveled "without the pomp, ceremony, and ordinary retinue, and without the usual indications of [his] grandeur."[26] This same play between invisibility and (at least initially restrained) visibility announced by the idea of the king *incogneu* is reflected in the actual activity of the king once on the island. For when he arrives there (and presumably still following the prearranged scheme), the king does not make himself visible: he does not look openly at his new queen (or his new father-in-law, whom he was also seeing for the first time). Rather, his actions are hidden by a louvered window (a jalousie). This position is transgressive in its voyeurism. But it is also powerful because it is unilateral.

The king sees, but is not seen, engaging in a scopic or one-sided viewing position.

The strategy echoes that of one of Louis XIV's predecessors, Charles IX, who first viewed his new bride from within a small chamber in a castle that the king had entered in disguise. In the case of Charles IX's 1570 marriage, "the King came by horse from two leagues beyond Mezières where he was staying: and not wanting to be seen at the entry of the castle had passed through a casemate and dressed in disguise, the face covered by his coat, in order to see his destined wife."[27] Charles looked out at a bride unaware of his presence. The organization of Charles IX's first view of his bride positions the king in a casemate, a fortified position or chamber from which guns are fired from embrasures. From this space, Charles shot his gaze at his bride. This panoptic and militaristic view provided a precedent for Louis's equally penetrating gaze from behind the louvered window.

Unlike Louis XIV's panoptic view from behind the louvered window, however, that of Charles IX was a position of satisfaction and closure: after the secret viewing, Charles returned to his court where "he found the Queen his mother, with whom he congratulated himself, that he had found the Queen his wife to his taste and satisfaction."[28] For Louis XIV, however, the scopic or one-way viewing perspective, one from which the king could see "all that he had a passion to see and without being seen," did not offer such satisfaction or closure. In fact, the text draws attention to the fact that the king was not content with his position of invisibility behind the jalousie when it notes that Louis XIV could see the queen "without being seen, but without being entirely satisfied." In the phrase, the idea of invisibility is associated with (literally placed next to) the sentiment of dissatisfaction. This juxtaposition offers a contrast to the experience of Charles IX. Louis XIV was not content to be invisible. He needed to be seen in his act. Such an association is not surprising since the voyeuristic impulse is intimately connected to that of exhibitionism, the two being linked to narcissism, according to Freudian theory.[29] Perhaps that is why Louis XIV moved to the door of the room in which the infanta was sitting.

Even if the king was still somewhat hidden (and thus constrained by his position) when standing behind the two ministers, the organizers of the marriage treaty who "also covered up his scheme," he was surely more visible than when he gazed at his queen from behind the jalouise.

Louis XIV's desire to exhibit himself (to put himself on show) is characteristic of the mechanism of representation of the absolutist king as Louis Marin has detailed it for the case of the Sun King well established in his power.[30] In the material examined here, however, Louis XIV had not yet begun his personal rule. He was not at Versailles, a space he mastered for self-display. Nor was he displaying himself uniquely to the public he habitually frequented. On the frontier between France and Spain, he performed not just for French nobility, but also for Spanish nobles and militia, and certainly for the Spanish king, Philip IV, as well as the infanta, María Teresa. As former adversaries and new members of the family, these last two may be the spectators whose attention is the hardest to attract and to hold. Indeed, successive versions of the story embellish this particular incident to embroider the details of the king's visibility and the infanta's reaction to it.[31] In *La Nouvelle Relation*, the reaction to the king is deferred to the conclusion of the description, where it becomes the central focus:

> And some time after the King stopped there, he left; & at the end of the bridge, getting back upon his horse, he went for a ride along the river's edge, waiting for the King of Spain . . . who got back into his boat to descend the river with the tide, & on the bank of the river, at the place where the river was narrow enough, he saw the boat pass near by, saluting it in passing, as did the 10 or 12 Lords who were on foot, but a little behind him; those in the boat did not recognize the King: Nonetheless the daughter of Louis of Haro and the Infanta's Attendants, wanting to stand up to salute this little troupe, the Infanta was seen making a gesture with her hand to them not to stand up: But after the boat had passed within 10 steps of the port where the King was, he said, *This isn't good enough, it is necessary to push the gallantry further*; in saying this he remounted his horse, and going at a little gallop along the river he stopped again, but without getting down off his horse, near a point of land which extended far enough into the river, and from there he again saluted the boat, at the moment it

passed; & the King of Spain taking off his hat, kissing it at the point where he held it, bent his knee, which are two circumstances to note; and at the same time, the Infanta, that is today the Queen, having stood up, made a deep bow to the King who continued to gallop his horse, & saluting with his hat the boat which was moving off, made a half turn to the right & came back to find the Queen Mother.[32]

The difference between what occurs on the Isle of the Conference and what takes place on the riverbank is significant. On the island, Louis XIV spies on his new wife (and father-in-law) from behind a jalousie and then through a door, over the shoulders of the ministers who negotiated the treaty. On the riverbank, he looks openly at the Spaniards, first on foot, and then while galloping on his horse. He is no longer behind a jalousie, a door, or two ministers; it is others (his men) who are behind him. The first space is marked by stability. The building was constructed specifically to fix and stabilize the relations of power between two dynasties during the negotiation of a treaty. Everything in it is measured. In such a controlled space, the actions of the king are limited and he has trouble making himself visible. The second space, on the other hand, is marked by instability and movement. Everything on the riverbank is in motion: the earth washing away on the banks which change with the tide, the Spaniards floating in their boat, the boat descending the river with the tide, the king galloping on his horse. The riverbank is a site where it is difficult to make oneself noticeable because everything is in motion and transitory. This is a site where the actions of the king are difficult to choreograph because the actions of the Spaniards, whose attention he wishes to attract, are not permanent or settled.[33] To get attention in such a space and in front of such an audience, Louis XIV must make himself even more remarkable. To be seen in such a place requires the greatest possible mastery over the situation by the young king.

In moving onto the riverbank and attempting to attract the attention of his new bride, Louis XIV replays the scenario of the first view enacted in the 1615 Bourbon–Hapsburg marriage of his parents, Louis XIII and Anne of Austria. Louis and Anne's encounter did not occur on the border, but well inside the country, in an urban space, Castres, near Bordeaux. As such, the king of Spain would not have been present. Perhaps for these two reasons the space of the viewing was more easily mastered. Satisfaction was not hard to come by. Louis XIII found it by adopting two reciprocal and satisfying viewing positions:

> The King, wishing to see the above mentioned Dame without being recognized, went all the way to the mentioned place, Castres, & went into the lowest room of a Hostelry waiting at the window where there were bars and leaning on the Archbishop of Rheims and the Marquis of La Valette. The Queen's carriage having arrived opposite the window mentioned, the Duke of Epernon, who had come with several Lords & Gentlemen of the court in front of his Majesty and saluted him in this place, where the mentioned woman had her carriage stopped. Meanwhile the King and the Queen looked at each other. Because she had not missed being forewarned and the two were in this manner for a fairly long time.
>
> After this and when the greetings were accomplished, the Queen had her carriage depart, & she being gone, the King got back in his, which he made drive away more quickly in order to overtake that of the Queen & arrive in Bordeaux before her. Approaching the carriage of the Queen, he cried out that it should be stopped & regarded awhile the Queen, and she him, then took off his hat and she saluted him taking off her gloves, putting her hands together, raising them a bit, and lowering her head.[34]

As in the marriage of Louis XIV, there are also two stages of Louis XIII's viewing of his new bride. In both stages, however, the king and his new bride gaze directly at each other in the perfectly predictable and controllable symmetry of two protagonists whose positions are fixed and secure (the hostelry and the stopped coaches).[35]

In comparing these two models, it becomes evident that if Louis XIV is finally able to gain satisfaction in the scenario described, it is because he also manages to achieve such symmetry. But his task was more difficult than that of his father. For he had to master the fluid space of the river border and not that of the city inside France. That he managed to master the border space is indicated by the gestures of recognition made by King Philip IV and his daughter, the infanta.

The first removed his hat and bent his knee, "two circumstances to note," according to the narrator of the pamphlet, and the second made a deep bow. On horseback in an iconic pose of virile kings (particularly those of Spain, if one thinks of Velásquez),[36] Louis XIV is recognized by his former adversary, the one over whom he would hope to triumph in the treaty. In the exchange of gazes, nuptial fictions portray the king of France as triumphant. For if Louis XIV went to see his new queen, it was not simply out of romantic urge, but rather because the scene of the first view would have drawn an audience (of viewers on the shore or readers of pamphlets) interested in the scene of Louis XIV being recognized by a former enemy—at least that is how the pamphlet uses one nuptial fiction to serve another. The voyeur king behind the jalousie was not "content." To be content, it was necessary to see. To see, it was necessary to be seen. To be seen, it was necessary to be remarked upon. And to be remarked upon, a second perspective was necessary: that of spectators. The choreographed and unilateral perspective did not fulfill these criteria for Louis XIV. Rather, he had to perform on (and dominate) the slippery terrain of multiple perspectives or views.

The close reading of this passage suggests a model for the way nuptial fictions are placed into view by the occasional pamphlet. For the passage examined describes the king first during his viewing of his new queen and her father, Philip IV, in the organized space of the island and then in the mobile site of the riverbank. Paradoxically, the king is less a master, less visible, and less able to make himself noticeable in the first space where there is only one clear perspective offered, his own. The need for variation in the perspective is as important for the king as it is for the spectators, the readers of the nuptial fiction, who, in the beginning of the scenario, ally themselves with the position of the king and follow his directed, scopic gaze. That perspective is not satisfying because it offers only an incomplete glimpse. The readers are not satisfied because they are missing details about the scene. The gaze of Philip IV seems to complete the spectators' view, but this enlargement of perspective is only illusory. The gaze of Philip IV does not actually expand the view. It only underlines the staging of Louis XIV.

The narrative strategy in this story of the first view may be compared to the modern cinematographic technique known as the "shot-countershot," wherein the film gives the spectator the illusion of completing an initially limited viewpoint by shifting the camera's perspective back and forth between two interlocutors. The film's viewer feels that he or she is getting more complete information when able to see the scene of the encounter through the eyes of its protagonists. According to theoreticians of the cinematic gaze, however, while the multiplication of perspectives seems to offer the spectator the sense of seeing more clearly and completely, it actually serves to reinforce and elaborate the first viewpoint. The spectator is thus seduced by the illusion of having seen everything when in reality he or she has seen only what the director makes available.[37] In the pamphlet, the reader, in the same position as the viewer of the film, is caught in the visual snare of the story. The reader looks first through the eyes of Louis XIV and then looks at Louis XIV through the eyes of Philip IV (and his daughter). The image of the French king is thus reinforced for the reader-viewer, whose attention is sutured or attached to the scene by the illusion of variation and sense of completion such variation offers. Unlike the case of Louis XIII in which there are only two gazes, scenes of Louis XIV's marriage stage at least three viewpoints. For it is not just the perspective of Philip IV that attaches the reader, but also the oblique glance of the infanta who lowers her eyes. As the reader momentarily shifts to "look" through the infanta's eyes, however, he or she moves from the shot-countershot format which may be likened to the "Interview" between two kings, to the more complex inter-view or glimpse of and/or between them. In shifting paradigms, the infanta's averted gaze does not complete the scene of the formal meeting, since her viewpoint is not quite accessible. The textual variations on this moment stress this inaccessibility. The infanta's gaze is too fleeting and partial a perspective. Reminding the reader that there really is no one viewpoint and that one "sees" only what the "camera work" of the pamphlet (and its narrator) make available, this incomplete (because unknowable) gaze is the most enticing of all.

Multiple Privileges and Partial Gazes

One might surmise at this point that if the play of perspectives offers the king satisfaction and reinforces his presence, it may not offer him the mastery that the pamphlet seems to set up. If the scene offers a model in which multiple perspectives are necessary for the creation of mastery, it also offers, albeit obliquely, other perspectives on such mastery. For even if the story stages the king as protagonist, he is nonetheless not truly the agent of his mastery in it. That is because the king's visibility is choreographed according to the traditions of royal marriages, the exigencies of geography or the reactions of the Spaniards on the one hand, and according to the words of the journalist and his publisher on the other. The latter two actually have the final word on all the actions of the personages since reports on the marriage do not offer the perspective of the king alone, but also offer that of the journalist and the publisher who describe him. In fact, there may be a parallel between the mastery of the pamphlet's producers and that of the king produced by the pamphlet. For if the latter in his story is the most noticeable in the large and mobile space of the riverbank, the former also emerge out of a milieu marked by variation and mobility, the Parisian scene of print culture.[38] Such movement and incertitude is characteristic of pamphlet literature, a quickly created, easily distributed, and potentially subversive form. Of course it is not simply the physical geography of Paris that makes the form (and its producers) difficult to control. Rather it is the commercial geography, the various perquisites and interests of the booksellers [*libraires marchands*], the printers, and their *privilèges* that comprise the bustling Parisian sphere of print culture.

The scene of the first view therefore offers neither exclusively the scene of the king's viewpoint nor that of the journalist, but includes as well those involved in the writing and producing of occasional pamphlets. It is thus that the king can display himself to the largest public possible on the condition that his story is written, published, distributed, and read.[39] The king would have a certain control over the dissemination of the story of his marriage since no text could be published in France without official permission. Indeed, no illegal texts are found in the extant marriage archive. Of course, official authorization not only policed print culture, but also granted the publisher the sole right to report the events and accorded him the power (and financial advantage) of a scopic perspective. The texts examined in this study all had such official permission. The scene of the first view, however, suggests that the unilateral perspective is not the powerful (or satisfying) one. Other views are necessary for satisfaction (and success). It is not surprising, therefore, that there should have been not one officially sanctioned text publishing the account of the events of the marriage of the king on the French–Spanish border, but several. Such multiplicity permitted the proliferation of perspectives on the event and raised the stakes of constructing its nuptial fictions.

The pamphlet studied in Chapter Two, *La Pompe*, offered at least one other viewpoint. Its vantage was so different that it did not even describe the scene of the first view. One might wonder how such a text could have been published if Loyson had received the exclusive privilege for reporting on the treaty marriage in December 1659. There are several explanations as to why *La Pompe* did not encroach on Loyson's *privilège*. First, it was published in Toulouse, outside the jurisdiction of the Paris Book Syndic. Second, it was printed by the "King's printers," so it was probably sponsored by Mazarin as a stopgap to keep information flowing from the border while Colletet and Loyson processed and produced the reports they were receiving in Paris. The Paris edition of the text was probably protected for this same reason. *La Pompe* thus seems to offer an example of multiple publications being promoted by the state to increase its visibility. Loyson's text provided a second viewpoint. It functioned like the gaze of the Spanish king and his daughter. Once Loyson began publishing on the events at the border, no other viewpoints could be offered in Paris since Loyson did have the exclusive right to offer views from the border.

Or rather, almost no other viewpoints. For, despite the decree of June 1659 revoking all general *privilèges* to authors,[40] and despite Loyson's *privilège* of December 5, 1659, on May 16, his collaborator

François Colletet was granted a *privilège* to "arrange publication of
his works in Prose & in Verse, Serious, Pious, and Burlesque, *and
his Historic Relations in leaflet form*, of the Voyage of the King and his
Eminence. The entirety conjointly or separately, in one or several
volumes, by whatever Printer or Bookseller that it pleases him to
choose . . . [emphasis in text]."[41] The *privilège*, ostensibly for the
author's works, but also for his relations of the king's and minister's
travels, put the journalist in direct competition with the bookseller,
Loyson. This was a beneficial situation for the journalist, since the
permission offered him independence from the bookseller-publish-
er by giving him the possibility of selling his stories to the highest
bidder. At the very least, Colletet was now able to cede the publisher
the *privilège* for each text separately and thus would be able to
negotiate for more money from Loyson (with whom he must have
had some initial agreement). Such multiplication of *privilèges* must
also have been beneficial to the regime, which effectively increased
its visibility. That seems to have been the ultimate result of the May
16, 1660, permission. On June 4, 1660, Colletet ceded his *privilège*
(initially for one text, but later for a second as well), to a printer,
Alexandre Lesselin.[42]

The pamphlet by Colletet that Lesselin printed was entitled *Le
Nouveau Journal Historique, contenant la Relation Véritable De ce qui s'est
passé au voyage du Roy et de son Eminence. Et aux Ceremonies du Mariage
de Sa Majesté. Celébrées à Fontarabie & à S. Jean de Luz.* On the first
page, Colletet announced this text as the continuation of the four
pamphlets on the negotiation of the treaty (*Les Journaux Historiques
. . .*) that he had written for Loyson in 1659. Loyson counterat-
tacked with the publication of *La Nouvelle Relation*, which was
situated in relation to "preceding accounts," but distinguished from
the Lesselin text by being presented as more complete: "There
appeared recently an Account entitled *The New Historical Journal*,
which contains only a small part of the Ceremonies of this happy
marriage. . . ."[43] In fact, *La Nouvelle Relation* embellished details that
the Lesselin pamphlet had provided only schematically.

Even if the officials awarding the *privilèges* may not have seen
an explicit contradiction between Loyson's and Colletet's 1659 and

1660 *privilèges*, the players involved did.[44] The field of print was tight and competitive in this period, at least from the perspective of the corporate players, the *marchand libraires* and the *imprimeurs*. And the topic of Louis XIV's marriage was a commodity worth battling over. Loyson therefore acted quickly against Lesselin and Colletet, bringing a legal suit against them on June 19. As a result of this litigation, the pamphlet Colletet published with Lesselin was seized and taken out of circulation; production and distribution of *Le Nouveau Journal Historique* was stopped entirely by the confiscation of the sheets printed and of the forms for printing.[45] For three weeks, Loyson's *Nouvelle relation* and its detailed description of the scene of the first view offered the Parisian public the predominant perspective of events at the border.[46] On July 10, 1660, the Civil Chamber of Châtelet delivered a judgment "against J. B. Loyson in favor of Monsieur Colletet and of Alexander Lesselin his printer." Having seen the *privilège* of Colletet and following the "sentences formerly rendered," the court terminated the seizure order on the copies of and printing forms for *Le Nouveau Journal Historique*.[47] Loyson's legitimate right to publish accounts of the marriage never seems to have been questioned. Shortly after the decision in favor of Colletet and Lesselin, the two published a second (and last) pamphlet together, *Seconde Relation Veritable et Fidelle de tout ce qui s'est fait & passé de plus remarquable dans les Conferences & dans les Adieux des deux Roys, jusques au depart de sa Majeste de la ville de S. Jean de Luz* (Paris: Chez Alexandre Lesselin, 1660).[48] At the beginning of this text, Colletet alluded to the quarrel with Loyson when he remarked that its publication had been delayed because of "the jealousy of a bookseller, by nature a lover of deception, and who seems to have been born only to contest the *Privilèges* of our Kings, having been opposed to my legitimate intent."[49] These remarks were reinforced in lines printed in the margin referring to ongoing litigation and by the publication of the abstract of the judgment on the last page of the pamphlet.[50]

The interest in this litigation over the *privilège* to report on the king's marriage—essentially a litigation of competing corporate and individual interests—is that the three pamphlets that were the

subject of the litigation were all, essentially, the same text, written
by the same writer, François Colletet. The first (published by
Lesselin) offered an outline of the events that the second pamphlet
(published by Loyson at the same time, or a little afterward),
paraphrased, adding some details—as, for example, the passage
analyzed here describing the king's voyeurism. The third pamphlet
(published by Lesselin) began with the story of the voyeurism and
offered an even more expanded version of its events.[51] It also
included allusions to what occurred in Paris between the bookseller
Loyson and the publisher Lesselin. The competition for the right to
tell the story of the marriage (and for the mastery of the field of print
culture in Paris) reproduced and multiplied the versions of the story
of the king's first view of his new bride. Nonetheless, in the
competition to exercise the privilege to tell the story of the king,
essentially a competition to make oneself visible, there was finally
(and despite the apparent multiplication of perspectives) only one
dominant point of view, that of the journalist Colletet, sole author
of three different pamphlets on the same subject.

The above interpretation dovetails with the reality of the
shot-countershot model. For while the pamphlets seem to provide
other views, they actually reinforce one view, that of Colletet. But
there is a difficulty with an interpretation that privileges the dominant point of view of the journalist. In the pamphlet published with
Lesselin (the one seized), Colletet denied the possibility of the single,
unilateral, perspective in the description of an event. As he described
it, his activity as a journalist depended upon the possibility of offering
diversity (of perspectives). That is the profession of the journalist or
nouvelliste, someone who collects and redistributes news items
received from others.[52] Colletet underlined this aspect of his practice
at the beginning of the text when he stated that he took up the pen
after having described the events of the 1659 negotiation only
because "from time to time Written Reports [*Memoires*] that contain
all the particularities of the most remarkable occurrences are passed
on to me . . . and I do not want to frustrate the public which is
naturally curious about new things . . ."[53] Colletet stated clearly
that he made himself visible in a field already crowded with other

authors for the sole reason that he had learned of more details about the events:

> The illustrious Author of the Gazette in prose and that of the Letter in Verse, both of whom in their own genre write so pleasantly the History of our century, have not forgotten anything of that which could satisfy the impatience of all of France. I will content myself only with telling in few words that which I learned one month ago from some faithful pens, whose manuscripts I conserve in my Library as a precious treasure.[54]

The existence of such sources, referred to by Colletet as "precious treasures" was signaled everywhere in pamphlets organized by the dates of the manuscript letters [*mémoires*] received from the frontier.[55] Colletet alluded frequently to this facet of his work, often underlining how his sources contradict each other. But in emphasizing the contradictory perspectives, the journalist did not stress his own mastery. He offered the reader the illusion that it was the reader who selected the true story from among all the possibilities that the journalist was presenting. Even if the journalist had already chosen the details that constituted *his* story, the strategy succeeded because the reader had the impression that he (or she) had all the (diverse) details possible to obtain.

Interestingly, when he began writing in 1659, Colletet had already chosen diversity as the trope of his pamphlets. According to the journalist, diversity attached the reader to the text. He announced this strategy at the end of the second pamphlet of his series of four on the negotiation:

> Already the fire of poetry carries me away & fires up my spirit; & I do not dream that I must Speak in prose & not in verse, This is not the style of History which demands the simple & not the heroic, naked truth & not Fable disguised. Therefore, I have not stopped myself from moving further, & I break free [from history] only to amuse my Reader, to whom a too long narration without some new & surprising diversity would be too boring.[56]

Although Colletet's initial relations were entitled *Journaux historiques,* he explicitly rejected history, or "naked truth," an association he picked up from the iconography of Truth, which was tradition-

ally depicted as a naked woman. In Cesare Ripa's *Iconologia*, a text
Colletet may well have consulted, the image of Truth is presented
as naked because "truth is a natural state and like a nude person,
exists without need for any artificial embellishment." Ripa adds as
well that "[o]ne arrives at truth by the study of science, of facts,
hence Truth holds a book."[57] In his opening pamphlet, Colletet
rejected the penetrating gaze of science, the gaze that undresses its
object in its straightforward look at nature, to choose instead "Fable
disguised" and "diversity," both of which indicate a dressing-up of
the story by embellishment. Such adornment would be true to the
idea of diversity as diversion, a diversion of the gaze from one
apparent center, the meeting between kings, to another, that
between queens, or kings and queens (from formal meetings to
novelistic scenes of reunion, passion, and desire). By valuing fiction
over history, Colletet foreshadowed his later rejection of the prosaic
and unilateral gaze at an accessible body, a rejection also enacted by
his protagonist, the king. He opted instead for the artifice and
diversion of the king's gallantry with its multiple perspectives and
slippery territory (the riverbank, the returned gazes of former
enemies) to attract readers to a new kind of journalistic, adorned,
history. This was not a project for the prosaic book (held in the hand
of naked truth), nor for the purely allegorical (remember, Colletet
had also rejected that style), but one for the fashionable flying sheets
of occasional pamphlets.

   It is perhaps not so surprising that Colletet's strategy breaks his
discourse loose from the fixity of the single *privilège* of Loyson to
unfurl in accounts that embroider and multiply fact, dress it up, and
disguise it in the pages of the occasional pamphlet. While such
diversity may seem paradoxical in the context of a regime that would
be characterized by privileging the absolute, unilateral gaze of the
monarch, it nonetheless made sense as an occasional (during the
marriage) tactic (or ruse) to attach the reader to the story (or stories)
for the greatest profit of all involved.[58] Indeed, even from the
perspective of Mazarin, the facilitation of multiple reader positions
(and connections to the story) could yield profit and power. In
working from two *privilèges*, both accorded him by the state, albeit

one indirectly and the other directly, Colletet worked along avenues and models provided to him by the regime to multiply information and visibility. Colletet's understanding of the necessity of dressing up naked truth, finally, suggests what was actually occurring. As indirect beneficiary of the first *privilège* and direct beneficiary of the second, he reenacted the movement of the king as he described it, first offering a gaze over the shoulders of Loyson and then offering his perspective more directly by engaging his own printer, Lesselin. It is only through gaining access to publishing multiple perspectives that Colletet finally could find "satisfaction," or rather the greatest profit (and recognition) for himself and his patron.

Inter-views of the New Queen

In discussing multiple perspectives in relation to the king and the journalist, the most compelling and diverting viewpoint of all, that of the new queen, has slipped out of view. Or rather, it has been relegated to the periphery of a homology drawn between the king's first view of the infanta and the agents of the description of that view. But images of the new queen should remain at the center of this discussion insofar as she was the object of the scopic gaze of the king (and the journalist) and the position that drew readers' interests. She was, as seen in Chapters One and Two, the driving force of nuptial fictions, providing momentum for them, and exerting force on the protagonist of the fictions, the king. She was the cog in the wheel that turned the nuptial fictions for all the agents and she offered a model for the way Colletet's pamphlets organize their fictions and themselves.

It is not surprising that as center of the king's gaze and site of the meeting of the gazes of the two kings, Philip and Louis, the new queen should drop from view. She slipped out of focus in *La Nouvelle Relation*'s description of the voyeurism as the gaze of her husband slid over her body to settle on the true object of his desires, the enemy king. It was, finally, the recognition of Louis XIV by Philip IV that was essential to the glorification and particularization of the absolutist monarch. If María Teresa did not disappear entirely

in this gesture, it was for two reasons. First, because her own deep
bow to the king served to complement the actions of her father,
placing her in parallel to the Spanish monarch whose visible recognition of Louis XIV was essential to the dissemination of an image
of Louis as powerful and absolute. Second, and more important,
because she offered a site of pleasing opacity in the play of perspectives. This facet of her was emphasized when the king first saluted
the boat from the riverbank. At that point, one of the infanta's
attendants, the daughter of the Spanish minister Haro, was described
as beginning to return the salutation. But she was stopped by the
infanta who "was seen making a gesture with her hand to them not
to stand up." In this case, the infanta resisted Louis XIV, refusing
to return his gaze, withholding the recognition so fundamental to
the Bourbon monarch's self-staging. Such opposition was short-
lived, however. For the king decided "*This isn't good enough, it is
necessary to push the gallantry even further*" [emphasis in text]. In so
saying, the king remounted his horse and exhibited his gallantry
even more visibly by galloping alongside the boat until the king of
Spain acknowledged him, an event the pamphlet writer underscored as truly exceptional. Indeed, it was only when this long-
sought and remarkable recognition by Philip IV occurred that the
infanta stood and acknowledged Louis XIV. As opposed to her
father, who removed his hat and bent his knee, the future queen
took a deep bow to the already-satisfied king. The infanta saluted
the king, but, as in the house on the island, and unlike her father,
she did not gaze directly at him. Her gaze was oblique and furtive.
A sign of modesty? Perhaps. But it was also one of opacity, a
perspective that did not offer a clear counterview as did that of the
king of Spain, but left ambiguities that gestured toward the diversity
Colletet used as the trope for his reporting.

It is interesting that when Colletet rewrote the description of
the scene of the first view in the second Lesselin pamphlet, he kept
the information unstable precisely around the issue of the king's
spectators. In this later version, Colletet embellished this passage,
offering, among other elements, the following description of the
excitement of the Spanish nobility who crowd around the king:

"He was no sooner outside that he remounted his horse, and walking along the prairie, all the guards of the King of Spain left their posts and their positions, and went in a crowd to the water to see the King, who they circled from all sides, making a thousand exclamations of joy."[59] At the same time the pamphlet multiplies audiences, it also embellishes the reaction of the infanta to seeing her new king, offering her reactions as a subject of speculation, making her perspective seem even more remote:

> As for the Queen, one can well believe that her eyes were not lazy, & that they had well wished that the boat had traveled more slowly than it did, in order to enjoy longer a so precious view: the King her father spoke to her at two or three different stages and one could judge well by his expression that Our Monarch was the true subject of his discourse, although it was uncertain if it was effectively he who was the subject, and also he did not salute him, & it was only the Ladies in waiting of the Queen who acquitted themselves of this civility.[60]

Does such speculation make the queen's perspective all the more tantalizing? Does the infanta's gaze thus offer a diversity than can never be pinned down and completed?

Certainly her oblique gaze is the most pleasurable because it is the least satisfying to the readers. Such a glimpse is all the king and the pamphlets can obtain from (and of) the infanta. Withholding and withheld, this glimpse or perspective of the infanta is the true object over which they fight and position themselves, the true object of privilege because it is the unobtainable territory, the real story to sell, the slippery object that occasions the narrative and draws in the reader by offering a subject position that truly seems to complete the public's view. Of course, because the infanta's gaze resists the move toward completion offered by Philip IV, it keeps the readers coming back for more versions, another look at the queen, and, more important, at the king (or kings).

Sandwiched between the two kings, the perspective of the infanta epitomizes the position of the multiple perspective as an "inter-view," a perspective that tantalizes but withholds, fueling the desire for information that keeps the narrative moving (and readers' attention riveted to it). In so doing, it underlines the insufficiency of any one perspective, and the partiality of all perspectives. Partiality can be taken here in both senses of the word, as the incompleteness or partialness of information and as the viewing (history) and its partiality, interestedness, or state of being partisan. For those two points are precisely the issue at hand in the small pamphlet war between Colletet, Lesselin, and Loyson, in which incomplete information becomes a premium in a power struggle of competing interests. In that war, the stakes lay in creating and holding reader interest, in finding a topic in which the reader could both partake and take more parts (because incomplete) without ever fixing one position, which might be the wrong one, one leading away from the king (and the texts). Such mobility increased visibility, but at the risk of undermining the scopic or absolute position of the king (and the absolute privilege of the pamphlet).

The dialectic between mobility and fixity also characterizes the position of the occasional pamphlet in the creation of nuptial fictions. For the form can be contrasted to the monumental works of official history. As noted earlier, in 1660 the pamphlet genre (and by extension its authors) was struggling to make its impact felt as legitimate or privileged. Its interstitial position is evident in the *Register of Permissions to Print*, the text where all official *privilèges* are recorded by the Syndical Chamber of the Book Trade. There one already finds evidence of the pamphlets that would be produced for the marriage in an entry next to the name Loizon [Loyson] under the date December 1st:

> Permission to print a book titled The Summary of the History of France by Monsieur Mathieu, historiographer of the King augmented by the most noteworthy things that occurred in the year [*sic*] 58 and 59, at the same time the list [*tableau*] of all the provinces of France, enriched by the blazons and coats of arms [*armoiries*], and as well as the list of departures of couriers of the mail, of messengers and wagoners by the Colletets, and a book entitled the Edicts, ordinances, proclamations, and regulations of the Kings of France from François the First up to the present for the benefit of Jean-Baptiste Loyson, bookseller of Paris as of the first of November 1659, signed, Maugevet.[61]

This *privilège* accorded to Loyson in November 1659, one month before the permission for the marriage pamphlets was granted, foreshadows his collaboration with François Colletet.[62] But it does not explicitly concern the marriage, or pamphlets. Rather, it allows Loyson to reprint the works of Pierre Matthieu, Henry IV's historiographer (and chronicler of his marriage).[63] It also gives him permission to print a volume of laws from the time of François I to the present. Note that in order to reprint existing works, publishers were required to add new material to them.[64] Hence the additions to Matthieu's text of "the most noteworthy things that occurred in the year [sic] 58 and 59, at the same time the list of all the provinces of France, enriched by the blazons and coats of arms, and as well as the list of departures of couriers of the mail, of messengers and wagoners by the Colletets." The material making the two books and republication possible was to be provided by the Colletets (Guillaume still being alive at this time). Such access to current information provided by the list of the mails and wagoners who brought it may have been what later made François Colletet a likely choice for writing the marriage pamphlets. Here, however, this material is interesting for the contrast it offers to the main text, an important tome of history. The addendum to Matthieu's work provided by the Colletets was the matter of current events, the kind of material reported in almanacs (such as schedules of mail departures) or published in the *Gazette* or other short pamphlets produced to provide information on noteworthy current events.

In the *privilège* to republish Mathieu's history, the Colletets' collaboration is barely glimpsed, seemingly inconsequential compared to the great tomes of history. But it provides the embellishment that makes the publication of the two monumental books legally possible. Such tomes offered information on accomplished, definitive acts about which all is known. The former, the reports ("of the departures, of couriers, of the relay, of messengers, and wagoners"), are texts defined not by their completeness, but by their seriality and by their nature as being in process, up-to-the-minute reports. They are the product of messages sent back and forth, a story glimpsed while under construction. The pamphlets' nuptial fictions are also descriptions under construction, serial narratives in which elements fall from sight, are recuperated, tried out, rearranged, part of a story already told (because choreographed according to prearranged ceremonies), but always partial and unpredictable, because their subject is an event in process. And yet, nuptial fictions are necessary to prop up or republish the larger history, that of the king who projects his power as accomplished and complete.

Within this context, it is not surprising that the infanta (and her gaze) should slip continually out of view. For the infanta is to nuptial fictions what nuptial fictions are to the king's history. Such complementary seriality also characterizes the print vehicle that most often conveys her image, the occasional pamphlet—serial, incomplete, under process, taken in and out of circulation to be renewed and retooled as the information is provided. Of course, such a format will not be the final version of nuptial fictions (or of the new queen's image). Neither will it go on to serve as the central form of portraying the mature king. As seen in the scenario, to obtain complete satisfaction, the French king needed to fix the gaze of others on himself. He required a gaze which was not only stable, but stabilized and completed, like that provided for Henry IV by Matthieu's volume of history (containing the naked, monological truth) approved for republication in the December 1, 1659, *privilège*. But such weighty tomes did not necessarily serve their purpose. They did not produce wide readerships, being less current and thus less profitable. In fact, Loyson never republished Matthieu's work, producing the more lucrative pamphlets with Colletet instead. He must have realized such histories of the already accomplished, would, finally, offer so complete and totalized a view of the king that they could not seduce the as yet unconvinced viewer, shut out by such finitude. A similar finitude may be ascribed to Rigaud's portrait of Louis XIV (Figure 7), initially painted to be sent to Louis XIV's grandson who had ascended the throne of Spain, but kept instead by the king in France.[65] The large tomes of history, stored on the shelves of private libraries, may be likened to this large portrait: impressive, but with limited mobility. Colletet's pamphlets, on the other hand, did travel. Like almanacs, they were widely distributed to a broad public for whom they diversified the king's portrait, adding the queen's focus to that of the king (and the nuptial fictions to the other fictions of sovereignty). The interstitial position of nuptial fictions and their icon, the queen, matched the economy of the pamphlet's corporate and generic interests (or perhaps the pamphlets reproduce themselves according to the logic of the nuptial fiction). Imitating the queen or producing her as their position, the pamphlets construct their portrayal as a series of inter-views that engage the reader.

This view of the nuptial events, offered via partial glimpses, served to yield the greatest interest to all involved—king, journalist, and bookseller. Such a strategy was fundamental to the production of the king's symbolic power. Yet it is significant that the central icon of this strategy, the queen, remains outside the loop of profit and agency generated around her representation. For according her the power she really exercised would be as dangerous as leaving the agents of nuptial fictions free to work outside the system of *privilèges*. And yet, such agency is clearly evident in the portrayal of the scenes from the border, in its images and vehicles. It is that dangerous agency and the issue of mastery that is examined in the next chapter, which looks beyond print culture to other technologies used to celebrate the marriage and project its fictions.

CHAPTER 4

Nuptial Technologies

Representations of the queen were crucial to nuptial fictions' displays of the king's prowess. In the story of the marriage treaty, the queen was both a subordinate symbol in the kinship exchange and a dynamic force or potential player in her own right. Nuptial images are thus both malleable signs and less predictable agents of signification. This dialectic is also a property of the vehicles used to project the fictions of marriage. The central purveyor of the nuptial fiction, the occasional pamphlet, was both a manipulatable (privileged) prop for displaying the king and an entity that could manipulate for profit. A figure from one of the central myths of the marriage—Medea from the story of the Golden Fleece—likewise typifies this characteristic dialectic of nuptial fictions. For Medea's magic initially serves and protects the riches of her (father's) state: the Golden Fleece. Later, however, the sorceress turns her talents against her father, using them instead to steal the Fleece to further Jason's political projects (and gain his love). Medea thus engages simultaneously in state building and in state unbuilding. She is an object manipulated by her father and by Jason for their own gain and an agent who destroys them both when she takes things into her own hands.

It is not by chance that the Golden Fleece was a central myth in the marriage celebration. As the dictionary of Furetière notes, "the Chief and Grand Master of the Order of the Golden Fleece was the King of Spain." The Gazette also mentions the association between the myth and the Hapsburg Empire, "every one knowing that it [the Golden Fleece] is the highest order of this kingdom [Spain]."[1] These associations probably explain the myth's utilization in celebrations of the treaty marriage. It was the theme of the fireworks set off in Lyon in December 1658 to celebrate the initial agreement to a marriage between Louis XIV and María Teresa. It was also the centerpiece of fireworks set off for the king and queen's entry into Paris in August 1660. And Pierre Corneille dramatized the myth in a machine play, *La conquête de la Toison d'or*, staged first in Normandy at the château of the Count of Sourdéac in the fall of 1660 and then in Paris at the Marais Theatre the following January. Medea and Jason are, however, not found in the allegorical arsenal used by the poets who wrote sonnets for the marriage. Nor are they found in Colletet's early allegorical reports on the treaty negotiation.[2] The story does not appear in the ceremonies of print except as reports of the fireworks and of Corneille's play. Rather, the myth was utilized by media that, like the sorceress, engage in technological wizardry. For both fireworks and machine drama used firepower, strings, and pulleys to defy logic and gravity in order to reshape matter, whether it be pyrotechnic, dramatic, political, or mythic.

That there should be an affinity between these forms and the celebration of the marriage is not surprising. The manipulation of dynamic forces was also the basis of kinship exchange, a practice aimed at containing, displacing, and mastering violent impulses via so-called civilizing or symbolic processes. There would be no call to exchange kin if there were no danger to resolve. Such refashioning was also the goal of the marriage treaty, which reconfigured national boundaries, dynasties, and international relations. In brandishing the figure of Medea, such spectacles rehearsed the symbolic activities of kinship exchange by explicitly staging danger and its containment.

"Fires of Joy"

In considering the pyrotechnic spectacle referred to at the time of the marriage as "feux volans" (flying fire),[3] this study moves away from the flying sheets [*feuilles volantes*] of print culture and into uncharted territory. For the role of fireworks in organizing political culture has not been studied in depth.[4] Louis Marin spends only two pages on the medium in *Le portrait du roi*. While Jean-Marie Apostolidès looks more extensively at court entertainment, he concentrates on thematics, not mechanics.[5] Indeed, there has been little serious twentieth-century scholarship on the symbolic potential of fireworks. In the seventeenth century, however, there was a developed and coherent discourse on the form. In fact, the first French treatise on fireworks as a form of entertainment was published in the context of the marriage treaty. It was written by Claude-François Menestrier, an erudite Jesuit who wrote extensively about such topics as the symbols of heraldry and the art of the emblem, as well as about public spectacles, ballet, tournaments, and jousts. Menestrier also authored a history of Louis XIV in medals, devices, and emblems. He was one of the seventeenth century's principal theorists of symbolic forms and activities and had keen insight into how representational forms and public spectacles participated in the project of glorifying the monarchy.[6] That is probably why Menestrier was chosen to organize the fireworks display in Lyon in December 1658 as well as the one in April 1660 that celebrated the peace treaty. Menestrier's treatise on fireworks appeared in his *Les Rejouissances de la Paix Avec un Receuil de diverses pièces sur ce sujet*, published in 1660.[7] Among the texts published with the 73-page description of the April festivities was a 32-page treatise, *Advis Necessaires pour la Conduite des Feux d'Artifices*.[8] The *Advis*'s commentary on the hermeneutic and practical dimensions of the genre serve to introduce and lay out the advantages and liabilities of employing the explosive medium of fireworks and, by extension, of utilizing the explosive theme of the sorceress Medea.

Fundamental to Menestrier's theoretical exegesis of fireworks is a hermeneutic related to contemporary theories of the elements.

According to Menestrier, earth, air, water, and fire, "four great workers of marvels of nature labor incessantly for the glory of our incomparable Monarch."[9] In his treatise on fireworks, Menestrier concentrates on the last element, fire, which, "since it holds the highest rank in the order of the world . . . has the advantage over all the others in these public festivities."[10] The unique advantage of fire (and therefore, as Menestrier will argue later, of fireworks) is linked to heat's particular elemental properties:

> Its explosive brilliance [*éclat*] carries first of all sparks of light into the eyes, which are the first projections of the light, which are the first advances of pleasure, & its heat opens the heart to the most beautiful flashes [*saillies*] of joy. There is nothing more bountiful than it [*feu*], it communicates its qualities to all that approach it, & makes continual profusion of its light. There is nothing more bustling, it is in continual restlessness, it attaches itself to all bodies, it works on all sorts of matter, & transforms the substance of everything it penetrates, its workings create miracles of art and nature. It changes sand into crystal, poisons into remedies, flowers into essence, & earth into gold.[11]

According to Menestrier, fire is a particularly powerful element (one that labors) because it "transforms the substance of everything it penetrates." The element works its tranformative power on all forms of matter, furthermore; that is, not just on the material it burns, but also on the spectators that witness its miracles of art and nature. It can change sand into crystal, but in a parallel, if apparently less noticeable operation, it also changes the constitution of those who look at it, entering their eyes to open up their hearts.

When Menestrier turns more directly to the form of fireworks, what he calls fires of joy [*feux de joye*] and their role in festivities, the workings of fire on the spectator become even more explicit. As he turns from elements to humors and their accompanying passions, Menestrier focuses on the "joy" of "fires of joy":

> Joy is not only magnificent in its profusion, it seems ingenious there; and however fervent it may be in its flashes, it is never immoderate. There is propriety [*bien-seance*] in its movements, & its richness [*luxe*] fastens the mind as much as the hands of those who serve it. In causing the heart to open out, it gives passage to sparks of blood, which serve in the formation of beautiful ideas; & the Fire that she [Joy] kindles,

does not only pass into the eyes to make them more alive; it also gives vigor to the imagination, & seems to make it fertile.[12]

Discussing joy, Menestrier conflates it with fire, elaborating on the comments he made in opening his account of the festivities about the effect of fire on the human body. This conflation is finally justified, and the comparison further developed, when Menestrier notes that fire is the element joy prefers in public festivities:

> It is Joy that presides at all public ceremonies, it makes their magnificence, it regulates the management of them; & the majesty that accompanies it in its dignified activities allows it the better part of its success. It utilizes diverse Artifices in order to insinuate itself into the mind; & often reverses the order of nature in making Birds swim, Fish fly, and mountains and rocks dance. There is no Monster that it does not imitate, no animal that it does not set its hand to. It is nonetheless more happy to utilize Fire than any of the rest of the Elements; & that is the reason why it is in the habit of using it [fire] at all public Festivals.[13]

There is an affinity between fire and Joy because both have an ability to transform; they insinuate themselves into the spirits of the viewer who will then accept the projected fantasies, illusions that upset the order of nature. Such power of transformation and seduction is never improper or out of control: Joy, and its handmaiden, fire, always function within the bounds of propriety [*bien-sceance*]. If joy (conflated with fire) disorders nature, it is never unregulatable. On the contrary, the very powerful forces of seduction that penetrate the heart and minds of its viewers are dignified. As such, they regulate the conduct of public festivities and do not unsettle it.[14]

While Menestrier proposes that joy's "diverse Artifices," the *feux de joye*, manage public ceremonies, he also stresses that joy's artifice is manageable: "however fervent it may be in its flashes, it is never immoderate." With all this emphasis on regulation and management—the title of his treatise is *Necessary Advice on the Management of Fireworks*—Menestrier is not talking about a form connected to bacchanalia. Despite the fact that fire's unique property is to reverse the order of nature, that same power allows it to penetrate the viewer in order to persuade and control him. Thus, as Menestrier points out, the form regulates and orders, guarding the bounds of propriety. As Menestrier conceives of them, fireworks are a "classical" art, one that controls and orders through its spectacular illusions. Fireworks do not produce liminal or chaotic events. They mark the ordering of chaos and the moving out of or beyond liminality.

Perhaps that is why there is little or no discussion of the destructive properties of fire's transformations in Menestrier's treatise. Rather, Menestrier emphasizes the generative and ordering properties of fire's force. But if fireworks are associated with celebration in general, and with festivities of marriage in particular, they are, nonetheless, inextricably connected with war and destruction, just as is the marriage.[15] In fact, prior to the publication of Menestrier's treatise, to learn about fireworks one turned to treatises on warfare that dealt with the military uses of pyrotechnic devices. In France, that source would have been Jean Appier Hanzelet's 1620 *Receuil de plusieurs machines Militaires, et feux Artificiels pour la Guerre & Recreation.* Divided into six sections, the topic of "recreational fireworks" appears in Appier Hanzelet's work only after four lengthy chapters devoted to the use of explosive devices in the attack on and destruction of military targets, in the protection of military positions, and in offensive actions, including psychological warfare. Anticipating that his militaristic emphasis will raise objections, Appier Hanzelet opens the treatise with an apology for the fires of war:

> Our military machines, our fireworks, & all the inventions contained in this little book, seem at first to be directly contrary to charity because the entire endeavor has no other goal than to ruin, demolish, overthrow, and reduce to ashes Cities, Castles, Villages, Fortresses, & other structures, to finally slaughter, kill, massacre, burn, dismember, & cruelly ravish the life from the bodies of men, women, & children, & thus pillage and unjustly make others' goods our own.[16]

But if Appier Hanzelet admits to the destructive nature of fireworks, he quickly offers as justification of his subject that "war was the wet nurse of Peace."[17] Later in his work he embellishes this image by stressing fire's connection to life, rather than to death, in reminding his readers of fire's role in humor theory as "necessary to human life" because "life itself consists in heat, and [fire] is the cause of all generation."[18] Appier Hanzelet thus stresses how fire, with all its capabilities for destruction, is also the sign of life itself since "everything is engendered & grows by heat and humidity: which is the Symbol of generation. It was considering this that Euripides said of the Troyades, that Vulcan had the charge of carrying the lighted torch to wedding festivities, when the lovers endeavored to couple."[19] The epitome of such generation was the marriage ceremony, the event that also produced France's first codification of fireworks as a genre of celebration apart from its uses in warfare.[20]

In the *Rejouissances*, Menestrier also passes quickly over the link between the fires of destruction and those of celebration. He underscores (as did Appier Hanzelet) the connection between the instruments of war and those of peace—"The fires that we light no longer lay waste to Towns & Provinces, & the noise of cannons offers presently more joy than terror"—picking up on a *topos* central to the marriage literature, that peace comes from war.[21] But Menestrier does not apologize for treating the topic of fire. For Menestrier, the power in fire requires no apology because as he uses the form it is always under control, regulatable, and utilizable for the public good.

Fireworks were such an appealing and appropriate form for celebrating a marriage treaty because, when associated with generation, fire embodied a terrific power of transformation (over matter), but one that could be manipulated and controlled. Through the display of such transforming power fireworks served as a reminder of the power of Louis and Mazarin, as well as of their agent, Menestrier, to transform the fires of war to those of peace.[22] Indeed, the recurrent suggestion of the link (explicit and implicit) between the generation of fire and the degeneration of the fires of warfare was a powerful mode of advertising not only a peace treaty, but all the transformational and contradictory aspects of it, oppositions at the heart of a treaty process reconciling not just fear and joy, or war and peace, but longtime enemies, the Spanish Hapsburgs and French Bourbons. Maintaining, even staging the contradictions at the heart of the peace process allowed the regime (and its public) to reinvoke the destruction of war, but this time in a controlled and forward-looking fashion in alluding to the future marriage and regeneration of the state by procreation.[23]

One might say, therefore, that fireworks reenacted and combined the two dimensions of the treaty marriage, the destruction of war that prepared it and the generativity (or fertility) meant to result from it. In so doing, they provide a sense of joyful mastery akin to that Freud observed in the play of his nephew when he threw a spool crying *fort* (away) and reeled it in crying *da* (here).[24] Freud understood that the little boy enacted loss in order to experience the pleasure and mastery of the return. Fireworks likewise allow the pleasurable *da* or reordering of the frightening *fort* or fear, now overcome. The pleasure comes from reproducing an unpleasant experience (throwing away the toy or lighting fireworks), and then mastering the fear (bringing it back on its string or staging fireworks, in which one can control and shape the thematics) to derive the pleasure of control. In this sense, fireworks are not a form of carnavalesque in which hierarchies are overturned in a bacchanal that maintains differences and places them side to side. They do not produce a liminal moment of chaos and disordering. Rather, they are a phenomenon that invokes mastery in effecting transformation; they stage the chaos of transformation to emphasize that it can be controlled.

Exploding Symbols

The illusion of mastery that fireworks allowed made its technology an appealing one for celebrating the marriage. With associations that range from being able to destroy life to being the source of life, fireworks' spool game between the fires of degeneration and destruction and those of generation and life suggests that technology can regulate all matter (including spectators). Taking the audience to the limit of fear and reeling it back in, attaching it via regulation and amusement, inspires awe and respect while exhibiting force and mastery. And yet to do so was literally and figuratively playing with fire. Menestrier did not shy away from recognizing this fact. He did not apologize for the danger of his form. That danger was integral to the process mastery. Without the danger of loss and destruction, there could be no experience of joyful recuperation.

Menestrier made this fact clear in the middle of his treatise. After reviewing the nature of fire and joy and listing suitable subjects for pyrotechnic displays (historic, emblematic, etc.), Menestrier addressed the practical quandaries faced in working with fire by relating the following two anecdotes concerning the destruction wrought by fireworks on the "machines" from which they are set off:

> One of the principal observations that it is necessary to make about the management of these Fires, is not to put any figure which one might have occasion to laugh at on the monument; & that as they are ordinarily burned, one should not be able to make the complaint that Monsieur Colletet did in one of his epigrams, on the occasion of a fireworks made on the Strand, where one burned the muses in 1649
>
>> In a glorious Century,
>> One cherishes the Daughters of the Gods;
>> But in a cowardly or ridiculous one,
>> They are taken to the Strand and burned.
>
> A few years ago the Gazette also remarked that the people of The Hague having erected a Pyre, where France was represented subjected to Spain; & and having set the Fire, it attached itself to the Image of Spain in such a manner that it reduced it right away to ashes, leaving the image of its Rival whole, & only a little darkened by smoke.[25]

In the passage, Menestrier deals with the concrete realities of the form he theorizes, moving from the abstract power of fire over the mind to its concrete force over matter. For he must admit that even if one follows all the precepts he has laid out as to what subjects, artifices, and ornaments to choose for each occasion, one is still utilizing a technology, fire power, to create "a pleasing confusion of variously distributed light, that does not please any less than it dazzles."[26] That is to say, this agreeable confusion of lights that dazzle requires an element that is powerful, even outside the mouth of a cannon.

In the example Menestrier offers in his treatise, the destructive power of fire does not display its author's mastery. Rather it makes him (and the object of celebration) appear ridiculous precisely because he cannot control the power behind the artifice. The first part of the anecdote concerns an epigram by Guillaume Colletet, father of the journalist François discussed extensively in Chapter Three. The elder Colletet's adage refers to the practice of decorating the monuments from which one set off the fireworks, here with allegorical figures, the Muses, that are presumably to be celebrated. Whereas in the northern tradition of fireworks, the devices were laid out in the open to be seen as they were set off, in France, where the Italian or southern tradition of pyrotechnic display was adopted, the devices were hidden in elaborate, decorated monuments called "machines."[27] While such machines ordered and arranged the display for its greatest effect, igniting the fireworks also set fire to the monument, burning and destroying (or at least radically transforming) the very objects one wished to celebrate. For the poet Guillaume Colletet, who was perhaps offering a critique of the Italian style, such a process was characteristic of an era that was "cowardly" or "ridiculous." Menestrier picked up on this reference to suggest that one might be ridiculing the celebrated object.

In the second part of the example, the anecdote of a celebration in The Hague, where France was represented as subject to Spain, Menestrier focuses less on pleasantries than on representational catastrophes. Here the political reference is obvious since The Hague would have been in Flanders, part of the territories France had recently conquered from Spain. The celebration in question was staged "several years ago," presumably during the Spanish occupation of the region. The implication of the story is that the presumably pro-Hapsburg organizers would also have seemed cowardly or ridiculous when, after the display had ended, the image of Spain on the machine was reduced to ashes, leaving that of the rival France only slightly blackened by the smoke, reversing the desired hierarchy of images.

In his treatise Menestrier offers a remedy to this debacle, noting, "if one is absolutely obliged to put the figures of Saints, of Princes, or of Virtues, & when it is the custom to burn the Machine, it is necessary to find a means to save them from being consumed."[28]

Menestrier's remedy for controlling the potential destruction wrought by his medium on its foundations or machines was to use "*fils*" or lines, both real and metaphorical. His solution was technical and thematic. He recommended choosing a theme that provided a mechanical solution: removal of the figure in question from the monument. The example he chose was the story of Saint John the Baptist. Menestrier suggested that just as the fire for the artifice was being set, the head of the saint should be "raised up along a rope" while his persecutors were reduced to ashes.[29] He suggested a machine and a thematic that would manage the destruction of fire. These were good solutions, but hardly applicable to the celebration of the peace treaty because the monuments that Menestrier described in his account of the Lyon celebration in 1660, as was traditional in such an event, were adorned by figures of past monarchs and their queens, in some cases topped by portraits of Louis, his new bride, the queen mother, and Mazarin. These are not figures to which one would appropriately apply a thematic (or machinery) of beheading![30] Given the impossibility of such a solution to the quandary raised for the celebration at hand, it is curious that Menestrier addressed the problem of burning revered figures in the context of an event in which such images were absolutely necessary to the iconographic traditions of the moment, that is, in the context of an event that would necessarily have to blacken sovereign figures.

The quandary here for representation and celebration is striking. For if one devised monuments on which one put revered images, the very medium that highlighted those figures, in this case the fireworks, could also potentially blacken them—not just figuratively, as would be the case in print culture, but quite literally, in the case of fireworks. And yet, the very activity of heating up the image, the very technology behind the metamorphosis of symbols, making fish fly or mountains move, is what attracts the viewer to the image. While machinery—strings, pulleys, themes—can help manipulate the medium when it gets too hot, it can also put into question the agency of technology in relation to the fictions of sovereign power. This paradoxical position as resolution and threat is also that of the new queen and the occasional pamphlet. While both the queen and the pamphlet can be mastered and fashioned to direct attention to the king, both also threaten to singe his image by drawing attention to themselves.

The alliance between a powerful display fashioned to serve the king and one that might explode or blast him (or his representation) is part of the deep structure of fireworks (and nuptial fictions) that is always linked to the potential destruction (and production) of war. What stirs up and thrills the audience is not just the power of fire as an element and joy as a humor. Rather, the juxtaposition of heat and light reminds the audience of fire's power to transform (for good or ill), even while—and especially because—it is being controlled and managed. It issues forth from the mouths of cannons (or the machines of the monuments) to kindle sparks in the citizens and not kindle them into sparks. One may wonder what particular thematic line might serve to both highlight power *and* control it in the context of royal marriage. What myth might offer the chance to pull the strings of mastery and pleasure? It would surely not be the story of Saint John the Baptist in which heads fly. Rather it would be one like the conquest of the Golden Fleece in which material goods, the wealth of a nation, fly. The story has, furthermore, the thematic affinity Menestrier recommends, one that allows for the seduction of illustrating technological mastery, namely the magical metamorphoses (or technologies) for which the sorceress is also known. These would lend themselves well to the medium. Such thematic affinity would allow the display of technological expertise, a prowess that would counterbalance the more problematic aspects of the story.

While it may seem that the myth of Jason and the Golden Fleece skirts a bit too close to real territorial issues of the marriage (theft, for example), these topics might also have been the attraction of the story for the celebration of the 1660 treaty marriage. Staging Medea's story allowed the French to externalize their fears and desires and thus put them in order. Perhaps that was why the myth first surfaced after the meeting of the Bourbon royal family with that of Savoy. That meeting was supposedly organized to seal an agreement for a marriage between Louis and the Princess of Savoy. The Medea myth may have reproduced the explosiveness of the actual situation, a feigned match. The match (one of the choices offered in the almanac engraving of *Les Estrennes*) was not to be. The meeting, as was most likely the intention, provoked the Spaniards into sending their envoy Pimentel to offer France the infanta and a treaty.[31] Certainly in that instance, the eleventh-hour arrival of the Spanish envoy Pimentel caused a stir, or rather an explosion. When the smoke cleared, the princess of Savoy, a first cousin of Louis XIV, had been replaced by another first cousin, the Spanish infanta, an act that could have potentially charring effects on the young king (also courting Marie Mancini at this moment)—or his minister Mazarin, who organized the political spectacle. At the time of the preparation for the pyrotechnic display, could it have been known that a deal would be struck with Spain and not Savoy? Planning a celebration around a subject that, as noted earlier, was associated with Spain, not Savoy, suggests that the outcome was never in doubt.

It is thus that the 1658 fireworks staged by Menestrier celebrated the theft of an object associated with Spain, underlining the French military victory over its enemy while foreshadowing (or illuminating) a facet of the treaty negotiation best kept in the dark, that the French would still have designs on stealing the "order" of Spain. That the same theme of the theft of the Golden Fleece served for the grand finale of the celebration of the couple's return to Paris August 26, 1660, suggests that the controversial interpretation of the story was not a deterrent. The explosive story-line was clearly convertible into positive symbolic capital. It is interesting to note in this light that the character Medea is absent from the Paris fireworks which, as critics agree, were also much more staid: they were a fixed tableau designed by Lebrun, quite different from the dynamic Lyon version organized by Menestrier.[32] Perhaps their transformation of the fiery story into a static set piece allowed the organizers of the Parisian celebration to advertise what was, by August 1660, a completed deal: the theft from Spain (of the Hapsburg power figured in the infanta's potential to inherit her father's throne) and the containment of María Teresa's agency (or rather its conversion for their benefit). They could thus bracket the sorceress, much as the royal entry celebrations could serve to subdue the new queen, placing her firmly into the king's collection, eradicating any potentially unsettling dimensions of her image. There is no need to practice mastery over an object that has already been mastered.

One can most clearly understand how this containment works in shifting attention from fireworks' exposition of the Medea myth, for which there is no thematic exposition, to Corneille's spectacular machine play, *La Toison d'or*. This technologically innovative drama offers the clearest understanding of the attraction of the story for nuptial fictions because it demonstrates how the myth, despite its more problematic angles, could be neutralized and utilized by the regime via a combination of dramatic machinery and narrative. In it, the two dimensions (explosivity and the display of mastery) work together to stage the agents of the spectacle, or rather its technology, in offering a pretext to illustrate the power of the newfangled machinery that Corneille and his sponsor, the Marquis of Sourdéac, an amateur "machinist," wanted to build.[33] The scenes of Medea on the dragon stealing the Fleece were particularly suitable to showing off the technical prowess of the two in a play that did not use strings to remove heads, but rather to move characters across the stage for the first time in theater history. Despite the advantages of the story for displaying this technical innovation, Corneille's version offers a clear view of the explosivity of the power of Medea, who helped Jason to acquire her father's or country's riches, the Golden Fleece (Spain?), even going to the length of cutting up her brother (heir to the throne of Colchis) and spreading his pieces in order to aid the escape of the Argo. Of course, the last (bloody) element of the narrative is absent from Corneille's version. Corneille chose instead an account of the myth in which Médée's brother Absyrte is already an adult at the time of the action.[34] Whichever narrative Corneille chose to dramatize, both parallel the history of the marriage with its presentation of male heroics, cross-cultural love, empire building, and stolen riches. Nonetheless, it is not that parallel that is of interest here. Rather it is the fact that even vaguely alluding to such a similarity, and certainly doing so soon after negotiating a treaty, was both potentially explosive and, in effect, containable. For the daring feats of the story attract the viewer to the valor of the male hero, but they also threaten to explode on him when one follows the traces of the story, theft of an empire's riches and a foreign princess whose powers will one day kill off the progeny of the match to punish her philandering husband. Indeed, the possibility of neutralizing that part of the story-line is doubly striking in the hands of Corneille, who had already staged the most gruesome end of the myth to popular acclaim in his 1635 tragedy, *Médée*.[35] With its hovering threat of infanticide, no story more clearly illustrates how the explosive heat of a queen (remember, Medea burns up her husband's new love interest before killing their own children) can cut to the core of the worst fantasies of dynastic aspirations. In the hands of Corneille, however, this prequel to the myth offers a finely developed program for manipulating explosive symbols, like Medea, and making them function in the service of the state.

María . . . Medea . . . Medusa

The exegesis of both the explosivity of symbols and the machinery of their manipulation offered by Corneille's *La conquête de la Toison d'or* begins in the play's prologue. This is the section of the drama that presents the connection between the entertainment of the story with its spectacularly innovative technology and the events of the year in which the play was produced. The current events behind the play are suggested by the prologue's characters, the same allegorical figures seen in the almanac engravings: France, Victory, Peace, Discord, Envy, Hymen, and Mars. Corneille explicitly associates his drama with the marriage and peace in comments about the decor of the prologue found in the program [*livret*] published in January 1661 to accompany the Paris premiere:

> The happy marriage of his Majesty, and the Peace that it pleased him
> to give to his People, having been the motives of the public rejoicing,
> for which this tragedy was prepared, not only is it appropriate that it

should serve as the subject of the Prologue that precedes it, but it was even absolutely impossible to choose a more illustrious subject for it.[36]

These prefatory remarks lay out the setting of the prologue, "a land ruined by wars," when the first scene begins with France lamenting the price of Victory whose "gifts are to be cherished, but whose consequences are to be feared."[37] According to France, even if Victory has assured the place in history of France's sons, War has left the king with a country of down-hearted subjects.[38] While Victory understands France's "cares," she nonetheless warns France that her ingratitude will stir Mars' wrath.[39] Indeed, Mars arrives in Scene Two of the prologue to confront the ungrateful France, who is yearning for Peace and disdaining Victory. When Mars suggests to France that with one or two more victories France will know no bounds, but would see "all Europe learn your language/ . . . all Europe under your laws," he raises the ugly (and unspoken) specter of that which underlies the treaty process: the firepower behind fireworks, that is, the Bourbon desire for hegemony over Europe, a desire inimical to the intent of a peace treaty, which is meant to erase enmity and resolve competition.[40] In the play, France refuses such glory. She voices desire only for Peace. In response to this slap in the face, Mars shows France he has placed Peace under house arrest in his palace:

> You renounce this glory,
> Peace has more charms for you,
> And you disdain Victory,
> Who I with my own hand attached to you
>   [*attachée à tes pas*].
> See in what irons under me Discord and Envy,
> Hold Peace enslaved.[41]

The fate of Peace, guarded by Discord and Envy, is shown in the third scene of the prologue. But if Peace is seen in chains, she is not silent. Indeed, Peace predicts that a god stronger than Mars will come to her aid, the god of marriage, Hymen, empowered by the recent conference between Mazarin and his counterpart, the Span-

ish minister Haro. With these references, Peace places the action of
the prologue firmly in the liminal period between war and marriage.

The end of this third scene of the prologue is particularly
striking. It presents the audience with a face-off between figures of
spectacular monstrosity and the spectacular power of a figuration,
when Hymen appears to confront Envy and Discord. For Discord
and Envy disdain Hymen, who carries in his right hand a spear
adorned with lilies and roses. They ask: "How can we fear a God,
who against our fury/Takes as arms only flowers!"[42] But Hymen
quickly sets the two straight. His weapon is not the spear in his right
hand, but the portrait on the shield in his left hand:

> Yes, Monsters, yes, fear this vengeful hand,
> But fear even more this great Princess,
>   For whom I have just kindled my torch:
> Could you endure the features [*traits*] of her face?
>   Monsters, Flee her image,
> Flee and let Hell, that was your cradle,
>   serve forever as your tomb.
> And you, miserable instruments of an undeserved
>   slavery,
> Fall, odious irons, in the face of this divine sight,
>   And render to it an immediate homage,
> Humble yourselves in shame, and in respect.[43]

Hymen uses as his weapon not a spear (not the fire of war however
transformed and adorned), but rather the shield with its figuration:
the lines [*traits*] of a face of "this great princess," a "divine sight"
that will be even more powerful than the spear. Indeed, the *traits*
are a weapon, since the term refers not only to lines (of the face or
the marks that designate it), but also to the cord pulled in a weapon,
or even, poetically, the shaft of Cupid's dart. The divine aspect is
thus the figure not just of the image of the infanta on the shield but
of the actual lines of her representation, small pieces that, when
taken together, comprise a divine and powerful appearance. The
association between the shield and the torch it has kindled furthers
the power of the image, reminding the literate audience of nobility
in Normandy (and later Paris) of the piercing power of light as

presented by Menestrier. It is thus not surprising that when Hymen points the portrait of María toward Discord and Envy, they fall down to the part of the stage representing Hell. Hymen then points the portrait toward the chains holding Peace. The stage directions indicate that with this act the chains break apart and fall away.

This vignette concretely stages the power of images in general and of the technology of figuring the new queen in particular. The gesture of using the portrait of María Teresa as a weapon against evil forces is not an innovation on the part of Corneille. The idea that the infanta brought peace was present in many celebratory poems published for the treaty marriage. The specific image of her portrait breaking the chains of peace had, furthermore, already been prominently displayed on one of the central entry monuments described and reproduced as an engraving in an occasional pamphlet by André Félibien[44] (Figure 13). But its use by Corneille, as on the entry monument, is striking for its reference to the story of another powerful head whose image, reproduced on a shield, also served as a deadly weapon: the Medusa's head. After slaying Medusa, Perseus attached her head to his shield, later using it to free Andromedus.[45] It is likely that Corneille was aware of the connection between María Teresa and Medusa (Marie and Méduse in French). Indeed, critics agree that when Corneille's Hymen asks the monsters if they can stand the traits of the infanta's countenance, the god is referring directly to Medusa.[46] Furthermore, the myth of Perseus and Andromedus, another popular story for royal celebrations and fireworks, had been the subject of Corneille's first, very successful machine play, *Andromède*. Corneille was not commenting on the beauty of the new queen.[47] Rather, he was commenting on the power of portrayal within the context of the machinery of representation. He was showing how to take a dangerous and horrifying power and refashion and reconfigure it, turning it to one's own advantage.

Indeed, the portrait of the "unknown" princess was used to organize the representation of the king in the almanac engravings dating back to 1658 and 1659. In the almanacs discussed in Chapter One, the princess was shown only as a cameo. The problematic, yet necessary, pieces of her body were circumscribed. In Corneille's play, the image is not of a Medusa head attached to a body moving on its own, but rather of a manipulatable image of the María *qua* Medusa placed on Hymen's *qua* Perseus's shield. As such, it is not a female whose power petrifies, but the image of one whose power, when placed in the right hands (that of the male mythic hero, Jason or Perseus, or even the androgynous Hymen), moves objects, tosses Discord and Envy into Hell, and breaks Chains. María Teresa *qua* Medusa is domesticated and pressed into the service of the regime. Like Saint John the Baptist in Menestrier's anecdote, the head has been removed and saved, to be wielded as an icon that will not subject a regime to ridicule, as Guillaume Colletet had warned, but that, like Menestrier's fires of joy, is proper [*bienséant*].

If the viewer of Corneille's play misses this point, he or she gets a second illustration of it when Peace, set free, orders France to celebrate: "Make your joy burst out in stately spectacles."[48] France, however, declares herself powerless to transform the ruined nature of the set when she asks how she can metamorphose the battered and scarred landscape of war into a suitable (theatrical) decor: "Has human effort ever extracted/Stately spectacles, out of such a rent breast?"[49] Once more, it is Hymen who saves the day when, wielding a portrait of the new queen, he proclaims:

> Arise at this sight, fountains, flowers, woods,
> Drive out this detritus, the baneful images,
> And form gardens, such as with four words
> The great art of Medée gave rise to at Colchis.[50]

If France is powerless before the burned set (or monument), Hymen, like Menestrier, has a thematic solution for stage technique. Making a parallel between his own transformation of the stage and the magician Medée's transformation of the deserts of Colchos, Hymen once more holds up his shield/portrait of María Teresa to generate the once impossible transformation. In so doing he sets the stage for the story of Medée and Jason, which is, on many levels, the story of equally impossible transformations (and births), the greatest being the equation made between the new queen and the story's main character. Hymen thus explicitly allies the power of wielding the image of the queen with the force deployed by Médée. He also makes Médée's story, the one about to be told, the exemplum of the power of representation. But as he does so, the domestication of Medusa as María Teresa is once more unsettled. For as the head of María *qua* Medusa is joined to a body, a third character, Médée, is added to the cycle of imagined queens. This joining of head to body to make a dramatic character is a representational act that threatens to put the firepower back into the pyrotechnics of spectacle. Like Freud's nephew's game of *fort–da*, it threatens to char the main players of the monument and subject the regime to representational ridicule, while at the same time restoring beauty (fire) to the smoldering ruins of the stage set.

The Agent / Object of Desire

Does Corneille's *La Toison d'or* concentrate on the ugliest and most frightening scenarios (war-ravaged landscape, frightening women like Medusa) in order to take those images and master them, just as does the portrait of the infanta in the prologue? Does it engage in the *fort–da* game in which the child wards off the most fearful thing (loss of the mother) by reenacting it? If so, the use of the myth in the marriage celebration, like the game (and kinship exchange, or symbolic processes more generally), allows the displacement of meaning from one activity or agent to another. In that sense it is interesting that the story of Médée as Corneille tells it is actually about shifting: the wavering interest of Jason and the changing ownership of the Fleece (and power). At the same time, it is about attempts to channel these shifts. This emphasis is already evident in the opening scene, in which Médée and her sister discuss Médée's change of heart (to Jason from a dead fiancé) and the probability of Jason turning from nationalist aspirations (and his departure) to desire for Médée. Indeed, one might say that it is, finally, the channeling of Jason's shifting interests (in Médée, in the Fleece, in the queen of Lemnos to whom he had already proposed marriage) that is the topic of the play's opening. For immediately after the scene between Médée and her sister, the action turns to King Aète's reflections on Jason's interests. That is because the time of the play is directly after Jason has helped Aète fend off the attempt of a neighboring king, his brother Perses, to steal the basis of Aète's power, the Golden Fleece, the object upon which the power of his kingdom depended. Because Jason has helped Aète to defeat his enemies and preserve power, some compensation is necessary. Since the same oracle that predicted that Aète's power would be linked to the Golden Fleece also predicted that his younger daughter Médée would marry a foreigner, the king automatically envisioned that the compensation would take place in the form of not just any gift, but that of his daughter, and with her, a share in the throne.

Aète is certain of the suitability of offering Jason a gift of kin, a gift that will bring with it part of his state. For he believes "[t]he Throne has its attachments as does Marriage," and such an attachment can domesticate the powerful warrior "when this double knot holds a person [âme] enchained."[51] It is thus that he does not explicitly offer Jason the "choice" of a spouse. Instead, Aète offers Jason the choice of anything he desires in the kingdom:

> But, if in my Lands, but if in my Palace,
> Something has been able to merit your desires,
> The choice that would have made of it an extreme
>   value,
> Would endow it with a worth that it would not
>   have on its own
> And I would believe I owed to this superior choice
> The happiness of having returned to you a little of
>   what I owe you.[52]

In the face of such an offer, Jason does not hesitate. He asks for what he has come in search of, not a bride, but the Fleece that will restore his rightful power. While both Médée and her father are shocked at the request, Aète is able to characterize the desire as an attack on his state and he is caught in a web of mimetic desire wherein the two men's wish for the same precious object becomes an explicit conflict over political power.

The rest of the drama concerns the working through of this rivalry between Jason and Aète via the playing out of their interest in the Fleece. It is important to understand Médée's role in the rivalry. For while Aète imagined he could placate the warrior who saved his kingdom by offering to share kin, Jason wanted not kin, but skin. This position maintains Jason's basic identity as warrior. That is because in his desire for the Fleece, he does not enter into the symbolic activity that displaces enmity from the battlefield to the realm of symbolic relations (that is, marriage). Instead he chooses a symbol, the skin, which does not adjudicate enmity and civilize warlike urges, but which generates enmity and rivalry. The manner in which that rivalry plays out, however, is directly related to the agency (and technological skill) of the spurned object of desire, the kin (Médée), who will adjudicate the fate of the skin. For she has an interest in that object as well.

Médée's connection to the Fleece is not one of ownership, but of guardianship: it was she, along with her aunt Circé, who helped devise the spells (or shields) that guard the Fleece. Médée does not (need to) own the object (or property) because she does not comprise the leadership of the state. She is the full-bodied version of Medusa's head. She shields an object from attacks, but she still has power over it as guardian. Nevertheless, if Médée has used her "learned magic" to help preserve her father's state, the very object she has helped guard has also displaced her. Médée must therefore attempt to displace the Fleece as Jason's object of desire, or barring that, she must join with the object to reappropriate it and thus use it to take control of the kinship exchange. Médée is an object utilized by those around her (kin) who transforms herself into an agent of power, a complete body able to join kin and skin, to move on its own, to exchange itself.

Another way to read the play is to see it as about the nature of kinship exchange, more particularly about a series of characters' attempts to control exchange and consolidate their state or status (or in Jason's case, to return home to status in his state). Characters who attempt to control exchange include Aète, who hopes the offer of Médée will placate and domesticate Jason; Juno, who comes to tamper with the events and help Jason obtain the Fleece by fooling Médée; Hypsipyle, a foreign queen, who comes to reclaim Jason, who had promised himself to her (in exchange for her crown); and Médée, who may be said to attempt to become the agent of her own exchange in the face of the competing (and at times complementary) desires of all the other agents, including the desire of her younger brother for Hypsipyle.

Médée's position in the exchange is crucial here. For as the story plays out, Jason, in the attempt to attain the Fleece, begins to articulate a complex desire not only for the Fleece, but for Médée as well, largely as a mode of gaining the former object. The adjudication and bringing together of these two competing desires takes up the larger part of the two central characters' interactions until Médée seems to become allied with the Fleece, not as a second object of desire, but as the only agent who can bring Jason the fabric of his (ever-territorial) desire. Jason states this fact openly:

> Yes, that which our Destinies order me to obtain,
> I want it from your hands, and not from my own.
> If this treasure isn't given me by you,
> My strength [*bras*] will punish me for having asked
> too much,
> And my blood in front of you on this sad shore
> From your just refusals will display the result.
> You will see me, Madam, accept the rigor of it,
> Your name in my mouth, and your image in my
> heart,
> And my last sigh by a pure sacrifice
> Save my glory [*gloire*], and render justice to you.
> What happiness to be able to say, in meeting my fate,
> "A loving respect alone caused my death!"[53]

In declaring that he can obtain the Fleece only from Médée's hand, Jason both attempts to seduce Médée into helping him and underlines the simple fact of his situation. Médée has set the spells that hold the object he desires, and thus only she can give it to him. Médée is the only player in the drama who can provide (or withhold) the object on which everyone's fate seems to rest. The secondary story line about Hypsipyle and Absyrte underscores Médée's agency because both seem to rely on Médée's moves and choices to get what they desire. As learned magician, Médée holds

all the strings in a drama of many directors, including the gods. Like
the portrait of María Teresa *qua* Medusa, only she seems capable of
untying the bonds that chain the characters, a power that lies in her
ability to undo the magical "knots" that hold the Fleece. She thus
appears to hold the power to transform the situation, just as her
magic transforms landscapes.

If Médée is the agent of the Fleece, neither Médée nor the
Fleece is the sole representative of the infanta in Corneille's use of
the myth to celebrate the marriage. Indeed, despite certain parallels
between the characters of the myth and the historical context, one
should avoid insisting on any absolute parallel between the mythic
characters and locales and the historic personages and places in
question (i.e., associating Jason with Louis, Medusa with María
Teresa, the Fleece with Spain or with the new queen, and so forth).
For in the period in question there was an intense vogue for the
phenomenon of the enigma, the interpretation of mythic and
emblematic images to find their meaning. Menestrier, who organized the 1658 Golden Fleece fireworks as well as the 1660 celebration, also codified the specific genre of the emblem, and that of
enigmatic images more generally, in numerous writings. He wrote
his first treatise on the emblem in 1659, *Dévises, emblèmes, et
anagrammes*, and continued writing about the subject throughout his
life in the 1662 *Art des emblesmes* and the 1694 *Philosophie des images
énigmatiques*.[54] As the title of his last work on the subject indicates,
the emblem was related to the enigma, a practice that originated in
the Jesuit colleges during the late sixteenth century. According to
Furetière, the emblem is "A sort of pictorial enigma, that, in
representing some known story with words at the bottom, teaches
us some moral lesson, or gives us some other knowledge."[55] As part
of the Jesuit curriculum of the exercise of rhetoric, students were
taught to look at the visual depiction of a story from sacred, secular,
or mythological history and find in it a subtle referential system
figuring an object or idea that was quite unlike the apparent
subject.[56] Corneille would have also been familiar with the genre of
the enigma since he was educated by the Jesuits. In fact, one of the
major sources he used for the story of the Golden Fleece was Natale

Conti's *Mythologie ou explication des fables* (Paris, 1627), a work that was also an important reference for the scenes used to create enigmas.[57] By the late 1630s, furthermore, the genre of the enigma had already migrated from the Jesuit Colleges to the salons of the *précieuses*, preparing for its appearance in the pages of the *Mercure galant* in the 1670s.[58] Just after the marriage, the genre was also utilized by the Académie Royale de Peinture et de Sculpture in prize competitions; in 1664 the prize went to Mosnier's *Conquest of the Golden Fleece*, the work considered to fulfill best the requirement for a picture symbolizing one of the battles that led to the 1660 treaty, the conquest of Dunkirk by Louis XIV.[59]

It was no enigma that Corneille's *Conquête de la Toison d'or* concerned the Treaty of the Pyrenees. Corneille announced as much in his prologue. What was more enigmatic was the connection between two apparently unrelated scenarios, the treaty and the dramatic story line. To understand that relation fully, it is important to appreciate that an enigma was not necessarily meant to depict one "object" or "moral" only. Indeed, although not all theorists of the genre promoted such polyvalence, when the Jesuits publicly staged presentations of their students deciphering enigmas, they often set up elaborate debates that showed more than one possible interpretation for an enigmatic image.[60] It was therefore not just the activity of deciphering meaning that was the goal of the enigma. The possibility of multiple associations, the chance to guess and generate interpretations, also provided pleasure and drew in the spectator or reader. Thus, while handbooks might be published with interpretations and while pamphlets described and interpreted the many emblems of the celebrations for the treaty marriage, that does not mean that there would be only one possible meaning for the enigma to be successful, of interest, and thus symbolically potent; at the very least there might be multiple pathways or readings to enjoy (or gain mastery over) the enigma.

In this climate of interest, both Médée and the Fleece may represent the infanta in Corneille's play. The Fleece and Médée are two sides of the same enigmatic image. One is the ultimate gift, a Fleece or skin on display that adjudicates power sharing. The other is the fully embodied figure, the agent that is necessary to get the gift or power. Seen in this way, the role of Médée seems to offer a resolution to the dilemma of what role the exchanged woman plays in her own kinship exchange. In this case the princess is not a passive, abstract object turned into the material on the market, as the feminist theorists Luce Irigaray and Gayle Rubin have characterized the woman's role in the process of kinship exchange.[61] Rather, she is a dynamic figure attempting (if not fully succeeding) to maneuver her own exchange and control the currency of the symbolic activity, even within the powerful precepts of the male power system of territoriality (or dramatic machinery).

Indeed, as the play continues and the rival Hypsipyle arrives to confront Jason with his infidelity, Médée becomes an agent of kinship exchange. For when she attempts to help her brother Absyrte obtain the queen of Lemnos for himself in Act Three, she takes on a position parallel to that of the goddess Juno, who is attempting to make a match between Médée and Jason. In this section of the play, Médée stages a scene that parallels the two vignettes of the portrait in the prologue. For after a long and conflictual exchange with her rival, Médée imprisons Hypsipyle, allowing Absyrte to "rescue" the queen he has fallen in love with. It is Médée who has built the prison and who breaks the spell, this time not as a portrait held by someone else, but as a fully embodied (albeit invisible) figure working in her own interest to remove Hypsipyle from the field of contention for Jason by promoting the interests of her brother.

The conflict between the two women is secondary. Both Hypsipyle and Médée are spurned for the Golden Fleece. The two more or less agree on this fact in the long exchange that precedes Hypsipyle's "imprisonment" in Scene Five, Act Three. In the exchange, they are set up as parallel figures. Later, Médée's position as agent is more central. It is a role most fully enacted in the final scenes of the play, which stage the theft of the Fleece and resolve Médée's apparent enactment of her own exchange. For the concluding scene of the drama demonstrates how Médée acts to adjudicate her own exchange, how she stages her relation to the

Fleece, and the difference in the goals of her own program of exchange from that of the men. It is no surprise that this scene should be the most spectacular of the play. It is the scene in which Corneille and his host, the Count of Sourdéac, are best able to show off their technical skills. It a particularly dramatic moment in which Médée, on a fire-breathing dragon, swoops down from above and then moves across the stage, Fleece in hand, to display Corneille's technical innovation as well as the Fleece and her relation to it.

As a scenario of female (and dramatic) agency, this scene is striking. For in it, Médée reunites with the object that seemed to split off Jason's desire from her body to her skin or cloth. She masters the scenario by bringing the desired object in and out of view as she flies backward and forward, visible and invisible in the smoke of the special effects of the machine play. The swaying of her body attracts her audience, almost as if she were in a dance of seduction that replaces the tensions of verbal sally found in Corneille's verse of Acts Three and Four. Indeed, if Médée had earlier told Jason that "he who wishes a gift should not insist on it," she concretizes this fact (and her power to give and take the ultimate gift) as she dangles the Fleece just beyond his reach when she flies, as the *Desseins* tells us, just at his height.[62] Interestingly, it is at this point that the ever verbal Jason withdraws from pursuit, saying:

> Madam, I lay my down my weapons at your feet,
> I make homage to your divine charms,
> And renounce with joy my highest glory.[63]

In his place, Jason sends the Argonauts, Orpheus in particular, to take over his role:

> If it is necessary by this combat to buy victory,
> I give it up, Orpheus, to the charms of your voice,
> Which drags rocks and makes forests move,
> Put the dragon to sleep, and cast a spell on the
> Princess.[64]

In substituting Orpheus (the very embodiment of seductive voice) for himself, Jason illustrates how his own dialogue has failed to match Médée's charms. But the preeminence of movement over voice is illustrated by the fact that Orpheus must also withdraw. He cannot approach the sorceress as she dips and sways in and out of the "clouds," and so he drops out (or up) of the pursuit, as Jason had indeed predicted.[65] Médée, like the infanta, is *infans*, without speech. It is not her words that draw attention to her. Rather it is her dancing body and clutch on the Fleece as she takes center stage that hold the gaze of all those around her, who wait expectantly to see in whose service she is dancing.[66]

If Médée is the master (or mistress) of her scenario, if she is a machinist pulling her own strings and levers, her mastery is short-lived (or merely apparent). For the audience soon learns what it already knew: if Médée is operating in the service of her own interests in order to attract Jason, the sorceress is also acting in Jason's interest, since she will deliver the Fleece to his ship. Indeed, the dance is not simply one of agency. Rather, it is the performance of an elaborately choreographed agreement between the two lovers. This prearranged deal may explain Orpheus' withdrawal from battle. If Médée seems to hold the strings, or fibers/Fleece, that fix the attention of the viewers, she is also a puppet on a string, a large and animate spool, pulled in and out of sight as its manipulator(s) attempt(s) to master anxieties of loss in a baroque version of Freud's grandson's spool game. For not only is Médée spun out between the desires of her father (whom she betrays) and Jason (who will ultimately betray her), but she is also manipulated by the wishes of the gods whose parallel universe is apparent throughout the play. This universe takes center stage in the play's last two scenes when three simultaneous decors or stage sets are revealed: the forest of Mars, from which the Fleece had been stolen, the Palace of Aète's father, the Sun, and that of Jupiter, the ultimate *metteur-en-scène*.[67] Standing in the forest of Mars, Aète appeals to the higher authorities for aid. In response he learns from Jupiter what his destiny will hold: he is powerless to stop his daughter. Thus, the gods are ultimately the playwright-technicians of this scene. They control the way the characters or spools spin or move.

But if Médée is finally only a puppet of Jason, the gods' and Corneille's (Sourdéac's) desires, she is nonetheless an "object" who causes some consternation. For her theft of the Fleece is fundamental to the destiny of Jason. Without her, Jason is powerless to attain his goal. As the sorceress flies about on the dragon-machine of theatrical technology, she embodies the very anxiety of presence and absence that underlies her importance to Jason's aspiration at state building (or recuperation). As such, she requires the stage designers to play out the *fort–da* spool game on an adult level, bringing the necessary yet frightening imaginary being in and out of view. With this movement, a new one in stage history, the technicians also attempt to master the vagaries of the symbolic moment that finally can be seen as an attempt to direct one of the most fundamental relations of all, that of the little boy to the object of his adoration, the mother.[68]

This relationship is inscribed in the play when it ends with the only comfort Jupiter can offer the defeated Aète, that of an heir who will avenge him:

> Make Lemnos your sanctuary,
> The heavens wish that Hypsipyle
> Should respond to the desires of Absyrte, and that a
>   dotal scepter
> Should soften the course of this fateful moment.
> Because finally out of your perfidious daughter
> Will come a Médus who will reestablish you,
> In returning to Colchos he will be your guide,
> And a thousand great exploits that will ennoble him
> Will be the remedy of all your ills,
> And will give birth to the Empire of Medes.[69]

Mentioning the heir, Médus, reinvokes through onomatopoeia Meduse, the petrifying specter of the female genitals, the fury that petrifies the male viewer.

Catherine Gallagher has associated the image of the Medusa's head with anxiety about what women can produce that men rely on. According to Gallagher, it is not only the fear of castration that Medusa represents (the traditional psychoanalytic reading of the image) but that of women's generativity as represented by the Medusa's head as the "mother's vagina."[70] In the case of Medea, her ultimate power will be the fact that she can provide heirs and, in a world reliant on blood lines (dynasty), she can also revoke them by committing infanticide (and fratricide), later producing another heir, Médus. But for Médée, that bringing forth and taking back is not a male child's game of *fort–da*, an activity aimed at mastering and orally articulating the relation with the powerful mother. Rather, it is a dance of a mother's mastery of her body. Such a movement is not surprising in the context of dynastic relations, where it is the real possibility of agency (or transformation of matter in the procreating mother) that threatens a sovereign power (i.e., a dynasty) that relies on progeny (dynastic continuity) and not just the sterile, albeit pleasurable [*jouissive*] relations between male kin. For in the myth, Médus is finally the person who will return to reinstate his grandfather on the throne in Colchos. But he is neither Jason's heir, nor Absyrte's. Rather he is Aète's grandson, the son of the treasonous daughter Médée, the result of a liaison she has with yet another foreign king, Aeges [*Egée*]. As such, the role of the bride (foreign princess or sorceress) in the generation of the state, even as Medusa's head, seems as ineluctable as the early jurists feared it might be.[71]

Explosive Technologies

One of the fundamental purposes of nuptial fictions was to stage and contain the anxieties of the treaty marriage. Limbs, frames, fashion, and *privilèges* were some of the strategies used to contain the frightening truths about state building, namely that sexuality, passion, foreign women, and even ceremonies of information played a central role in the generation of the absolutist state. Corneille's play offered a particularly striking version of that "truth," one that may have been difficult to neutralize. Indeed, one might ask how Corneille could stage the truth about female generativity and its foundational (albeit nefarious) role in state building? His machinations and their images, while mythological, seem to hit too close to home for comfort. That they were staged may have exempted them from the kind of "policing" practiced on print culture. *Privilèges*

were not necessary to stage plays, money was. And Corneille did
not lack the latter, having the support of the rich Sourdéac,
interested in trying out his new technological experiments. When
Sourdéac donated the machines constructed for the play at his
château to the *Théâtre du Marais* actors, he effectively underwrote
the play's Paris run. Corneille was thus freed of the rigors of the
theatrical economy even if he was reliant on the eccentricities of his
host.[72] Corneille's machine play seems as explosive a spectacle as the
fireworks Menestrier organized and theorized. Yet, being free from
economic strictures may have allowed Corneille to develop a more
explosive parallel between Medea and Jason and the marriage of
Louis XIV than was possible in the civic celebrations in Lyon and,
more particularly, in Paris.

Of course, Corneille did attenuate his staging of the Golden
Fleece myth somewhat by removing Jason and Médée from sight
at the end of a play that had opened by invoking the most frightening
of images: Medusa, María, and Medea. As in Menestrier's theoretical
example of John the Baptist (or even in the anecdote Freud tells
about his grandson), Corneille used strings and pulleys to remove
problematic images. At the play's conclusion, the couple Jason–
Médée is replaced by another less threatening duo, when, after the
smoke clears, Hypsipyle is shown gladly accepting her suitor Absyrte. This kinship match also provides Aète a new homeland in the
face of invasions predicted by Jupiter, who announces:

> Persès in Scythia equips a sovereign arm;
> As soon as he appears, leave this place, Aète,
> And by a prompt retreat
> Spare all the blood that would flow in vain.[73]

The ending is a defeat for the male ruler Aète, and one that
underlines female "primogeniture" to be certain (is it a coincidence
that the threat comes from the Scythie, land of the Amazons?). It is,
nonetheless, a reassuring conclusion. For Jupiter informs Absyrte
and Aète that they will get Hypsipyle's kingdom and power while
they await their savior, the issue of Médée. The perfidious Médée,
infanticidal (and fratricidal in some versions of the myth) though she
may be, will leave progeny who will return to avenge the clan,

founding an empire issuing out of the explosive daughter and not the compliant son. Of course, the couple composed of Hypsipyle and Absyrte is, to be sure, a less exciting and dramatic one than Médée and Jason. Their story line is much less spectacular. In fact, they are barely dramatic and one could argue that the new couple is together and visible only because of Médée and Jason's explosion. One might say, therefore, that the couple left on stage recall the fiery explosive couple Médée–Jason, stirring the old sparks, now insinuated in the viewer's imagination, much as Menestrier would have predicted. They are, however, simply the emblem of that explosivity, the spool or text that replaces another more frightening story line or agency.

A second reason why the myth of Medea could be fashioned acceptably by Corneille may be found elsewhere. As mentioned, fireworks first utilized the story of the Golden Fleece before the treaty negotiations in 1658 and then repeated the myth precisely to master or contain it, perhaps by eliminating the figure of Médée from the Paris entry's version, leaving Jason alone as the agent over her now dismantled explosivity. Corneille's spectacle, the most detailed (and therefore most unsettling) version of the Golden Fleece myth, was not staged during the marriage celebration. It was staged in its aftermath, in November 1660, after "the Golden Fleece" had been "stolen" and taken to Paris (along with territorial concessions, a bride, etc.). And the play did not premier in Paris, but in the provinces, in Normandy. It was not staged in Paris until January 1661. Due to the death of Mazarin, furthermore, it was not seen by the court until 1662. By this time, Louis XIV was firmly in control. He no longer needed Médée's agency to enrich his state. Indeed, the birth of a dauphin in late 1661, like the Médus of Corneille's play, displaced the queen in importance, shifting the story away from potential loss and putting mastery and gain in sight. The impact of Corneille's technological innovation had, moreover, been displaced by the production of court spectacles constructed to stage the power of Louis XIV. Anyone attempting to pull the strings of mastery would suffer the fate of Fouquet, brought down by his spectacular upstaging of the king in September 1661. As such, the unsettling staging of female power (reproduction) lurking (as the fuse) at the site of the representation of royalty could be defused by Louis in control as sire of his offspring and his spectacular stage.

Of course, traces of danger always remained. Despite Louis' attempts to hide the strings producing his scenario, court spectacles relied on a team of artists.[74] So too the dauphin recalled the role of his mother. Likewise, the power of theater (and fireworks) could be recalled by their traces in print culture. Print was a simulacrum of staged performance, to be certain. Its relation to the original drama mirrored that between the couple of Hypsipyle and Abysyrte and the more fiery Jason and Médée. But the print version did keep nuptial fictions available just as the presence of the queen at court, however marginalized, was a constant reminder of her agency in state building. Nuptial fictions did not fade from view after the treaty marriage. As with the story of the Golden Fleece and the intermittent birth of heirs, they resurfaced, hinting that Louis XIV would be ever reliant upon the spool-game gestures of those painting his portrait or those machines or monuments upon which his portrait hung, or out of which his portrait was generated . . . or reproduced. How this explosive reliance (and its mastery) was subdued by the regime and how it was understood (and exploited) by a public outside those working for the regime is the topic of the final chapter.

CHAPTER 5

Curiosity and the Art of
Collecting a Queen

Symbolic displays of power would be meaningless without a willing and avid audience. Representations of the queen (or her homologues, such as Medea) created such a public. The daughter of a former enemy, an unknown princess arriving from a foreign land to capture a gallant young king's heart and provide future rulers for the dynasty, she was an object of intense curiosity. Without her there might not have been a story. Or, at the very least, there might not have been such a good story. Even before the marriage agreement, broadside almanacs such as "The Celebrated Assembly of the Court" (Figure 5) created suspense about who would be Louis XIV's bride. In so doing, they advertised the military victories in Spanish-occupied Flanders that would lead to the treaty marriage. During the actual negotiations with Spain, descriptions of a diplomat's reactions to seeing the infanta published in pamphlets such as the *Relation la plus fidelle & ponctuelle* attached readers' interest to news of the diplomatic mission to Madrid and then to the even more prosaic, albeit spectacularly advantageous to the French, treaty negotiations that followed. Arriving in France, the new queen's movements were placed at the center of the narrative developed by officially designated journalists and publishers reporting on the treaty signing and marriage ceremony. In *La Nouvelle Relation*, for exam-

ple, the images of the queen provided a story line that could create
a pleasing tension to draw reader interest toward the more mundane
details of the treaty signing, the king's meeting with Philip IV, and
the court's journey home to Paris in triumph.[1] Of course, such a
central place in the marriage "plot" accorded the new queen a large
role in how the king was seen. Nuptial fictions are distinguished by
how they facilitate the staging and management of that power as it
is manifested in both the images and the various media that create
and disseminate them.

In an age without the free circulation of discourses that characterized the establishment of a public sphere during the Enlightenment, the only access to the images and processes of this political
fairy tale were via apparatuses of the state: royal rituals, civic
celebrations, and, of course, their reporting by "privileged" print
culture. Michèle Fogel has characterized the kinds of print culture
examined here, almanacs, news pamphlets, etc., as "ceremonies of
information."[2] Anthropologists generally agree that ceremonies are
myth makers, and indeed marriage itself is considered by anthropologists as a myth-making ritual of passage that processes and
transforms reality via symbolic acts.[3] Print-culture reporting on
those rituals was no less ceremonial or transformative. Indeed, one
might argue that print culture in the age of absolutism was always
dealing in myth; even if the pamphlets reporting on the marriage
presented themselves as the surrogate eyes of the public, they
actually constructed and disseminated knowledge (information) at
the will of Mazarin, that is, according to a system of royal prerogatives (*permissions* and *privilèges*). As was seen in Chapter Three,
pamphlets offering apparently diverse views of the king were
actually representing one "privileged" position. The central entryway into all the images and media of nuptial fictions, these pamphlets
were a biased source for understanding the nuptial fictions and the
role played by the queen (and the supporting media) in them.

To gain another perspective on how the queen functioned as
an object of curiosity fueling nuptial fictions (both as image and as
a model for the technologies that construct that image), it is
necessary to look beyond official reports and activities to material

not usually included in the marriage archive. A play by Pierre Corneille has already provided one such "outside" perspective on the appeal of nuptial fictions. A different kind of external insight is provided by Madeleine de Scudéry in a novel, *Célinte*, published in Paris on January 25, 1661, almost five months to the day after the royal entry into Paris. The text is of interest because it provides a gloss both on the nature of the royal entry and on the material produced to report and describe it to the public. Perhaps it is not chance that a work of prose fiction provides crucial insight into how nuptial fictions (and the absolutist power they support) resolve their reliance on curiosity about the queen. The genre of the novel was gaining in popularity in 1660, but it was not yet a legitimated form. Indeed, it has been linked by literary critic Joan DeJean to opposi-tional politics during the Fronde.[4] As such, Scudéry's novel does not simply reproduce the perspective of the king and Mazarin. It turns the eye of the *salonnière* on the construction of nuptial fictions.

Curiosity about the Marriage of Louis XIV

It is not the plot that is of interest in Scudéry's *Célinte*. The novel is a fairly conventional (except for its short length) Scudérian tale of love and jealousy. Rather it is the novel's introductory prologue that is relevant to a study of nuptial fictions. It is an account of a long exchange between *mondains*, worldly Parisians participating in salon society, whose discussion of the recent events of the royal entry turns into a philosophical debate about the nature of curiosity. Since Scudéry herself was an active and visible figure among the Parisian intelligentsia in this period, and since "elite" urban culture centered around salon life with its oral readings of written texts and its philosophical debates about enigmas such as curiosity, it is not unreasonable to conjecture that the prologue originated in the oral discussion of the salon. Most likely, the text circulated widely in that milieu in manuscript form in the months just after the entry (at the same time the occasional pamphlet descriptions of the entry would also have been circulating there).[5] Indeed, it is clear that in her treatment of the entry, Scudéry drew heavily on the many occasional pamphlet descriptions circulating before, during, and after the entry, not only because she cites them extensively, but also because that literature relies heavily on the very *topos* Scudéry herself links to the entry: curiosity.[6]

Scudéry probably picks up on the rhetoric of curiosity because it is omnipresent in the largest series of pamphlets produced to report the wedding, those discussed in Chapter Three, the texts written by the journalist François Colletet. From the very beginning of his reporting, during the treaty negotiations in 1659, Colletet used the trope of curiosity as a legitimizing frame for his narrative, underlining repeatedly that his pamphlets were a response to the legitimate impatience of the curious public to learn about events of such great historical import. Indeed, Colletet framed his very first relations of the negotiation of the peace treaty with a remark about the public's curiosity: "But in waiting for this important business [the treaty] to be entirely concluded, & and the peace proclaimed in one and the other Realm, in order to satisfy the curious who desire to know the particularities of the voyage of Our Monarch, & of his Eminence, I will take up the task of making a succinct and faithful Relation."[7] The trope changes somewhat in the re-edition of this text one year later: "But to perpetuate the memory of a business of such great importance, upon which the People & all the Nations have their eyes fixed, & to satisfy even the Curious of this century [*les Curieux de ce siecle*] who desire the particularities of the voyage of Our Monarch, & of his Eminence, I will take up the task of making a succinct and faithful Relation."[8] Reprinted after the completion of the marriage and entry of the queen into Paris, Colletet's second edition of his report on the treaty negotiation shifts into the discourses of monumental history, invoking the importance of memorializing the events on both the local and national levels.[9] Keeping the earlier version's reference to the "curieux," Colletet elevates the group in the second edition by characterizing them as "Curieux de ce siècle," alluding to an audience of collectors of rare items. This shift is striking, since the phenomenon of collecting nuptial images will be an important aspect of how nuptial fictions are preserved for posterity. Colletet's references to the curious reader are a mode of legitimizing both the pamphlet and the curiosity of his public. Indeed, Colletet engages in such legitimation of curiosity elsewhere in his reporting, as, for example, in the *Nouveau Journal Historique* where he remarks: "I do not want to frustrate the public, which naturally is curious about new things, and *which has the right to be curious about things that in effect cause all our happiness and all our joy* [emphasis added]."[10]

Given the prevalence of the *topos* of curiosity in the marriage literature, it is worth reviewing the traditional views of the notion that Scudéry and the pamphlet writers would have been familiar with. As a negative impulse, curiosity was linked in the period to wanting to know about things that are none of one's business; it was associated with a kind of hungry avidity for illicit knowledge. The example of such improper curiosity most often given is women's proclivity to gossip and their delight in inappropriate information, an image repeatedly invoked in the skirmishes of the *querelle des femmes* during the Renaissance. Negative curiosity was likewise connected to sexuality (the inappropriate gaze, for example) and all forms of transgression or excess, including Eve's insatiable curiosity for the apple from the Tree of Knowledge and the inability of Lot's wife to contain her curiosity and not look back (both being severely punished for their curiosity). Juxtaposed against this negative view of curiosity was the more secular and stoic position in which the impulse was linked to a desire for knowledge construed as positive. For example, in early modern Europe, science was considered a legitimate curiosity, and, within the Christian tradition, the desire to know God would also be acceptable. As an activity of the mind linked to increasingly legitimized science or already legitimate philosophical investigation, curiosity could be construed as a positive, even natural activity for mankind (literally "men," since so few women devoted themselves to scientific or philosophical study in this period).[11]

This brief discussion serves to establish two important aspects of the notion of curiosity as it would have been understood by those using it at the time of the marriage. First, curiosity was considered a dangerous impulse, one needing regulation because it was likely to spawn the kinds of impulses and interests that would lead to an independence of mind and a public sphere, as posited by Habermas for the period of the Enlightenment.[12] Second, curiosity was a highly gendered notion. Scudéry's treatment of the topic is thus interesting because the free discussion of the public sphere did indeed have roots in the salon society organized by women in seventeenth-century Paris.[13] Her perspective on the events of the royal entry offers an outside view of nuptial fictions by someone who is both an observer of the ceremonies and a reader of their reporting, but who is only tangentially part of the official economy of their generation.

Indeed, Scudéry did not travel to the border and she did not write up reports. Rather, she commented on both scenes in the context of her fiction. Unlike Menestrier and the pamphleteer Colletet, she was not paid (and did not receive patronage) to advertise and popularize the events of the treaty marriage. As a woman, she would not have been given such a task. Rather, her realm was fiction, the genre Colletet imitated in his reports. If Colletet imitated Scudéry, the novelist profited from the journalist's reports to make her own fiction more contemporary. As a writer of novels, she was singularly positioned to offer not necessarily an objective interpretation of the nuptial fictions Colletet constructed, but at least an alternative take on those stories. As a female intellectual, her perspective on how the entry ceremonies were shaped by (and shaping of) the new queen was likely to differ from those of male commentators. Indeed, unlike Colletet and the pamphleteers, she did not simply offer a hermeneutic interpretation of its monuments, but provided an in-depth analysis of the ritual and its fictions.[14]

Curiosity about the Royal Entry

The prologue to *Célinte* is similar to the kind of philosophical debates Scudéry made famous in her earlier novels and in her later moralist essays.[15] These debates always take place among a group of exemplary individuals who, finding themselves together in an idyllic spot, stumble, as if by chance, upon a topic of conversation. The group then spends a few hours (and many pages) inventorying the subject as characters offer examples and anecdotes that allow them to demonstrate the various issues of and positions on the question at hand.[16] The prologue to *Célinte* is no exception to this model. It stages a group walking in the Bois de Vincennes outside Paris a few days after the entry. The topic of conversation is chosen when Lysimène, a woman, turns to one of her companions, Meriante, a man, and asks him if he is happy to be away from the chaos of the Parisian entry ceremony, a ceremony to which curiosity had attracted such a large crowd: " 'Admit the truth,' she said, turning towards Meriante, 'you are very happy to be away from the noise and tumult after having been forced to be in it these past days[,] finding yourself there by the universal Curiosity [*Curiosité universelle*] that everyone had to see the Entry of the Queen.' " Meriante's reply begins the debate when he turns Lysimène's question into a chance to declare himself not just an enemy of the tumult of the entry, but of the curiosity that drives people to such unpleasant scenes: " 'It is true,' he replied, 'that I am a great friend of repose, of silence, & of solitude, & a great enemy of this Curiosity that pushes so many people to seek so eagerly all the things that cannot be seen without a crowd, without disorder, and without confusion.' "[17]

Note here that for both Meriante and Lysimène, curiosity is clearly linked to a kind of hectic, urban sociability of disorder and confusion, the carnavalesque tumult of the entry. Both contrast this environment to the pastoral calm of their current location. Nonetheless, the two will ultimately take different positions on the phenomenon. Indeed, when Meriante declares himself to be a "great enemy of curiosity," his announcement stirs up general consternation as the interlocutors take stands on the issue. Meriante declares, on the one hand, that "curiosity ordinarily harms much more than it benefits and gives more pain than pleasure," while the other speakers generally defend the search for knowledge as "very necessary to the world" and to "sociability."[18] The narrator of the prologue then mediates the discord by asserting that "[c]uriosity is like water, there is good and bad according to the ground it passes through."[19] The group generally accepts this idea that curiosity and the impulse for knowledge may be good or bad depending on the media (the persons or the milieu) through which they pass. But only Meriante believes that the curiosity behind going to see the entry of the queen could ever be construed as negative because then it would be necessary to condemn too many people, the entire public of Paris and the world. Indeed there is a flurry of reactions to this effect in the face of Meriante's absolute position against curiosity:

> "But," admonished Artelice, "at least you will not place the universal Curiosity that everyone had to see the Queen's entry among the ill-founded Curiosities, because you would be condemning too many people." "As a matter of fact," continued Lysimène, "in Paris there are currently people not only from all the Provinces and all the Towns of France, but from all the Villages of the Kingdom." "It is necessary to add," chided Philinte, "that there are people there from all the neighboring countries; & that since Paris has become the premier city of the world, she has never had so many foreigners within her walls." "Indeed," said Artelice, "it is curiosity that brought them here, it is curiosity that keeps them here, and it is curiosity that provides their pleasure."[20]

The group largely agrees that the curious crowds that come to see the entry are good people, hence their curiosity is good. Before Meriante can muster a reply to this barrage, Cleandre arrives on the scene. Having overheard that they were discussing the entry, and not having been able to attend due to an illness, Cleandre approaches the group and expresses curiosity about what they have seen.

This interruption shifts the conversation more directly to the relation between curiosity and the entry. For when Lysimène is chosen to respond to Cleandre, she notes that she will not repeat what "several people will be describing very exactly," referring to the many pamphlet descriptions of the events as well as to engravings of the monuments that were also appearing in Paris.[21] Lysimène proposes instead that the group focus on what she calls the "Story of the Loggia, the Balconies, and the Scaffolds, [which] would be a more entertaining Curiosity for an invalid."[22] In so doing, Lysimène sets up what appears to be a fundamental opposition between the processions and ceremonies already described in official literature and the curious public, an unofficial dimension of the entry not fully accounted for by print culture. Cleandre requests that the company inform him of both scenarios because he feels the two are not at all inconsistent or contradictory, but rather are necessarily connected. As the prologue progresses, however, it becomes difficult to see how the two spheres are compatible, since they appear to function according to different logics of curiosity.

For the events of the entry, the eight hours of parade that pass without "a single moment of boredom," the indisputable and legitimate object of fascination is the king, since as one interlocutor notes, "it must be admitted that the king was a thousand times above the others [marchers] by his prepossessing appearance, his grace, distinguished looks, majesty, and magnificence."[23] Second to the king was his bride, "who by the whiteness of her complexion, the sparkle of her eyes, the beauty of her hair, and the sweetness and modesty of her glances, & all the charms of her person, conquered the hearts of all those who saw her, *to lead them like captives she had chained with new ties, to the service of the great king who gave her to us as queen* [emphasis added]."[24] In the face of such superiority, the interlocutors find it hard to see how Meriante could disapprove of their curiosity: "Yet I do not believe that Meriante could say that curiosity in this encounter could be censured, because could there ever be a more well-founded curiosity than wanting to see the most beautiful spectacle that had ever been seen, the most beautiful Princess in the world, and the greatest King in the land." Note the hyperbole here, as if the repetition of the superlative singles out the object of curiosity as unique and thus legitimizes the gaze. Both the king and queen are objects of curiosity precisely because they are so great or mythic as to exceed description; not some petty topic of private interest, they serve to create an awe that safely and respectfully positions the viewer before the object of curiosity. As such, they belong to the category the interlocutors term "Universal Curiosity," curiosity about what they call "the big news items of the world [*les grandes nouvelles du monde*]." The best example of such universal curiosity is the recent marriage of the king. Other examples offered are the peace accord that led to the marriage, the death of the king of Sweden, and the restoration of the king of England.[25]

Such news is characterized as universal because it belongs to the permanent record of history. According to one interlocutor it would be shameful to be ignorant of such information.[26] It is also information controlled and manipulated in the public record in the interest of the state.

Opposed to the heroic information of universal curiosity are the particular details about the carnivalesque crowd that draw in the viewer to what Lysimène refers to as the "story of the loggia, the balconies, and the scaffolds." These scenes are apparently no less absorbing than those of the parade. What elicits curiosity about them, however, is not awe but amusement, even disdain of the disorders seen (not great news items, but ephemeral events such as fights between lovers, people falling from balconies, foreigners who do not comprehend what they are seeing, and glimpses at other ignorant and disorderly viewers). Such disdain before the fleeting event allows the interlocutors to feel superior and perhaps, even in telling the stories, to be a little less exact, that is, to exaggerate for narrative effect. As such, this kind of curious scene or "news item" that can exceed "the appropriate limits of Curiosity" is called *la grande curiosité*, which will be translated here as "excessive curiosity."[27] When Meriante summarizes this type of curiosity, he associates it with malicious gossip, " 'it should not be doubted,' replied Meriante, 'that slander is very often the result of excessive curiosity and that ordinarily, curious people do not want to know things in order to report them as they were said to them, but *in order to add everything that could harm those of whom they speak* [emphasis added].' "[28] Such negative or excessive curiosity is dangerous or ill-founded precisely because the curious person is not in awe of the information and thus feels free to supplement it at will (manipulate or deform it) to the harm of others and the aggrandizement of him- or herself. This impulse is different from the more monumentally oriented "universal curiosity," both in its interest in particularities, as opposed to grand events, as well as in where it orients its gaze, inward towards the cabinets (loggia or balconies) and private spaces of a world often associated with the ephemera of the female, instead of at the great vistas or galleries of the permanent or monumental (male) historical event.[29] One might characterize the difference between these two kinds of curiosity as oriented toward two different spheres, an official ceremonial arena controlled by the king and an intimate one, also public, but not official, and so less easily constrained.

The relation between the official and the intimate is part of what was described earlier (in Chapter Three) as the logic of the "inter-view" in which private details of the marriage help keep interest fixed on the public scene. Likewise, Scudéry does not set up a clear opposition between the two kinds of curiosity, but rather sees them in a dialectical relation. For details about the king and queen in the citations chosen by Scudéry, mostly details about their demeanor or appearance such as the queen's milky complexion or the king's grace, are not the "great news items of the world" or information about which it would be "a shame to be ignorant." Rather, these details seem to be similar to those focused on by the excessively curious, details constructed or created to chain people (as the queen's role is described in the citation above) to the service of their creator. The only difference between the two cases, therefore, is that the great news items work in the service of a king (a figure not normally construed as a slanderer) while the second function in the service of less important people.

The opposition between the stories of the entry and those of the "loggia" thus seems to be a red herring designed to throw the reader off the track of what Scudéry is really saying about the entry and its reporting, that even if the official literature about the entry hardly deals with the scenes of the loges, that arena is still crucial to the deployment of nuptial fictions. But of the over 150 texts produced around the marriage, the only ones dealing with the vilified dimension of the "loggia" are three or four pamphlets that satirize naive provincials, and approximately eight ordinances issued by the government about the building of viewing stands (scaffolds) that had collapsed in the past because of poor construction.[30] Scudéry's irony here is heavy-handed. To the reader familiar with pamphlets still circulating in Paris when her novel was published, she certainly would have driven home the fact that curiosity is difficult to monitor, even among the most enlightened, and the notion that it could be otherwise is only an illusion of naive officials who write edicts and of official journalists who are out of touch with the streets, or their loggia.

Despite Scudéry's irony, it is important to keep in mind the dichotomy between the loggia and official events of the entry (and its potential for collapsing) when reading the conclusion of the prologue's debate, which essentially underlines the need to monitor curiosity. Such oversight is necessary because the two logics of curiosity can converge when what seems controllable can too easily get out of hand. This possibility had already been suggested when one of Scudéry's interlocutors wondered whether the ever-dogmatic Meriante "will find that it is a reasonable curiosity to want to see extraordinary persons who distinguished themselves from the common man by a thousand noble qualities," moving the conversation in the direction of what really determines the appropriateness of the curiosity, the nature of the audience and not that of the object. For the group decides that curiosity about great people would always be praiseworthy as long as the persons who are curious are capable of judgement. Nothing could be more troublesome than an ignorant person who wants to see the most learned man in the world.[31] Meriante advises such bores to limit their curiosity to seeing "these extraordinary monkeys, such as the famous Fagotin, so celebrated among animals, exhibited at the Saint Germain Fair, or to see those Bears that dance so well. . . ."[32] What is the difference between the monkey and the extraordinary person, between the world of the balcony and that of the king? Was Scudéry, via Meriante, suggesting that the entry made the king and queen into magnificent monkeys, the object of the gaze of ignorant persons? One Scudéry scholar, Alan Niderst, editor of the edition of *Célinte* cited here, wonders if this section might be a reference to the fact that the curious crowds who came to Paris from the provinces and abroad may have also wanted to see the famous writer, Scudéry? Niderst suggests Scudéry was expressing some exasperation at such attention.[33] It seems more likely that Scudéry was expressing sympathy for the new queen, who had become a kind of object of curiosity in the zoo of the entry, a legitimate if necessary evil of the state apparatus. Nonetheless, if there was a difference between the two scenes, it is clear that it did not lie in the impulse, curiosity, or in the object of curiosity, but in the agent (or agents) of curiosity, the viewing public, whose massive size had allowed one interlocutor to justify not condemning the "universal Curiosity that everyone had to see the Queen's entry among the ill-founded Curiosities, *because you would be condemning too many people*" [emphasis added].[34]

It is Meriante who finally rules on this issue of audience (and thus concludes the debate) by offering one last striking image of the danger of curiosity (even in the hands of reliable individuals). His example is an apparently innocent one, that of "certain people called *Curieux*," collectors of curiosities who engaged in a practice that came into vogue in the mid-sixteenth century and was still popular throughout the seventeenth century.[35] Such collectors were known for constituting *cabinets de curiosité*, collections both of exotic objects arranged in small rooms often known as *cabinets*, in or around an actual cabinet, or, in the case of certain collections, in a large space such as a public gallery, in which a collector, particularly one of engravings, might spread out the treasures of his collection. One might characterize collecting, therefore, as a phenomenon oriented inward into the space of the cabinet and outward toward the great vistas of history. Or rather, it was an attempt by learned men and nobles to place objects of universal curiosity into small spaces of particular interest, while also taking objects of particular interest and displaying them in galleries, as being of universal import. Of course, this intersection occurred not only on the level of display, but also on that of what was displayed, since collections were often composed of objects of historical import (antiquities, medals, engravings of great men) and objects more ephemeral in nature (exotic plants, shells, and unicorns' horns, for example). One might say, therefore, that the collection is an attempt to establish, as fundamentally acceptable and legitimate, a relationship between universal and excessive curiosity, at least within the site of the *cabinet*. Meriante, of course, condemns the practice, merging its two populations, those *curieux* with scientific leanings whose objects of curiosity—butterflies, caterpillars, and spiders—he finds frivolous and those

curieux with a historical orientation whose objects of curiosity—statues, paintings, and medals—he admits are "more noble things."[36] In
Meriante's opinion, even those who are learned and whose objects
of curiosity are noble are subject to a dialectic of desire that is always
volatile and unpredictable "[B]ecause whoever accustoms himself
to desire too strongly an indifferent thing, can in some other
encounter desire a criminal one with equal ardor."[37] In so doing, he
underlines that the two logics of curiosity, the universal, which
seems to seek knowledge indifferently and in awe, and the excessive,
which seeks knowledge avidly and with little respect, are intimately
and inextricably related. Playing with curious objects, even in the
name of science (or political fictions), is a dangerous game, one that
can too easily lead to disorder.[38]

The image of the *cabinet*, wherein even a desire for indifferent
and awesome knowledge can go awry despite the best attempts at
organization, is an apt closure to Scudéry's discussion. For the logic
of the *cabinet* is a logic that, like the two scenes of the entry,
highlights the unsettling compatibility between the vistas of history
with its collection of medals, antiquities, and engravings and the
world of avid self-aggrandizement through the manipulation of the
curious object within the *cabinet*. As critics have pointed out in the
wake of Foucault, such displays as the *cabinet de curiosité* amassed and
arranged by powerful people were never meant simply to display
objects, but also to display the power and wealth (or intellect) of
their owners. In his book about collectors and collections in
seventeenth-century France, Antoine Schnapper sketches the relation between the viewer of the *cabinet* and its owner as one of the
primary functions of the collection.[39] It is thus not surprising that
Louis XIV would have reorganized and rebuilt his royal collections
as part of his program of self-aggrandizement. One can also see why
collecting might have appealed to Mazarin. For even if, as Schnapper
notes, collecting was not limited by traditional social stratification—
collectors could be scholars, military officers, doctors, and lawyers
as well as nobility—the enterprise was linked to stirring up nation-
alism insofar as collecting, particularly that of the antiquarians, could
be associated with patriotism in its inclination toward items of

historical interest.[40] This orientation was surely at play in the entry wherein the history of the French monarchy was put on display for patriotic reasons, using curiosity for state building. Thus, even if, as Schnapper notes, collections could not rival great spectacles of power (he gives the example of the painted decor of a castle, but one might think of the entry in this way), the *cabinet de curiosité* did serve to reproduce and transmit values, making them available to the bourgeois process of self-legitimation.[41]

In this context, it is not surprising that the image of the *cabinet* would be a central rhetorical trope of reporting on the entry. The entry ceremony allowed Mazarin to make forms and ideas available to a broad spectrum of the French public via the ceremony and its reporting. As the work of Lawrence Bryant has established, royal entries were traditionally about the ordering of relations between the city and the king. According to Bryant, "The *entrée royale* flourished when corporations, cities, and kings shared authority." It is thus that Bryant calls the 1660 entry "the last great royal entry ceremony."[42] For Louis XIV's absolutism marked the end of sharing power. The 1660 treaty, insofar as it laid the foundation for the rule of an absolutist monarch who would not share (even, and especially, symbolic) power, offers an especially interesting example of the adaptive nature of ceremonial that Hanley has described in her work on the *lit de justice*.[43] Although the 1660 entry seems to conform to old rules, it is really about using existing structures to enact a new set of rules. As such, the logic of the cabinet is an interesting trope. It masquerades as a display of sharing and showing, but it is really about the manipulation of the collection in the service of the glorification of one collector, Mazarin, creating and setting up Louis XIV as absolute collector.[44]

Scudéry, writing out of the tradition of the salon, a tradition of collaboration, might well have been particularly sensitive to such a shift between sharing and dominating. Indeed, a quick overview of how the trope of curiosity appears in the pamphlets suggests this shift. The initial image of the curious reader mentioned above is replaced in the entry descriptions with a characterization of Paris as a *cabinet de curiosité* when the city is characterized as "[t]his mighty city . . . where all the wonders were collected in order to make this celebrated ceremony striking."[45] In another text, Paris is characterized as "the summary of all the wonders of the World [*l'abregé de toutes les merveilles du Monde*]."[46] Like the rhetoric of curiosity more generally, language characterizing Paris as a *cabinet de curiosité* is also found in other pamphlets, as for example, in one panegyric poem that refers to Paris as *l'abregé du Monde*. The description of *La France curieuse* to see the new court, particularly the queen, its newest addition, found further on in the text reinforces the initial image.[47] In this metaphor of Paris as *cabinet de curiosité*, France is cast as the curious collector and Paris as the cabinet for the collection.[48] The shift takes power away from Paris, making it one more collectible in France's cabinet, or at the very least suggesting it is the cabinet, part of the collection, that which holds, orders, and displays it. This portrayal begins to suggest, as does Scudéry's preface, that such images are about the shaping (taming and domestication) of the entry ritual. In this context, it is not surprising that nuptial fictions, initially about the joining of Louis XIV and María Teresa (about the joining of France and Spain), would ultimately shift that relation of collaboration to one of mastery in order to portray the monarch as absolutely powerful.

Curiosity About the Queen

Construed as functioning in the service of mastery (and not sharing), the trope of curiosity in the pamphlets has none of the negative associations proposed for it by Scudéry's interlocutors. For Colletet, the entry is part of the more noble (male) dimension of curiosity, that which is regulated and regulatable. For example, the legitimacy of curiosity is evident from the title of one of Colletet's pamphlets: *Description des Arcs de Triomphe Esléves dans les places Publiques pour l'Entrée de la Reyne. Avec la veritable explication en Prose, & en Vers des Figures, Ovales, Termes, Portiques, Devises & Portraits qui sont tant aux Faubourg que Porte S. Antoine, Cymetiere S. Jean, Pont Nostre-Dame, Marché-Neuf, Place Dauphine, &c. Ensemble diverses Remarques Curieuses & particulieres pour les amateurs de l'Histoire*.[49] In its title, the pamphlet offers its curious remarks as a guide for understanding the city's monuments by invoking one of the principal tropes of the tradition of collecting in utilizing the term "amateur." In the seventeenth century, this expression was a synonym for the *curieux*, that is, the person who collects things.[50] In this pamphlet's title, the reference is to the *amateur* of history; indeed, as Schnapper has noted, the practice of collecting in its relation to antiquarians was also often linked to history and to patriotism insofar as the conservation of artifacts, as noted earlier, was linked to preserving and glorifying the nation's past.[51] The pamphlet that uses the term *amateur* in its title presents itself as such a patriotic historical project when the narrator states: "I cannot refrain from giving a particular account, *in order to preserve an Everlasting Memory. . . .*" [emphasis added].[52] The Loyson pamphlets thus firmly place the curiosities of the entry in the category Meriante labels noble or universal. As seen in Chapter Three, Loyson and Colletet were established players in the game of state building. It is therefore not surprising that they might construe their texts on the entry as legitimate catalogues of a collection of universal interest.

In focusing on the king as object of curiosity, the entry pamphlets situated him as the object of the universal curiosity of respectable *amateurs*. This is the same position Scudéry seemed to ascribe to the king in her prologue. Indeed, *La Description des Arcs*, mentioned above, describes a "gallery" of portraits of the kings of France displayed on the Pont Neuf, a gallery at the end of whose series Louis's portrait is found, placing the young king firmly into the seriality of history and the domain of the awe-inspiring.[53] Of course, even positioned as such, the king's role in the *cabinet* is not really as a collected item. When the rhetoric of collecting as possession in the seventeenth-century sense of the verb, *posseder*—"[t]o know well, to have studied something well,"—surfaces in the pamphlets that anticipate the family's return to Paris, it is the queen and not the king who is the longed-for object of study.[54] This distinction is seen in such passages as, "I trust that we will soon have the good fortune to be in possession of them, and to see this Queen who is the joy of the whole world."[55]

This attitude toward the queen as collected item echoed the focus of the pamphlets Colletet wrote describing scenes from the border. It also projected the notion that the king belonged to the permanent part of the collection associated with the seriality of history, while the queen occupied another part of the collection, not the gallery of history, but the small *cabinet* of exotica, shells, unicorns' horns, and other such ephemera (such as pamphlets). These are the objects that draw the viewer to the collection, as the pamphlets repeatedly assert in expressions such as "everyone is naturally curious to see new things."[56] Remember, however, that for Meriante, this part of the collection, while tempting, is not as noble as that which includes the more familiar paintings, statues, and medals, the memorabilia of history. Of course, collections normally consisted of both objects and images, the latter supplementing the former which might be, at best, ephemera, especially for a collection oriented toward botany or zoology.[57] The engraving in the *cabinet* can also be used to replace ephemera that could not travel, to bring home a curiosity seen only in exotic lands.[58] In this schema, the king is associated with the gallery of paintings or permanent collection (the seriality of history). He is presented as the object of curiosity that will endure and travel, while the infanta is allied with the ephemera that remains at home in the *cabinet* (and wilts).

Of course, despite their ephemeral nature, exotic objects are the center of the collection. They are the big-ticket curiosities that draw the viewer to the more familiar and mundane, albeit more noble, parts of the collection. They are the stories of the loggia (inter-views) that draw the reader to those details of apparently universal, and possibly less compelling interest. They are also the queen's charms that Scudéry insists "chain" or captivate the reader to the service of the king. Thus it is the queen who is ultimately the focus of the collecting, and not the king. For even if there is an attempt to legitimize the curious gaze at the king who occupies the permanent collection of the Pont Neuf history gallery, how could Paris actually ever "possess" or know its divine monarch? Close study of the king is surely a dangerous activity, one not necessarily always functioning in the service of universal (public) curiosity, but rather an activity that might easily, even in the hands of the serious amateur of history, and with the help of the pamphlet catalogue, lead to avidity, to taking liberty with the arrangement of the knowledge garnered about the king. Indeed, how can a "public" ever put a king in its collection as a known and studied object and still honor him with the awe of universal curiosity? Meriante would argue that even in the case of such an apparently appropriate kind of curiosity, the danger of transgression is too great. Meriante would argue against the liberty of the public sphere.

It is thus that if, in the entry pamphlets, the king is at times associated with the gallery of portraits, that part of the cabinet that holds engravings of famous men, he is ultimately depicted as associated with the position of powerful collector. This image is foreshadowed in the king's public display of his first view of his new bride. It is refined in a text from the entry ceremonies that describes the processions of the king and queen organized at Vincennes before the larger and more formal cavalcade on August 26. In this pamphlet, the king is depicted as a valiant warrior who "as Father of the Country having a true tenderness for the faithful bourgeois, wishing to give them some mark of it, would not settle with honoring them with his presence, he wanted, furthermore, to make them see the treasure which is most dear to him and the most precious in the world."[59] With this image, the king moves out of the gallery or monumental space of the Pont Neuf with its cameos of all the kings of France to take his position as live collector in a display that he owns and (purportedly) arranged. The pamphlet thus attempts to create a new relation between the king and the audience, making the shift in the entry from power sharing to asserting power.[60] The image, however, masks the actual manipulation, insofar as it presents the king honoring his curious public by making the magnanimous and necessary gesture of the collector to display his greatest treasure. Of course, if the king's display of his bride creates implicit sympathy with his fellow *curieux*, it also simultaneously enforces the distance that is between them in presenting the queen as "a very valuable treasure," something always inaccessible because she is part of the king's treasury or collection.[61]

This last facet of the entry is highlighted graphically when the queen is marched through the streets of Paris several days later:

> . . . so richly dressed that it was a marvel when one looked at her: she had only a simple headdress of crepe on the top of her head which floated at the will of the wind, in order that everyone could see her more conveniently. Her dress was of a gold brocade, entirely covered with embroidery embossed with gold and silver and so heavy that all Paris was amazed to see this great Princess carry this load so freely because besides these riches she was bedecked with rubies, pearls, and precious stones, which shone like as many stars and that were not of a light weight, because they were, in effect, the elite of the most beautiful of the crown jewels.[62]

Encrusted with precious metals and the best of the crown jewels, the infanta is literally turned into a jewel (another element in a procession that displayed many jewels, including those on the harnesses of various horses and even those held in the queen's own *cassette*), paraded through the streets of Paris to glorify her collector, the king.[63] This image is fascinating because while it purports to place the queen in the monumental or permanent side of the king's collection as one in a series of gems paraded through the streets of Paris, it really does not highlight the new queen as much as it displays the monarchy's manipulation of her. The pamphlet stresses that the public does not marvel at the infanta's importance. The infanta, so encrusted with jewels that she can barely stand, is not what attracts the crowd's attention. What attracts their attention is the way the king (or Mazarin) demonstrates his power to transform the new queen, to place her in the permanent collection by fossilizing her, by replacing her volatile (and dynamic) molecules with stones from the royal treasury. It is thus that Apostolidès notes that the infanta's dress "metamorphosed her into a dazzling *statue* [emphasis added]."[64] As such, the audience is not actually awed by her very weight and importance, but by the way that position is constructed, one might say overconstructed. They are no longer drawn to the obliqueness of her gaze as organizer of the king's visibility, but to his role as fabricator of hers. It is, finally, this staged manipulation of the infanta, her transformation into collectable jewel (or nuptial fiction), that serves to aggrandize the king in much the same manner as "excessive curiosity" aggrandizes the slanderer. For it is the king who now manipulates information insofar as the infanta is not presented "exactly" as she is, but rather as she is constructed as the ultimate object of curiosity: "the most beautiful and the most perfect Princess in nature," the princess of the fairy tale or nuptial fiction.[65]

Interestingly, the very uniqueness that draws the crowd to the new queen also separates her from them. When the pamphlets arrive at the moment of describing the new queen in their entry, they use the same ploy of not being able to describe that Colletet used in *Nouvelle Relation contenant La Royalle Entrée.* If the queen is indescribable and overwhelming, it is because while she is offered up for the gaze of the public, she also belongs to the king. The very uniqueness that makes her his, makes her at once an object of curiosity, of display, and an object that is not accessible. She becomes accessible only when the public looks at her through the eyes of the king, looks with him at his collection. This structure creates both awe of the king and (respectful) sympathy with him and resolves the tension created by her look at the king in Colletet's *La Nouvelle Relation Contenant L'Entreveue et Serments des Roys* discussed in Chapter Three. It also shifts the relation from showing to dominating.

One might say, therefore, that the logic of the entry and that of the cabinet are, finally, similar. Both take the dimension of excessive curiosity associated with the female (literally and figuratively) and exploit it for the sake of (absolutist) history. Of course, the idea of indifferent, somehow pure, universal curiosity is also shown to be a myth when universal curiosity and the "great news items of the world" are, finally, produced by manipulation of the female (position), now shown to be a male position as well. That fact is driven home by the last public event of the entry, the publication in 1662 of a large luxury edition description of the events: Jean Tronçon's *L'Entrée Triomphante de Leurs Majestez Louis XIV Roy de France et de Navarre, et Marie Therese D'Autriche son Espouse dans la Ville de Paris Capitale de leurs Royaumes, au retour de la signature de la paix generalle et de leur heureux mariage, Enrichie de plusieurs Figures, des Harangues & de diverses Pieces considerables pour l'Histoire. Le tout exactement recueilly par l'ordre de Messieurs de Ville.*[66] This folio replaces the occasional pamphlets, now relegated to the realm of ephemera. Not surprisingly, however, the luxury edition reproduces the rhetoric of curiosity found in the pamphlets, explicitly offering itself up as a catalogue to the entry, a final monumental version, utilizing materials about the entry that the anonymous writer had, out of curiosity, conserved.

   Not unlike the kinds of volumes produced to catalogue actual *cabinets de curiosité*, *L'Entrée Triomphante* links itself to the tradition of the cabinet by noting that its writer had conserved materials from the entry in his cabinet, materials he had now decided to put in order, transforming and correcting all the previous pamphlet descriptions of the entry to produce a luxury folio, the ultimate guide to the ultimate display.[67] Indeed, the text in question draws heavily on the pamphlet material. It is not the correction and reorganization of the curiosities of the entry, however, that finally legitimize its publication. Rather, it is the dauphin, born thirteen months after the entry and safely one year old at the time of the volume's publication (actually on the dauphin's first birthday), who is the jewel in the collection the folio describes. Indeed, the volume follows the entry to his birth, which it celebrates in its final pages. As the emphasis shifts from the new queen to the new dauphin, it becomes clear that she can assume her position in the collection only by adding to it, by getting pregnant, reproducing the dynasty's power by supplementing its collection. Or, rather, the official print report has illuminated the fact that, with a little manipulation of the female (and its various homologues such as the pamphlet, fireworks, the entry, etc.) on the part of the king, excessive curiosity produces universal curiosity in the royal *cabinet*.

   This is the point Scudéry illustrated (and satirized?) in her prologue, which merged a discussion of the entry with an analysis of curiosity (as well as the two logics of curiosity), and in her choice to write about the entry in a novel. She did not use journalism or the folio form (admittedly two opposite ends of the spectrum of state-sponsored print culture). Rather she tucked her description into her cabinet, the front of her novel, thereby allying it with salon conversation and the more private, less regulatable (and more collaborative), femino-centered genre of fiction and not with the monumental gallery of history, as did the journalistic pamphlets. In so doing, she concretized the greatest fear of Meriante, showing that one can supplement the great vistas of universal curiosity from the corners of the female *cabinet*. Her contribution to the entry might, finally, be compared to that of the new queen. While clearly never of monumental import, her text is nonetheless ineluctably compatible with and attuned to the functioning of (male) universal curiosity, or the ceremonial construction of its nuptial myth. Scudéry uses the myth as nuptial fictions utilize the queen (and the pamphlet utilizes nuptial fictions), namely, to fashion her own agenda out of a dialectic between the official and the intimate.

Scudéry's Cabinet and the Deconstruction of a Myth

It is important to clarify what Scudéry accomplishes in her discussion of curiosity about the entry by asking why she chose to stage this discussion in the prologue of a novel and not in the apparently more official venue of the pamphlet literature. In her initial categorization of curiosity, Scudéry played down the traditionally gendered distinctions of curiosity as linked either to universality or excessive avidity by focusing on the image of the cabinet with its parallel distinction of stability and ephemerality. With this distinction, Scudéry was able to show the interconnection or compatibility between the two dimensions. She was able to demonstrate how the female or less official position as ephemeral (malleable if not avid) was necessary to the reproduction of the ultimately more respectable male or public position of universal history. Following this logic, she chose to formulate her discussion in what would have been considered in 1660 to be an ephemeral form, the cabinet of the novel, which one could contrast to what became the apparently more monumental gallery of the journalistic pamphlet.[68] In so doing, she stressed the importance of her literature in the cabinet, a point reinforced at the very end of her prologue when the narrator announces she has just been given a book (*nouvelle*) about which she is very curious. At this point, Scudéry's interlocutors, who had been so logical and orderly in their debate about the dangers and advantages of curiosity, and who had so glibly excluded themselves from those who are overly curious, avidly jumped at the chance to hear a reading of the new novel. Initially, it seemed that Scudéry was being playfully ironic when she had her exemplary interlocutors give in to the excesses and avidity of curiosity. Reading between her text and the pamphlet literature, however, the irony seems less innocent. For Scudéry has surely shown that she knew how to reproduce and exploit the (femino-centered) logic of excessive curiosity. Or rather, that she understood the power of such a logic, be it in the balconies of Paris, on the body of the queen, or in the pages of print culture, tucked away out of sight of the permanent collection or its luxury edition, in the powerful space of ephemera that is the (female-) constructed fiction—which always generates excessive curiosity. In so doing, she deftly demonstrated that the power of nuptial fictions (the political fictions of 1660) is dependent on the collaboration of women, however ephemeral and excessive, and that "historical knowledge," like the performance of the king as absolute collector, is ultimately a fiction that is always constructed, composed of many collaborating and interacting elements and figures, no one of which can ever be completely dominated and contained.

The Queen Is Dead,
Long Live the King

Examining scenes from the marriage of Louis XIV highlights the dialectical nature of images, ceremonies, and media that contributed to the political fictions of absolutism just prior to Louis XIV's "taking of power." Because these representations of the young Bourbon monarch before his formal ascension to the throne were produced in combination with other images, it is no longer possible to think about the relation between representation and empowerment in terms of the kind of singularity or unicity that characterizes the Kantorowiczian (funereal) framework of substitution. While Kantorowicz's framework has for so long guided scholarship on the representation of Louis XIV, this study demonstrates that the logic of royal fictions is not always (or only) one of substitution and singularity. Nuptial fictions are fashioned according to a logic of combination and multiplicity homologous to the ritual of kinship exchange out of which they arise.

Such combinatory logic more accurately accounts for the symbols of political culture. For it is just such a dialectical symbolics that founds Lévi-Strauss' definition of culture:

> Any culture can be considered as a combination of symbolic systems headed by language, the matrimonial rules, the economic relations, art, science, and religion. All the systems seek to express certain aspects

of physical reality and social reality, and even more, to express the links that those two types of reality have with each other and those that occur among the symbolic systems themselves. The fact that the systems never can achieve that expression in a fully satisfying and (above all) equivalent form, is, first, a result of the condition of functioning proper to each system, in that the systems always remain incommensurable; second, it is a result of the way that history introduces into those systems elements from different systems, determines shifting of one society towards another, and uneven intervals in the relative evolutionary rhythm of each particular system.[1]

Nuptial fictions, be they fictions of print, ceremonial, or political culture, constantly come up against such differences in the realities of the treaty between France and Spain, an event aimed at combining systems that were fundamentally incoherent and incommensurable. The Hapsburgs and Bourbons, the alliances behind print, the myth of the Golden Fleece, the king and queen, are all examples of such incommensurable systems. As has been shown in this study, one important function of nuptial fictions was to display and then master such incoherence in order to work through and profit from dissonances inherent in the process of the treaty marriage.

As we have seen, representations of the queen epitomized the clash of systems that characterized the symbolics of the treaty marriage. For the new queen was the physical and symbolic site on which the multiple symbolic programs of Bourbon and Hapsburg cultures converged in the late 1650s and early 1660s. It is thus that her portrayal relied on many signifying systems (such as Spanish, female, and ephemeral) against which the French marked and measured their own power in constant comparisons between differing cultural, sexual, and logical systems. Insofar as one goal of the French in the marriage ceremonial was to come to terms with the multiplicity introduced by such alterity, rituals of marriage and their ceremonies of information were aimed at absorbing that difference in making the Spanish princess a French queen and displaying to the French people and the larger European political arena that the Bourbons were capable of absorbing Hapsburg Spain. Figuring the bride was figuring Spain (its economy, culture, clothing, language, etc.). Absorbing and appropriating her otherness was supposed to demonstrate that the king was the unique and powerful ruler of Mazarin's aspirations. Multiple and incommensurable symbolic systems were thus necessary in order to assert French hegemony, even as there was an attempt to erase such difference to assert the absolute power of the Bourbon king.

The process of making the queen symbolize one thing and then mastering her difference was impeded by her physical reality and that of her culture. The impact of her sweat, her clothing, etc., was not just described, but rehearsed by the media (and the myths) celebrating and reporting the marriage. Stated in another manner, as sign, the queen was both a malleable signifier and intractable matter that exerted force. This plurality did not contribute to state unbuilding as it would during the Revolution. Rather, the queen's "resistance" helped constitute Louis XIV's portrayal. It helped underline the king's force by providing opportunities for staging his mastery, however dependent on her that mastery was. This dialectical dynamic was homologous to (perhaps providing the model for) the vehicles that portrayed, disseminated, and commented on nuptial fictions. Print culture, its ceremonies of information, as well as other, more explicitly explosive media, all rehearsed and exploited the danger of nuptial fictions, developing and displaying techniques of mastering that dangerous dynamic.

While this study focused largely on the representation of sovereignty in one little-studied ritual, royal marriage, the last chapter considered another ceremony, the royal entry. It examined how the queen was transformed into a curio that could be placed into the royal collection. In her entry, the jewel-bedecked queen took on attributes of the funeral effigy, a device that Ralph Giesey has argued was meant to draw emphasis away from the king's dead body and shift focus from his mortality to the immortality of his status.[2] The queen as curio-effigy, however, was made immortal only by the deadening (or petrification) of her symbolic volatility. Indeed, after the entry, María Teresa would become an empty symbol, a domesticated and catalogued figure to be trotted out in place of the living person. Placed into the king's curiosity cabinet, her particular symbolic dynamic also waned, leaving the king in a more autonomous (less pluralistic) ceremonial position.

In making such a shift from marriage to entry, this book came full circle in an inquiry meant to open new perspectives on the fictions of Louis XIV's monarchy. But, in concluding with a discussion of the marriage entry, this study paradoxically returned to one of the origins of the very paradigm it set out to counterbalance: the Renaissance funeral. The triumphal entry of María Teresa was a kind of funeral for her powerful symbolic presence. In recognizing this phenomenon, one recognizes the reverse of what Ralph Giesey noted in studying the funeral procession, that it adapted elements of the triumphal entry.[3] According to Giesey, when the funeral procession emulated the royal entry, it shifted emphasis away from the fact that the king was dead by recalling an important activity of the living ruler.[4] It substituted the living for the dead. Note that while anxieties about the king's death in the Renaissance were managed by patterning the funeral procession after the entry, anxieties about a queen's function in the absolutist regime were managed by transforming an entry into a parade of the death of symbolic power by returning to rituals of substitution.

Such symbolic passing of the infanta did not unsettle the absolutist regime. But the death of her actual mortal body apparently did cause some problems. For, despite the fact that there would be no political implications for the regime in the death of a queen, when María Teresa actually did die in 1683, Louis XIV was said to have remarked that it was the only trouble she had ever given him.[5] This story is only anecdotal and its truth value is of no concern here. That it circulated at all attests to the perception that the queen, or thinking about the queen, was perceived as able to unsettle the image of the mature ruler. Indeed, one might speculate that if a king more often linked to his mistresses than to his queen consort was imagined as bothered by the death of his wife, it was probably not because she had disappeared. She was already largely invisible at his court. Rather, it may have been because of the visibility death might afford her. In dying, María Teresa recovered part of her dynamic influence. She became notable by the very production of the ceremonial of her demise. The processions, the laying of her heart at Val-de-Grâce and her body at Saint Denis, the writing and delivery of eulogies and the printing and dissemination of numerous commemorative pamphlets describing the funeral and praising the deceased queen renewed her visibility at the court of the fabled Sun King. These rituals and their reproduction by the "ceremonies of information" were María Teresa's funeral effigy. They recalled the nuptial fictions in providing her a status and presence she had attained at only two other moments in her reign, during her marriage in 1660 and during the birth of the dauphin in 1661. Such notoriety perturbed (albeit momentarily) the smooth surface of the king's own image as absolute.

It should be made clear that the death of a queen (especially one who died before her king) in no way equaled that of a king. Unlike the king who was both dead and reborn upon his demise, the queen's death did not necessitate fictions about her immortality. At María Teresa's funeral, therefore, the cry was "the Queen is dead, the Queen is dead, the Queen is dead, pray to God for her soul."[6] There was no cry akin to "the King is dead, long live the King," because the queen's dead body posed no liability for the state. Indeed, her value to the state had already been fulfilled in providing heirs. It follows from this study, however, that the visibility in ceremonial and in print afforded the queen upon her death inevitably reasserted her impact on the dynasty and highlighted her effect on the representation of the king's power. The death of the queen did not affect political stability, but it did revive a certain reflection on her life that reasserted the combinatory logic of nuptial fictions in the face of the substitutional logic of mature absolutism.

It is not surprising that in reiterating and reviewing the life of the queen, funerary imagery and discourses should choose the marriage as one of the primary moments of her life, a moment to be revised and resituated. Nonetheless, the reference to the marriage is introduced with some hesitation by her most influential eulogizer, Bishop Bossuet. In the first part of his funerary oration for María Teresa, Bossuet wonders if it is acceptable to intermingle a discussion of the pomp and ceremonies of marriage with those of the funeral, to associate the ceremonies of joyous beginnings with those of termination: "sacred festivals, felicitous marriage, nuptial veil, bene-diction, sacrifice, is it permissible now to intermingle your ceremo-nies and pomp with these funeral rites, to mix the highest of grandeurs with their downfall?"[7] If Bossuet hesitated to invoke the calculus of addition characteristic of nuptial fictions and ceremonies, he did so nonetheless in returning to the image of the queen as the instrument of reconciliation between two enemy nations.[8] Of course, from 1660 on the French saw the queen as instrumental not in reconciliation with Spain, but in usurping its throne. As seen in Chapter Two, however, nuptial fictions both unveiled and veiled that impulse in their transformation of the infanta from Spanish to French. In the revision of the queen's life, any anxiety about her transformability is erased. This erasure is particularly striking in a pamphlet Menestrier wrote describing and explaining the funeral decoration he organized at Saint Denis. In it, Menestrier returned to the scene of the Spanish infanta's transformation to French queen, remarking that "[f]rom the moment that she was married to the King, being an infanta who became Queen of France, she cast off the customs of her country to adapt to our ways: A Spanish Pistole, which under the coin-press changes form, and becomes a *Louis d'or*."[9] The metaphor underscores the Spanish infanta's value to the state in returning to the economic metaphor for the nuptial body of the queen discussed in Chapter Two. Reinvoking the image of currency recalls how the sticky residue of the infanta's sexual body was neutralized by the hard currency of commemorative coinage. Here the funeral commemoration once more illustrates the attempt to press the queen continually into the service of the state (or Louis). This time, however, the dead queen offers no resistance to her coinage. After her death, the queen's representation can continue its valuable contribution to the iteration of Bourbon hegemony. In the funerary oration's review, María Teresa is easily transformed from Spanish to French in an economy of substitution (of one set of customs for another) that belies the combinatory realities of state building revealed twenty-three years earlier in nuptial fictions.

A potentially more problematic *topos* invoked around the queen's death is that of her piety. One of the striking images used to convey this characteristic is the parallel set up between María Teresa and her namesake, the Virgin Mary. The comparison is apparent in a common funeral decoration for María Teresa that showed an angel taking her to heaven, suggesting the bodily assumption of the Virgin Mary.[10] Of course, the funeral lends itself to this association since one of the crowning moments in the life of the Virgin was her death. But the imagery also serves another purpose. Invoking the Assumption of the Virgin associates the queen with the king in reminding us of Mary's similarity to Christ; both can be resurrected without delay because both are perfectly free from sin.[11] It is thus that reviewing the queen's exemplary life (and celebrating it) also provides the opportunity for reviewing and celebrating the king (and his perfection). In Bossuet's funerary oration, a discussion of the Peace of the Pyrenees slips so easily into a celebration of Louis' military prowess that images of the king threaten to displace those of the queen.[12] But if the queen's funeral provides one more pretext for glorifying Louis in ceremonies and in print, it also potentially compromises him when Bossuet uses the occasion to allude to his marital infidelities. The allusion is subtle and serves to underline the queen's piety. The association of the king and queen provides the opportunity for underlining their differences, her saintliness, his yielding to mortal urges. While not necessarily flattering to the king, this contrast fits easily into the Christic model. For the Virgin's ascent to heaven was an easy one. She slipped effortlessly from her mortal body to heaven and immortality. Christ, on the other hand, lingered, dying in agony, being resurrected, but then returning to his disciples before his final ascension to immortality. Split between two spheres that pull him equally, the king/Christ is also split between his mortal and divine body. Ironically, the queen, who technically has no divine dimension, is the one able to leave her mortal body behind and accede to divinity with ease.

If Christ is often depicted returning to guide Mary to heaven, Louis XIV was not similarly associated with the queen's dead body (as if he were Christ). He did not attend the funeral ceremonies and memorial masses even though there was no expressed legal or theological prohibition on his doing so. The king was neither contaminated nor implicated by the death of his spouse in the way he would be by that of his predecessor. Although forbidden from wearing mourning, kings could attend the funerals of relatives.[13] Indeed, even the king's absence from his predecessor's funeral was a practice introduced rather late into the French tradition. Why then did Louis refrain from attending María Teresa's funeral? Did his absence indicate disinterest? Respect? Fear of drawing attention to the ceremony and away from himself?

While it would be impossible to answer these questions, one might hazard that since Louis XIV was the first king in generations to die after his queen, he would have had no clear precedent for a king's role in his queen's funeral. There were no ceremonial fictions established for this event. Moreover, by the seventeenth century, the use of the funeral for disseminating juridical fictions had largely shifted to another ritual, the *lit de justice*, the ceremony in which the queen asserted her authority as regent by bringing her child to parliament.[14] Interestingly, the relation between mother and son highlighted in the *lit de justice* ceremonial is alluded to in the prominent role played by the dauphin in his mother's funeral. It was the dauphin and not the king who went to Saint-Denis and to Notre Dame as the central mourner in his mother's funeral ceremonies. Substituting the dauphin for his father reinvoked the mother–son scene of the Assumption. In so doing, however, it reminded the public that Christ died before his mother! The king's absence may have thus served to attenuate the awareness that Louis may have also been symbolically dead in 1683 when the major successes of his regime had already begun to degenerate into ever more exaggerated excesses. Nonetheless, while the king's absence from the funeral may have served to avoid the invocation of a problematic plot narrative—Christ returning from the dead to bury his mother—the role of the dauphin as primary mourner linked the queen more closely to her offspring than to her husband, highlighting her role in reproducing the state. Shifting to an alliance of mother and son also underscored the king's absence, perhaps hinting at the potentially competitive relation between father and first-born son during a king's life. The prominence of the mother–son dyad stressed, finally, that it was the queen's body, and not the king's juridical (salic) empowerment, that reproduced the state. It emphasized the combinatory dimension of such political reproduction.

This excursus into print accounts of the last ceremonial of the queen suggests ways in which symbolic events and the fictions (nuptial, sexual, maternal, or funereal) produced by them cannot and should not be analyzed simply in terms of one ritual's symbols. For while it has been the assumption that the regalia and ceremonial of royal ritual in France are most often wrapped around the figure of the absolutist monarch, it is clear from this study that other figures, events, and places also contribute to the system that signifies sovereign power. If the king was said to have been bothered by the death of the queen, perhaps that was because the rituals and the ceremonies of information around her death stirred up the memory of plural fictions behind his power and suggested that his absolutist politic culture, like all cultures, could never be independent of other "realities," symbolic or otherwise.

Invoking the imagery of and anecdotes about the queen's death underscores the limitations of taking the king's funeral as the hegemonic moment for articulating fictions of sovereignty and suggests once more that fictions of absolutism depended on shutting out the incommensurable. Reading this imagery also imposes upon scholars the task of looking for what is shut out of or obliterated by the fictions of unity and singularity that have up to now founded mature images of Louis XIV. It dictates that we extend and modify the important inquiries of Ralph Giesey, Ernst Kantorowicz, Jean-Marie Apostolidès, and Louis Marin by endeavoring to recover sites (borders outside Paris, curiosity cabinets), rituals (marriage, childbirth), figures (queens, king's brothers, king's legs, Spanish soldiers), and media (almanacs, pamphlets, fireworks, machine plays, even prose fiction) not formally associated with generating significant fictions of sovereignty. Such an exploration and expansion of the horizon cannot help but enrich the understanding of the fictions that helped construct and maintain the complex absolutist culture, political and otherwise, and the activities and symbols that supported it.

REFERENCE MATTER

Notes

Introduction

1. For an overview of the treaty see *New Cambridge Modern History*, 4: 411–34, and 5: 198–221. For the treaty from the Spanish perspective, see J. H. Elliott's discussion of the last years of Hapsburg hegemony (particularly the analysis of political factors that led to its decline) in *Imperial Spain*. The text of the treaty itself was widely available in the seventeenth century, republished at various stages in the French campaign for the infanta's right to succession—as, for example, in 1668, after the War of Devolution when it was published as *Contrat de Mariage du Roy Tres-Chrestien*. For easy access to details of the treaty, see: Mignet, *Negociations relatives à la succession d'Espagne sous Louis XIV*, 1: 3–57, and Morel-Fatio, *Recueil des instructions données aux ambassadeurs et ministres de France*, 11: 139–53. For a technical analysis of the legal issues of the renunciation as related to succession from both the French and Spanish perspectives, see Stuers, *Etude historique sur les droits successoraux de la Reine Marie-Thérèse*. A very different perspective on the treaty is offered by P. Sahlins in *Boundaries: The Making of France and Spain in the Pyrenees*, which analyzes the notion of political boundary and the emergence of national identity by exploring the geopolitical history of the Pyrenees border. A brief history of the Treaty of the Pyrenees is found in Sahlin's first chapter.

2. The first steps in this direction were taken during the War of Devolution, in 1667. See Bilain, *Dialogue sur les droits de la reyne*, for an example of the rhetorical maneuvering that occurred around the infanta's

rights to the Spanish throne in this period. The Bourbons did finally accede to the Hapsburg throne in 1701.

3. There are three studies of the marriage. Ducéré, *Bayonne sous l'ancien régime, le mariage de Louis XIV d'après les contemporains et des documents inédits* (1903); Taillandier, *Le mariage de Louis XIV* (1928); and Dulong, *Le mariage du Roi-Soleil* (1986). There is also a work of historical fiction, Cortequisse, *Madame Louis XIV: Marie-Thérèse d'Autriche* (1992). Ducéré's detailed version, which cites copiously from contemporary sources, and Dulong's more recent study are the most serious of these works. But neither takes critical distance on the nature of their sources nor probes the functioning of the symbolics of marriage.

4. Burke, *The Fabrication of Louis XIV*, 45.

5. The fictions of these periods have been studied in depth. On the Fronde, see especially Jouhaud, *Mazarinades: la Fronde des mots*. On the portrayal of the mature Louis XIV, see Marin, *The Portrait of the King*, Apostolidès, *Le roi machine*, and, most recently, Burke, *The Fabrication of Louis XIV*.

6. The year 1660 is often used to divide chapters and volumes. An excellent example of this phenomenon is found in Chartier and Martin, *Histoire de l'édition française*, which uses the year to divide volumes one and two. In this division, Chartier and Martin simply reflect an accepted chronology.

7. Turner, "Betwixt and Between: The Liminal Period in *Rites de Passage*."

8. Marin, *The Portrait of the King*, and Apostolidès, *Le roi machine*.

9. Elias, *Court Society*, and *Power and Civility*.

10. Lévi-Strauss, *Elementary Structures of Kinship*, 483.

11. See Kantoriwicz, *The King's Two Bodies*, and Giesey, *The Royal Funeral Ceremony*.

12. Hanley, *The Lit de Justice of the Kings of France*.

13. See Rathé, *La reine se marie*, 31, on this point.

14. Claude de Seyssel, *The Monarchy of France*, 48. Loyseau also treats the topic in a chapter on princes where, citing Bodin's *République*, he notes the danger of recognizing "matrilineal descendents of sovereigns." See Loyseau, *Treatise of Orders and Plain Dignities*, 140. For an overview of the thinking about queens in the corpus of early modern jurists, see Barry, *Les droits de la reine sous la monarchie française*, and Rathé, *La reine se marie*.

15. Kantorowicz, *The King's Two Bodies*, 212.

16. Marin's two articles, "Le corps glorieux du roi et son portrait" and "Le corps pathétique et son médicin," both follow this model, as does Reichler's chapter, "La jambe du roi," in *L'Age libertin*. Both focus on the

king's sexual (mortal) body in moments of decay, not victory. See Chapter One of this study for further discussion of this point.

17. See Hunt, "The Many Bodies of Marie Antoinette," and Maza, "The Diamond Necklace Affair Revisted," both published in 1991, and Thomas, *La reine scélérate* (1989) for fuller discussion of the representation of the queen's sexuality. These essays, as well as Laqueur's "The Queen Caroline Affair" (1982), which deals with a later British queen, are the principal revisionary works on the representation of queenship.

18. See also *American Heritage Dictionary of Indo-European Roots.*

19. Irigary, "Women on the Market," in *This Sex Which Is Not One.* Rubin also offers a similar framework for understanding Lévi-Strauss in her essay, "The Traffic in Women."

20. For a discussion of the symbolic system generated around the marriage of Louis XIII and Anne of Austria, see Zanger, "Making Sweat: Sex and the Gender of National Reproduction in the Marriage of Louis XIII."

21. Chartier and Jouhaud, "Pratiques historiennes des textes."

Chapter 1

1. See, for example, Roberto Rossellini's *The Rise to Power of Louis XIV*, a film that has served to anchor many cliches (true and false) about Louis XIV. Marin, in *The Portrait of the King*, and Apostolidès, in *Le roi machine*, also work from the premise that the king is the absolute center of his representations, even while they demonstrate how those images are constructed.

2. See Thomas E. Kaiser, "Louis le *Bien-Aimé* and the Rhetoric of the Royal Body," in *From the Royal to Republican Bodies: Incorporating the Political in Seventeenth and Eighteenth Century France*, Melzer and Norberg, eds.

3. See also other writings on liminality, Douglas' *Purity and Danger* and Van Gennep's *Rites of Passage*, discussed by Turner in his essay "Betwixt and Between: The Liminal Period in *Rites de Passage*."

4. Turner, "Betwixt and Between," 97.

5. Ibid.

6. One example of such an almanac is the often-reproduced "Le Jansénisme foudroyé," Bibliothèque Nationale, Département des Estampes, Qb^{5}P68493.

7. All the almanac engravings discussed in this section can be found in the Bibliothèque Nationale's Département des Estampes Qb series and in the Collection Hennin. For information on the commerce of engravings in the seventeenth century and in particular for a discussion of almanacs, see Grivel, *Le commerce de l'estampe à Paris.* For general information about

almanacs, see Champier, *Les anciens almanachs illustrés*, Saffoy, *Bibliographie des almanachs et annuaires*, Bollème, *Les almanachs populaires*, Grand-Carteret, *Les almanachs français*, and Jean Adhémar, et al., *Imagerie populaire française.* See also Christian Jouhaud, "Readability and Persuasion: Political Handbills," in *The Culture of Print*, Roger Chartier, ed.

8. Bollème, *Les almanachs populaires*, 122.

9. Ibid., 13–17.

10. Martin, "Information et actualité: de la feuille volante au journal," in *Livre, pouvoirs, et société*, 1: 253–75. Martin uses the term "feuille volante" to refer to broadsides as well as short *livrets* such as *factums*, occasional pamphlets reporting on natural wonders, and almanacs.

11. Furetière, *Dictionnaire universel.*

12. The image of the king in his chariot is a common *topos* linked to triumph and peace, as, for example, in the Belgian painter Pierre Claeissens Le Jeune's 1577 *Allegorie de la Paix aux Pays-Bas*, Groeninge Museum, Brugges, Belgium. Dating from the period of Philip II's occupation of Flanders, the painting features a chariot (of allegorical women) crushing Envy. This imagery is also available in engravings from the marriage of Louis XIII, such as "Le Roi conduit par les vertus terrasse la discorde et l'envie de ceux qui avoient traversé son Mariage" [Dép. des estampes, B.N., Qb¹M89113]. And it is found in engravings from after the marriage of Louis XIV, such as "Le Triumphe de la Paix et du Mariage" [Dép. des estampes, B. N., Qb⁴P69268], echoing images from the military battles that led to the peace, such as in "Le Triomphe Royal de la Victoire obtenue par les Armes de sa Majesté à la Bataille de LENS" [Dép. des estampes, B.N., Qb¹M91723].

13. See Ripa, *Iconologie* (1644), II: 152–53 and 70, and *Iconologia* (1758-60), plates 57 and 130.

14. See Jeffrey Merrick, "The Body Politics of French Absolutism," in Melzer and Norberg, eds., *Embodying Power in Seventeenth and Eighteenth Century France*, and Lewis Seifert, "Eroticizing the Fronde: Sexual Deviance and Political Disorder in the Mazarinades."

15. The full text reads:

The Magnificent Triumph

Where our August Monarch is seen mastering himself and his enemies because he places his passions among his war trophies. The duke of Anjou his brother, the Prince of Conti, his Eminence, Monsieur de Turenne and Monsieur de Ferté increase the brilliance of this Triumph by their presence. One sees as well the Soldiers who march in front, laden with the spoils of the enemies, and carrying on their shoulders in the Roman manner, the Cities of Montmedy, St Venant, Bourboug, and Mardic represented in relief, which had been conquered by the very great King with all the [military] standards carried off in the various battles with the Spaniards as well as their shameful retreat from Ardre.

All translations of materials from the marriage are provided by the author. Titles and citations from early modern texts retain the original spelling, capitalization, and punctuation whenever possible. The only exception to this practice is the modernization of *i* and *v* to *j* and *u* when applicable. English translations reflect this early modern French orthography.

16. For example, the *topos* appears in Puget de la Serre's *Panégyrique de Louis Quartième*, a pamphlet that, judging by references in the text, probably dates to the same period as the almanac. The text's frontispiece is an engraving in which the king's portrait is held by an angel in a chariot. The third engraving in the text shows the king on a throne and is accompanied by the following verse:

> Who would be able to oppose the Illustrious projects
> Of a Prince to whom heaven has promised all glory:
> He prevails over himself [in] his first victory
> And devotes his passions to his subjects.

> [Qui pourroit s'opposer aux Illustres projets
> D'un Prince à qui le ciel a promis tout le gloire:
> Il emporte sur luy la première victoire,
> Et met ses passions au rang de ses sujets.]

The verse refers to the king's tireless military endeavors. That Louis focuses his passions on his subjects suggests he might have focused them elsewhere. This idea is repeated later in the text: "And certainly this great King has made us understand that he would prefer the repose of his people over his own repose, because since the day after his arrival in the Louvre he prefers the fatigues of a new voyage to the pleasures of his Court without considering the inconvenience [*incommodité*] that he could risk" (ibid., 19).

17. Foucault, *History of Sexuality*, vol. 1.

18. Foucault, "Power and Sex," an interview from the *Nouvel observateur*, March 12, 1977, republished and translated in *Michel Foucault, Politics, Philosophy, Culture, Interviews and Other Writings*, 110–24.

19. I thank my research assistant, Elizabeth Hyde, for helping to speculate on who the other two courtiers might be. Despite examining a large number of engraved images, however, we found it difficult to be sure of exactly who is in the picture. Note, as well, the addition of Anne of Austria to the group.

She was not present in the battle scene depicted in "The Magnificent Triumph."

20. Schama, *The Embarrassment of Riches*, 433–34. Schama notes that legs are seen as lower-order, a sign of fallen woman and wantonness in Dutch painting of the period.

21. There is not a great deal of work done on portraits in this period. Perhaps the most useful overview of the genre of the portrait within a larger engraving is the third chapter of Harth's *Ideology and Culture*. For an interesting discussion of the nature of portraits of women in Renaissance Italy, see Simons, "Women in Frames: the Gaze, the Eye, and the Profile in Renaissance Portraiture." Although it is disappointing that Simons does not actually fulfill her proposed agenda to offer not only a social and historical analysis of the female gaze but also a psychosexual one (7), her readings of portraits of women, particularly her analysis of the use of such portraits for dynastic purposes (marriage, displaying riches) and the way women were positioned within the portraits, are quite fascinating and suggestive for understanding the portraits within the portraits of the almanac engravings. For information on portraiture in classical France that is not specifically concerned with the issue of portraying women, see Dowley, "French Portraits of Ladies as Minerva."

22. Mauss, *The Gift*. For Mauss, gift exchange functions similarly to kinship exchange, as presented by Claude Lévi-Strauss in *Elementary Structures*.

23. In this light it is interesting to consider a contrasting image of a woman circulating in France in roughly the same period brought to my attention by Sarah Hanley in a talk given at Harvard in 1993. In the lecture, Hanley showed several engravings illustrating the adage "femme sans teste tout en est bon," including one by Jacques Lagnet that dates to 1657 (no. 3819 in Hennin, B. N. Dép. des estampes). Weigert discusses this engraving in *Inventaire du fonds françois*, 55. The illustrated proverb seems to suggest that if you can separate women's bodies from their heads then they are rendered harmless. In the proverb, however, the idea seems to be to get rid of the head. In the almanacs it is the bodies that are missing. Since there is no other information available about this proverb, it is impossible to comment further except to suggest that the contrast merits further consideration.

24. They are almost like caryatids, except these are not draped female figures, but male figures.

25. On the iconography of Flanders see Schama, *The Embarrassment of Riches*, 52, 55.

26. Millen and Wolf offer the most recent comprehensive study of Rubens' Medicis cycle in *Heroic Deeds and Mystic Figures*.

27. Fagon, *Journal de la santé*, 52.

28. Ibid., 54–57.

29. Montpensier, *Mémoires*, 2: 53.

30. *La Gazette*, no. 82: 642.

31. Fagon, *Journal de la santé*, 52.

32. For a more complete analysis of the passages about the 1658 illness, see Zanger and Goldsmith, "The Politics and Poetics of the Mancini Romance," 343–46.

33. Pascal, *L'amant du roi*, passim.

34. This is the argument made in Zanger and Goldsmith, "The Politics and Poetics of the Mancini Romance."

35. On the commemorative convention, see Harth, *Ideology and Culture*, 83.

36. For information on the petticoat breech and other aspects of men's fashions, see Boucher, *2000 Years of Fashion in Europe*. One important point to make here is that although this clothing may seem quite effeminate by our standards, silk stockings and high-heeled shoes were the norm at Louis XIV's court. It is generally accepted that the adoption of such excessive style helped Louis XIV to transform his noble class into a court society (from a warrior class).

37. As noted in the introduction to this study, both Marin and Reichler seem to have internalized Kantorowicz's own blindness to the king's sexual body, focusing on sexuality only in terms of the mortal body in decay, seen in the tension between the representation of Louis XIV's iconic leg and his aging face in the painting. See Reichler, "La jambe du roi," and Marin, "Le corps glorieux du roi et son portrait." Marin has also written on the rhetoric of the king's physicians in discussing his mortal body in "Le corps glorieux du roi," (also published in a slightly different version in 1985 in *La Revue des Sciences Humaines*, No. 198). Again, Marin focuses on the mortal body as decaying, not victorious.

38. See Hanley, *The Lit de Justice of the Kings of France*, on the ritual of that ceremonial in which, upon the king's death in the case of a regency, the young minor king took the throne publicly in Parlement. Hanley's discussion of Anne of Austria's transgressive role in Louis XIV's own *lit de justice* is particularly interesting in light of the idea that the queen understood her symbolic impact on legitimizing her son's ritual activities.

Chapter 2

1. Mazarin, *Lettres du Cardinal Mazarin*, 46.

2. This pamphlet offers one of very few concrete portraits of the infanta in publications describing the marriage. In its entirety, the text reads: "Here

I will tell you that we were somewhat surprised to find the Infanta more beautiful that she had been portrayed in her portrait, she resembled the Queen, I mean by that ours, she seemed to us tall enough, she has a broad forehead, eyes blue and very beautiful, a full face, a nose which is a bit big, a beautiful vermillion mouth, and a neck of a very great whiteness, her hair color is between blond and chestnut brown . . . ," *Relation la Plus fidelle & ponctuelle*, 5–6.

3. Grammont writes: "As for the qualities of the body, they could not be, to my sense, more agreeable: it is of a whiteness that cannot be described, piercing and lively eyes, a beautiful mouth. As for her teeth, I could not speak of them, because our conversation was too short for me to be able to remark on them, no more than on her size, which the height of her shoes and the large size [two ells] of her farthingale conceals; having only seen her enter and leave the theater, she seemed to me very guileless, the tone of voice agreeable, the hair of a beautiful color, and finally to finish a portrait that should satisfy your Eminence, I will assure him that it is the perfect resemblance to the Queen [Anne of Austria]," reprinted in Ducéré, *Bayonne sous l'ancien régime*, 94–96. The size of the skirt is actually given in the citation, two ells, which is a unit of measure 27–45 inches, so the infanta's skirt was likely 60–90 inches in breadth. Other elements besides clothing that impeded the Mareschal's "view" included language problems (the infanta did not speak French and few of the French understood Spanish), the cloistering of women in Spanish culture, and the infanta's modesty. His attempt to describe the body is, furthermore, somewhat risky, not just because of Spanish cultural attitudes toward women, but also because the infanta is, of course, a virgin, and should not be on display, even to those acquiring her. In Ducéré's discussion of the various letters Grammont wrote to the king, queen mother, and Mazarin, he comments that Grammont was under strict orders not to give too many details to the king. Ducéré notes that the letter to Mazarin contains the most concrete details available: *Bayonne*, 93–94.

4. For the text of the story, see Cosnac, *Mémoires*, II: 26–27. There are two versions of the memoirs given in this edition and the anecdote figures in both, although it is slightly more detailed in the second. The story is fascinating, since it concerns a description given by a woman, but recounted after the fact by a male witness. As such, it occupies the delightful gray area of memory-fiction.

5. Indeed, correspondence was rarely private, and Mazarin himself often used code words, indicating he assumed his letters were read. Since he utilized secretaries to rework his French grammar and to make the necessary copies, it is not unlikely that there was a clandestine circulation of his official

correspondence. In an analysis of the letters Mazarin wrote during this period concerning the passion between his niece, Marie Mancini, and the young monarch Louis XIV, I argue that Mazarin may have even utilized the letters to pressure the Spaniards into accepting his terms for the alliance. See Zanger and Goldsmith, "The Politics and Poetics of the Mancini Romance."

6. Furetière, *Dictionnaire universel*.

7. See Godefroy, *Dictionnaire de l'ancienne langue françoise. The American Heritage Dictionary of Indo-European Roots* also demonstrates this connection.

8. Furetière, *Dictionnaire universel*.

9. *Relation la Plus fidelle & ponctuelle*, 6.

10. See Mauss, *The Gift*, and Lévi-Strauss, *Elementary Structures*.

11. "Rite of passage" is used here in the sense utilized by the anthropologist Van Gennep in his book, *The Rites of Passage*.

12. Douglas, *Purity and Danger*, 115.

13. A translation of the title is: "The Pomp and Magnificence arranged for the marriage of the King and of The Infanta of Spain, Gathering Together the interviews that took place between the two Kings, & the two Queens, on the Isle of the Conference and the Relation of everything that occurred even after the Consummation." It was published in Toulouse by the Imprimeurs ordinaires du Roy, 1660. The text was also published in two editions in Paris by Jean Promé, 1660. The popularity of this text is demonstrated by its multiple editions.

14. I thank Roger Chartier for helping me to understand the relations between the provincial and Parisian editions of these materials.

15. The infanta's silence is a leitmotif of her description. In Grammont's letters reporting on his mission, he notes the modesty of the infanta, which he places in the context of Spanish culture in which women were cloistered and submissive (linked to their roots within Muslim culture). In some accounts, the fact that the infanta does not speak French is also offered as a delicious detail. Indeed, the infanta, even before she crosses into French territory, does not participate in the world Kristeva or Lacan would call symbolic. She does not herself exchange language, but is simply a symbol or object exchanged by the "language" of others. The queen mother, in reclothing her, is attempting to move her "daughter" into that realm. Whether she is able to do so remains to be seen. On Kristeva's notions of the symbolic, see Grosz, "The Body of Signification," in *Abjection, Melancholia, and Love*, as well as Kristeva's early books, such as *The Revolution of Poetic Language* and *Desire in Language*. On Lacan's notion of the symbolic, see MacCannell, *Figuring Lacan*, 121–54, and Ragland-Sullivan, *Jacques Lacan and the Philosophy of Psychoanalysis*, 130–95.

16. This is a delicate process, since to assert that the infanta needs to be refashioned is a manner of criticizing her and her country and thus might potentially unsettle the tenuous détente between France and Spain. That may explain why the idea of refashioning is placed into the mouth of the queen mother, herself a former infanta, in a move that the sociologist Pierre Bourdieu refers to as "cross-censorship," when a member of a social group guards and indeed enforces a code he or she may not experience as totally positive. Bourdieu introduces this concept when he discusses the "work of euphemization" and notes "the *cross-censorship* to which each agent submits with impatience but imposes on all the others," *Outline of a Theory of Practice*, 196. The idea is further developed in Bourdieu's *Distinction*.

17. This particular engraving was one of many images from the war that appeared on almanacs (discussed in Chapter One) or as caricatures. Other images are less subtle, including a caricature of a Spaniard being castrated of the cities captured by the French [B.N. Cabinet des estampes, Qb[1] M92102]. There existed, as well, a Flemish tradition of Lady Belgium being territorialized by invaders. For this tradition, see McGrath, "A Netherlandish History by Joachim Wtewael."

18. Carroll, "The Erotics of Absolutism," 5.

19. Ibid., 18. Norman Bryson also offers a reading of similar rape paintings, and his discussion of Poussin's two versions of the *Rape of the Sabines* is particularly interesting for its analysis of the relation between rape and the founding of political dynasties. See Bryson, "Two Narratives of Rape in the Visual Arts."

20. It is interesting that it is the queen mother who facilitates the rape. Perhaps because the king is not yet the absolutist ruler, the concerns of state building are still imagined in the hands of the regency. Here the king is displayed as young and ardent, but still in need of guidance by those more versed in statesmanship. Another possibility is cross-censorship, as mentioned in note 16.

21. This notion of resistance offers the new queen some agency in the scenario of her conquest. Feminists have criticized Lévi-Strauss' model of kinship exchange because it suggests women have no agency. The critique of Lévi-Strauss' model first appeared in Rubin's "The Traffic in Women," the first discussion of the role of women in various models of exchange. In her "Women on the Market," Luce Irigaray argued against Lévi-Strauss' model precisely because "when women are exchanged, woman's body must be treated as an abstraction" (175). Lévi-Strauss seemed to be aware that his model reduced women to an abstract position (what Baudrillard would call "symbolic capital") when he noted almost apologetically at the end of his study that "woman could never become just a sign and nothing

more, since in every man's world she is still a person . . ." (*Elementary Structures*, 496). It is not the goal of this study to resolve the debate, but rather to move beyond the polemic to explore how the infanta's symbolic status might still contain some possibility of agency. Indeed, Chapter Four will argue that such threatening agency was a crucial component of the nuptial fiction.

22. *La Pompe*, 8. A farthingale, as will be obvious in the ensuing discussion, was the large support system, usually hoops, worn beneath the skirt, creating a large, rounded appearance. It was popular in the sixteenth century in Europe, and persisted into the seventeenth century, especially in Spain.

23. It is difficult to find information about coaching etiquette. One source of information is Taar, *The History of Carriages*. The Spanish citation comes from a 1660 pamphlet, *Relación del Casamiento de la Señora Infanta*, 28.

24. Kleinman, *Anne of Austria, Queen of France*, ix.

25. *Mémoires*, 5: 87–88.

26. For the connection between women and monsters see, for example, Grieco, *Ange ou Diablesse, la représentation de la femme au XVIe siècle*.

27. This large skirt revolutionized the line of dress when it came into fashion. A contemporary parallel that might help us understand the impact of this new fashion would be the mini-skirt, which so radically transformed our notion of clothing and the body in the late 1960s. The popularity of the farthingale in seventeenth-century Spain is surprising, given its excessive and exaggerated line and the rather strict sumptuary laws of that country. For an excellent overview of the shifts in fashion in Europe during the early modern period, see Boucher, *2000 Years of Fashion in Europe*. This study is particularly attentive to the larger economic, political, social, and artistic context of the shifts in fashion.

28. Madame de Motteville is using "monstrous" in much the same vein as a contemporary playwright, Pierre Corneille, used "monster" to describe his play *L'Illusion comique* as "a strange monster . . . a bizarre and extravagant invention." Corneille described his 1636 play-within-a-play in this manner because it contained elements that would seem overly complicated in a milieu rejecting the excessive ostentation of the baroque for an aesthetic based on discretion or hidden art. The farthingale would also have been seen as a baroque remnant, out of date in the new aesthetic. See Corneille, *Oeuvres complètes*, 1: 614. The remarks are found in the Dedication to Mademoiselle M.F.D.R., written for the published edition of the play.

29. For the etymology of "machine," see *Webster's Seventh New Collegiate Dictionary* and *The American Heritage Dictionary of Indo-European Roots*.

30. Furetière, *Dictionnaire universel*.

31. Ibid.

32. Interestingly, all Spanish Dictionaries consulted offered an etymology that suggested this. See, for example, *Diccionario de la Lengua Espagnola* (Madrid: Real Academia Espagnola, 1984): "From to keep or hide [*guardar*] and baby [*infante*], because it is a garment with which women could hide their pregnant state." I thank Mary Berg for drawing my attention to this fact and Kathleen Ross for her assistance in translation.

33. We know that compositors slipped many errors into texts in early modern printing. For the processes by which such errors could occur, see Gaskell, *A New Introduction to Bibliography*, 43–49 and 110–16.

34. The entire citation is:

> A whirlwind strike off these bawd farthingales,
> For, but for that, and the loose-bodied gown,
>   I should have discover'd apparently
> The young springal cutting a caper in her belly.

See Webster, *The Tragedy of the Duchess of Malfi*, II, ii, 200. For the anecdote about Juana of Portugal, see Boucher, *2000 Years of Fashion in Europe*, 205. There are other anecdotes about farthingales in this vein cited in Waugh, *Corsets and Crinolines*.

35. This double heritage made Madame de Motteville important to Anne of Austria, who was herself a former Infanta, i.e., both French and Spanish. Anne of Austria was the sister of Philip IV, the monarch with whom the French were negotiating in 1660. That she was of Spanish origin was a liability throughout her reign, as she was often suspected of having sympathy for the Hapsburgs. In anecdotes concerning her reunion with her brother, she is said to have apologized for being too good a Frenchwoman during the years the two nations were at war.

36. Later on in the same section of the memoirs treating the 1660 marriage Motteville makes this connection explicitly when she notes that the "Infante Reine" (as she calls her) "was attractive [*aimable*] in that manner of half undress; because the guard-infanta was so monstrous a thing, that when the Spanish women did not have it on, they were much better," *Mémoires*, 5: 106–7. With these remarks, Motteville seems to be expressing relief about the infanta's physical body; she is underlining that the monstrous clothing can indeed conceal, but that she has seen the infanta's body, as has the royal family, and it is indeed pure and desirable. That Motteville should be the figure policing the infanta-queen's body is not surprising. As mentioned above, the sociologist Pierre Bourdieu has argued that it is often the member of a social group who suffers (or has suffered) most intensely

from a code of behavior who will go on to enforce the governing ideology most dogmatically.

37. Indeed, one goal of the marriage was to gain access to the Hapsburg throne. This goal was ultimately attained, and today the king of Spain, Juan Carlos de Borbón, is, quite ironically, the only Bourbon to retain a throne, albeit in title only.

38. One can see, as well, a possible connection between those slender, pliant shoots and the materials used to construct the hoop skirt. One final connection to note is that *vertugadin* was also a gardening term for which Furetière's *Dictionnaire universel* offers the following definition: "It is a slope of lawn in tiers of which the circular lines that comprise it are not parallel." This usage is no longer current, but one can see the linkage between the definition and the notion of fertility. These references to the garden and to the incipience of the young shoot connect the infanta back to the symbol of the lily which, in the eleventh century, represented both the virgin and fertility. Later it was associated with the Virgin Mary, who was both pure and fruitful. As the abstract symbolism of this flower evolved over the centuries, and as it was adapted as a symbol for the French monarchy, it also became linked to the allegorical image of France, swathed in the robe adorned with *fleurs-de-lys*, the same figure we saw in the 1659 engraving. This figure was related to the image of a garden in which France was often pictured. This garden, a popular image by the mid-fifteenth century, made the king the gardener of his territory. The infanta in her farthingale, inaccessible and yet suggesting fertility, would fit into this image, especially given the etymological connection mentioned above. For a thorough discussion of the evolution of the imagery of the lily, especially as related to the notion of nationhood, see Beaune, *The Birth of Ideology*, Chapter Seven, "The Lilies of France," and Chapter Eleven, "France and the French."

39. For a discussion of the potential danger of sharing the queen's body with outsiders, see Louis Marin, "Le roi, son confident et la reine ou les séductions du regard." The essay offers a reading of Herodifus' story in which the king wants to convince his servant that his queen is the most beautiful woman in the world and thus displays her naked body to him.

40. See Douglas, *Purity and Danger*, Chapter Seven, "External Boundaries." Douglas begins the section by citing Van Gennep's *The Rites of Passage*, Victor Turner's "Betwixt and Between: The Liminal Period in Rites de Passage," and Mircea Eliade's *Rites and Symbols of Initiation: The Mysteries of Birth and Rebirth*.

41. *La Pompe*, 9.

42. Ibid., 12.

43. Ibid., 15.

44. See Vigarello, *Concepts of Cleanliness*, for a discussion of the evolution of hygiene in the classical period.

45. Kristeva, *The Powers of Horror*, 4.

46. The pamphlet was published in Bordeaux in 1615. In English its title would read: "The Royal Reception of their Very-Christian Majesties in the city of Bordeaux, or the Golden Age restored by the alliances of France and Spain, collected by order of the King."

47. Ibid., 107–8. It is useful to examine the original French of this citation: "Le Roy la regardoit souuent en sousriant: elle [la reine] quoy que chargée du pois de ses robbes & brillãs suant à grosses gouttes, ne se pouuoit tenir de luy sousrire, & au Duc de Monte Leone Ambassadeur d'Espagne auec vne grace & Majesté merueilleuse." At a conference in Blois, France, in October 1995, Nicole Pellegrin of the CNRS raised the issue of what was sweating in this passage, the infanta or the gems, "brillãs suant," there being some precedent for such an image. Danielle Hosc DuBosc pointed out, however, that the hierarchy of the grammar supported the original reading, that it was the infanta who was sweating. Such ambiguity does not exist in the passage from the marriage of Louis XIV. For a detailed discussion of the Garasse passage, see Zanger, "Making Sweat: Sex and the Gender of National Reproduction in the Marriage of Louis XIII."

48. See Kleinman, *Anne of Austria*, 26, and Dulong, *Anne d'Autriche*, 11. In her *Le mariage du Roi-Soleil*, Dulong does not mention María Teresa's sweat, although she would surely have read the pamphlet in which it occurs and made the link with the previous marriage. Note, furthermore, that the many occasional pamphlets produced at the time of the marriage do not mention the sweat. See the LB[36] rubric of the *Catalogue de l'histoire de France*, vol. 2, for the year 1615 for a list of these sources. Neither does the historian Théodore Godefroy make reference to sweat in the account of the marriage he includes in *Ordre des cérémonies*, 57–59. On the other hand, an almost verbatim synopsis of the passage from Garasse was published in 1617 in the *Mercure François*, 4: 339–41.

49. Citation from the English translation of this text published in Oxford in 1640, 113. As noted, the work was first published in Toulouse in 1610 and then in Paris in 1623. It is thus likely that Garasse would have been aware of such contemporary erotic writings. In fact, by 1615 he had already begun writing the virulently satirical texts against Protestants and libertinism that later gained him what the author of the article on Garasse in the *Biographie universelle* refers to as a "triste célébrité." Indeed, his 1615 pamphlet, *L'Anti-Joseph, ou bien Plaisant et Fidelle Narré d'un Ministre de la Religion pretenduë, rendu publiquement à Clerac ville d'Agenois, ayant esté enfermé dans un coffre par une honneste dame de Ladite Ville, laquelle il faisait l'amour,*

published in the same year as the *Royal Reception*, is a text that seems overly familiar with the kind of libertine discourses it attacks. For more on the complex career of Garasse, see the entry under his name in *Biographie universelle*, 522–24.

50. Ferrand's example is taken from the story of Antiochus as told in Plutarch's *Life of Demetrius*, so Ferrand is actually quoting Sappho via Plutarch. In Plutarch, when Antiochus saw the woman he loved, "those tell-tale signs of which Sappho sings were all there in him—stammering speech, fiery flushes, darkened vision, sudden sweats." See *Plutarch's Lives*, 9: 93.

51. See Venette, *Conjugal love*, 56–58. I quote from a reprint of the English edition. In French, the text was titled *Tableau de l'Amour considéré dans l'état du mariage* (Amsterdam: Jansson, 1687). The text was very popular and underwent a large number of editions and translations. While this work dates from much later in the century, it drew on an association between sweat and ripeness dating back to antiquity that was not limited to notions of human fertility. The association can be found, for example, in Virgil's *Eclogue IV*, an interesting example since it was written at the time of an important treaty in 40 B.C. that involved a royal marriage. Virgil's text thus links peace to the fertility of the fields, bringing together the themes of cultivation, empire, and fertility also present in the alliance between Hapsburg Spain and Bourbon France. The exact lines are: "Soft spikes of grain will gradually gild the fields, /And reddening grapes will hang in clusters on wild brier, /And dewy honey sweat from tough Italian oaks," in Virgil, *The Eclogues*, 57. The cultivation of Empire is also one of the messages imprinted on queens when they don the royal robe strewn with *fleurs-de-lys*, as was traditional at weddings; the antique legend about the origin of the lily is that it is drops of Juno's milk that fell to the ground. See Beaune, *The Birth of Ideology*, 204.

52. Ferrand, *De la Maladie d'Amour*, 88.

53. If the sweat on the body of the infanta queen in the 1660 marriage is not as luscious and does not occur during the mass, but in the relative privacy of the queen mother's quarters, it may be simply a question of expectations about the taste of the readership. Indeed, in 1615 the reigning aesthetic would have highlighted baroque details that drew attention to the processes of the body, while in 1660 taste would have favored classical simplicity and a Horatian ideology of hidden art. That may be why in a translation of Longinus' *Treatise on the Sublime*, most likely written not long after the marriage of Louis XIV, Nicolas Boileau saw sweat as inappropriate language for translating Sappho's *Sonnet 31* discussed in the treatise. Boileau explains in a footnote that he translated the Greek, "a cold sweat," as "a

shiver seized me" because the word "sweat" was unacceptable in French: "In the Greek one finds a cold sweat: but the word *sweat* [*sueur*] in French can never be pleasing [*agréable*], and leaves a nasty idea in the mind." Just as changing Spanish skirts to French clothing makes María Teresa "pleasing" to Louis XIV, translating sweat as shiver makes the poetic language more "pleasing." In both cases it is a question of creating acceptable language. I would suggest, however, that it is not the actual word *sueur* that is disagreeable to Boileau, but the highlighting of the reaction of the body to passion that was not acceptable or *bienséant* in an aesthetic predicated on hiding art or effort. For Boileau's discussion of Sappho and the ensuing note on his translation, see Boileau, *Oeuvres Complètes*, 356–58, 416.

54. For an accessible overview of the state of medical thinking about women and procreation in the early modern period, see Berriot-Salvadore, "Le Discours de la Médecine et de la Science." Laqueur's *Making Sex: Body and Gender from the Greeks to Freud* is also particularly useful in the context of this discussion for its analysis of the history of sexuality in terms of the social construction of that history. See especially the chapter, "Representing Sex," 114–48, in which Laqueur explores the way the biological body is constructed by Renaissance science. Other sources to consult on this topic include Gélis, *The History of Childbirth, Fertility, Pregnancy, and Birth in Early Modern Europe*, and Maclean, *The Renaissance Notion of Woman*.

55. Laqueur, *Making Sex*, 66.

56. Ibid., 35.

57. See Giesey, *The Royal Funeral Ceremony*, and Hunt, "The Many Bodies of Marie Antoinette." Note that I do not ask here why the depiction of a queen's biological-mortal body does not unsettle her own portrayal for the simple reason that the queen did not have a divine dimension in the early modern French monarchy; she could not inherit property and thus could not participate in the divine rite of succession so fundamental to the political fiction of the king's two bodies. Such an assertion, however, is too formulaic and insufficiently nuanced. Indeed, the interdiction against female succession to the throne was not operative outside France. As Marie Axton has argued in *The Queen's Two Bodies*, Elizabeth I regularly invoked the dual status of her royal body in the rhetoric of her political propaganda. One appealing aspect of the alliances with the Spanish Hapsburgs was the fact that in Spain, as in England, women could have a divine body. The Spanish infanta could inherit the Hapsburg throne. This aspect of the match was especially true for the case of Louis XIV's marriage, which did ultimately place a Bourbon on the Spanish Hapsburg throne in part by means of the appeal to María Teresa's right to succession.

58. A Foucauldian reading would contrast this productive heterosociality of royal marriage in the service of state building to a kind of coupling Foucault has associated with the gratuitous pleasure [*jouissance*] of nonreproductive sex. See Foucault, *History of Sexuality*, vol. I.

59. Note that Garasse's publisher, Simon Millanges, was a member of a well-known publishing family in Bordeaux, mentioned by Henri-Jean Martin in connection with the Jesuit practice of printing "textbooks" in the cities near their establishments. See Martin, *Livre, Pouvoirs, et Société*, 1: 195.

60. As noted above, the classical aesthetic was predicated on a Horatian notion of hidden art in which all effort is concealed to make the work of art (or public demeanor) appear as natural and spontaneous as possible. Such artistry would have obvious advantages for political actions. Both Marin's *Portrait of the King* and Apostolidès' *Le roi machine* describe the relationship between hidden artistry and the portrayal of the strong king. My essays, "Classical Anxiety: Performance, Perfection, and the Issue of Identity," and "The Spectacular Gift: Rewriting the Royal Scenario in Molière's *Les Amants Magnifiques*," also describe the power of hidden art in both the scenario of the actor and that of the king.

61. For the role of fluids in rites of passage, see Van Gennep's description of the practice of throwing water at the legs of newlyweds in *Manuel de Folklore*, II: 578–79. See also Eliade's discussion of initiation rites in *Rites and Symbols of Initiation*. Interestingly, these water rites of transition are often associated with fertility. At times, reclothing is also part of the ceremonial, as Eliade recounts in his discussion of a rebirthing ceremony where "To be wrapped in a skin signifies gestation, crawling out of it symbolizes a new birth," ibid., 54–55. For an overview of water symbolism in fertility rites, see Gélis, *The History of Childbirth*, 24–33.

62. Douglas, *Purity and Danger*, 115.

63. *La Pompe*, 15.

64. For information on the use of medals by Louis XIV see Divo, *Médailles de Louis XIV*, and Jacquiot, *Médailles et jetons de Louis XIV*. On the symbolic nature of medals and money, see Goux, *Symbolic Economies*.

65. *La Pompe*, 15.

66. Furetière, *Dictionnaire universel*.

67. Allegory may be seen here as a form of metaphor, not of metonymy. This idea is of interest in relation to the history–allegory opposition seen in the almanacs examined in Chapter One where the allegorical representations may ultimately be less threatening than the historical ones. The queen, of course, floats between the two registers.

68. Irigaray, "The 'Mechanics of Fluids,'" in *This Sex*, 106.

Chapter 3

1. For the almanacs, see the Bibliothèque National Dép. des estampes Qb[1] series for that year. An engraving made from one of the Lebrun images is reproduced in Chapter Two.

2. See Falk, *Les privilèges de libraire sous l'ancien régime*, 195.

3. One of the Syndic's primary jobs was to keep records of permissions granted to publish. See Falk, *Les privilèges*, 54–55. For further information on the organization of the book trade in this period, see Martin, *Livre, pouvoirs, et société*, and Caille, *Histoire de L'Imprimerie*.

4. On pamphlets in the Renaissance, see Chartier, "La Pendue miraculeusement sauvée: Etude d'une occasionnel," in *Les Usages de L'Imprimé*. On the Fronde, see Jouhaud, *Mazarinades*.

5. Duccini, "Regard sur la littérature pamphlétaire," 313.

6. The phenomenon of scribal culture has not been adequately studied for the French case, perhaps because the form was so censored after the Fronde. For an interesting discussion of scribal textuality in the case of England that may have ramifications for thinking about the French context, see Love, *Scribal Publication*.

7. The last decree was published by Sebastien Cramoisy and may be found in folio 91 of "Collection Anisson-Duperron sur la Librairie et L'Imprimerie," Ms. Fr. 22071, Bibliothèque Nationale.

8. *Contrat de mariage*, listed in the bibliography as published in Paris in 1668, was first published in Toulouse by the *imprimeurs* and *libraires du roi*. See the *Catalogue de l'histoire de France*, 2: 207. Note that, like *La Pompe*, the contract is first published in Toulouse and then in Paris.

9. Promé published only one other pamphlet for the marriage, a short guide to the figures and paintings of the royal entry, *L'Explication des Figures et Peintures qui sont Représentées pour l'Entrée du Roy et de la Reine*. For information on this publisher, see Martin, *Livres, pouvoirs, et société*, 1: 357.

10. While we can explain the relation of the two editions of *La Pompe* and describe their differences, this information does not shed much light on what Roger Chartier would call the "history of reading."

11. For these titles, see the *Catalogue de l'histoire de France*, 2: 211–16. Note that the *Catalogue* identifies certain pamphlets incorrectly as reprints when there are notable differences between them. Other bibliographical sources providing information on these pamphlets, such as André and Bourgeois, *Sources de L'histoire de France*, or Ducère, *Bayonne sous l'ancien régime*, reproduce the *Catalogue*'s errors. I list all the pamphlets as separate in my bibliography and follow the publication information found in the copy studied. I place Colletet's name in brackets for certain pamphlets I

believe strongly are by the journalist because of the style, publication circumstances, or other evidence, but that I cannot absolutely attribute to him.

12. Found in *Journal Contenant La Relation Véritable et Fidelle du Voyage du Roy* . . ., among other pamphlets. The *privilège* states it was granted on December 5 and registered by the Syndic on the 12th. This *privilège* for the pamphlet is not officially recorded in the records of the Syndic. As Falk has noted, however, such books were not very carefully kept. See Falk, *Les privilèges de libraire*, 76. Christian Jouhaud has suggested to me that if there were some official record, it may have been attached to the book and thus have fallen out in the course of the centuries. Another possibility is that the *privilège* was not registered in order to keep the project secret. Registering the *privilège* would protect Loyson's monopoly, but might in fact let others know of his project. At any rate, Loyson would need only have applied to the local prefecture for permission to print such a short pamphlet.

13. Falk, *Privilèges*, 195.

14. It is unusual for writers to be named in *privilèges* accorded to a publisher. The fact may indicate that Colletet could provide the publisher access to something he could not get otherwise. This is speculation, but it is not far-fetched. Also, it attests to the importance of Guillaume Colletet. In this period, only very powerful authors (Molière, for example) received *privilèges*, and even then they needed to cede them to publishers. For more on the relation between authors and the profession of writing, see Viala, *Naissance de l'écrivain*. For examples of *privilèges* awarded to authors in this period, see the Bibliothèque Nationale manuscript, "Registres de permis d'imprimer (1653–1664)."

15. He probably turned to these tasks for practical reasons since his father left him no inheritance. For information on François Colletet, see the entry in the *Biographie universelle* as well as Heulhard, *Le journal de Colletet*, and Sgard, *Dictionnaire des journalistes*.

16. Correspondence between Mazarin and Gabriel Naudé confirms the ongoing relationship between the Colletet family and service to the state. In fact, Naudet explicitly recommends François Colletet to Mazarin as *secretaire* in 1651. See Kathryn Willis Wolfe and Phillip J. Wolfe, eds., *Considérations politiques sur la Fronde: la correspondence entre Gabriel Naudé et le Cardinal Mazarin*, 17, 32, and 62–63, among other references. I thank Christian Jouhaud for pointing out this source.

17. In English, the titles would translate roughly: *Journal Containing the True and Faithful Relation of the Voyage of the King & His Eminence for the Treaty of Marriage of his Majesty, & of the General Peace; Continuation of the Historical Journal Containing the True and Faithful Relation of the Voyage of the King & of His Eminence; Historical Journal Containing the True and Faithful*

Relation of the Voyage of the King . . . Third Journal; and *Fourth Historical Journal, Containing the True and Faithful Relation . . . .*

18. *Journaux Historiques, Contenans Tout ce qui s'est passé de plus remarquable dans le Voyage du Roy et de son Eminence, depuis leur depart de Paris, le 25. Iuin de l'an 1659. Pour le Traitté du Mariage de sa Majesté, & de la Paix Generale, jusqu'à leur retour. Avec une exacte recherche de ce qui s'est fait dans les Conferences des deux Ministres, & dans le Mariage du Roy avec l'Infante d'Espagne à Fontarabie, & à S. Jean de Lus. Et leur entrée dans toutes les Villes de leur passages, & leur Triomphe dans leur bonne Ville de Paris.* In English, the title would translate roughly: *Historical Journals, Containing all the most remarkable things that have occurred during the Voyage of the King and his Eminence, from their departure from Paris June 25, 1959 for the Marriage Treaty of his Majesty, & of the General Peace, up to their return. With an exact study of everything that occurred in the Meetings of the two Minsters, in the Marriage of the King to the Infanta of Spain at Fontarabie and at Saint Jean de Luz, and their entries into all the Cities of their passage, and their Triumphant return to their good City of Paris.*

19. In English the titles would be: *The New Relation Containing the Interview and Sermons of the Kings for the Entire Execution of the Peace. Together all the Particularities & Ceremonies of Marriage of the King & the Infanta of Spain. With all the most remarkable events that took place between these two powerful Monarchs up to the time of their departure* and *The Continuation of the New Relation Containing the Procession of Their Majesties for their Return to their good City of Paris: With all the particularities that took place during their Welcome in magnificent Entries into the Cities of their passage up to the present. Together with the Presents that his Majesty, the Queen Mother, Monsieur, and His Eminence gave to our Incomparable Queen.*

20. It is also possible that it was just the most retained pamphlet, the one for which we have the most surviving examples. But I think it was the most reproduced text even though the survival of such materials does not necessarily reflect the actual historical reality. Nonetheless, assuming that all such items of marriage ephemera survived in amounts roughly equal to their production, it seems likely this text's four editions outnumbered the editions of other surviving pamphlets.

21. Furetière, *Dictionnaire universel.*

22. Rousset, *Leurs yeux se rencontrèrent. La scène de première vue dans le roman,* 7–8.

23. See Masson, *Entier Discours des Choses qui se sont passés en la reception de la Royne & marriage du Roy,* for a description of the marriage of Charles IX, and T. Godefroy, *L'Ordre et Ceremonies Observées aux Mariages de France,* for that of Louis XIII. See the *Mercure François* for a description of the marriage of Henry IV.

24. Colletet, *Nouvelle relation*, 100.

25. Ibid., 11–12. Note here that as was the case in *La Pompe* the infanta is referred to as the queen even though the king has yet to meet her. That is because, as was customary, they had been married two days earlier by procurement on the Spanish side of the border.

26. The full citation from Furetière is: "Incognito [*incongneu*] is said of Noblemen who enter a city, who walk in the streets without pomp, ceremony, and their usual retinue, & without the marks of their importance." See the *Dictionnaire universel*. The king's visit to the reunion between his mother and uncle is not the only such "incognito" appearance of a noble during the marriage ceremony. Indeed, there are other cases of such visits by French nobility to the Spanish court in Fontarabie, the most notable one being that of the king's sister, who attends the marriage by procuration held there.

27. Masson, *Entier Discours*, Ciij. For an interesting analysis of this text see Nordman, "Charles IX à Mézières: mariage, limites, et territoire."

28. Ibid., Ciij.

29. Freud, "Instincts and Their Vicissitudes."

30. Marin, *Portrait*, "La Guerre du Roi," and "Le Corps du Roi."

31. For example, Motteville spins an elaborate conceit about the emotions of the queen mother, who is described as blushing when her son appears, and of the infanta, who is queried on (and described as refusing to give) her opinion of the young unknown. See *Mémoires*, 5: 93–101. See also Colletet, who embellishes the reactions of the Spaniards to this scene in *Seconde Relation*, 19–20. The passage is cited in note 60 below.

32. Colletet, *Nouvelle Relation*, 11–12.

33. Indeed, Sainctot, the master of ceremonies for the marriage, does not deal with this event in his own manuscript memoirs. See Sainctot, "Memoires autographes de M. Sainctot," 3: 155–79.

34. Godefroy, *L'Ordre et Ceremonies Observées aux Mariages de France, et d'Espagne*, 48–49.

35. In the 1615 alliance, the two sides in the treaty were bargaining from relative positions of equality. Perhaps the mutual and symmetric gaze replays that political balance. Such could not be said for either the alliance of 1570 or that of 1660. In the first case, it was the Hapsburgs who held the advantage; in the second, it was the Bourbons.

36. For an overview of the *topos* of the king on horseback in this period, see Liedtke, *The Royal Horse and Rider*.

37. This phenomenon is accounted for by suture theory, first adapted from Lacanian theory and applied to the cinematographic model by Oudart in his essay, "La Suture." The notion was taken up again quite actively in

the 1980s by American theoreticians of cinema and more recently by feminist theorists of cinematic representation. The latter, studying both the relation of the female body to the male gaze and the status of the female gaze itself, have brought their ideas into play with the paradigm of suture theory. See Silverman, writing on the topic as it concerns semiotics in *The Subject of Semiotics*, 194–236, and Mulvey's "Visual Pleasure and Narrative Cinema."

38. Viala in *Naissance de l'écrivain*, and Jouhaud in "Sur le statut de l'homme de lettres au dix-septième siècle," and "Histoire et histoire littéraire," have both described such a complex and active network of intersecting interests in the intellectual field of seventeenth-century France. Their notion of such cultural movement is taken from the work of Pierre Bourdieu on the cultural field found in such essays as "Champs intellectuel et projet créateur."

39. Note that the scene is actually described by other means, most particularly in letters of nobles and in their memoirs, but these forms would have a more restrained reception. Indeed, for the case of the description found in memoirs, most particularly those of Madame de Motteville and Madame de Montpensier, it is difficult to say whether their writings served as the source of the journalist (written accounts sent to him by these women) or if the women, in writing their stories later in life, may not have used the occasional pamphlets they may have had on their shelves. On female memorial writers as historians, see Beasley, *Revising Memory*.

40. See the Bibliothèque Nationale's "Collection Anisson-Duperron sur la Librairie et L'Imprimerie," Ms. Fr. 22071: 91.

41. Colletet, *Le Nouveau Journal Historique, contenant la Relation Véritable De ce qui s'est passé au voyage du Roy et de son Eminence. Et aux Ceremonies du Mariage de Sa Majesté. Célébrées à Fontarabie & à S. Jean de Luz* (Paris: A. Lesselin, 1660). In English, the title would be *The New Historical Journal, containing the True Relation of everything that occurred on the voyage of the King and his Eminence And at the Ceremonies of the Marriage of His Majesty Celebrated at Fontarabie and at Saint Jean de Luz*. The permission is printed in the beginning of a pamphlet. According to that notice, the permission was accorded on May 16, registered on May 22, and ceded to Lesselin on June 4. Colletet cedes only the right to one pamphlet to Lesselin. That is because he maintains the general *privilège* for all his works. Like Loyson's *privilège*, this one is not entered in the register. That may be because it is for a pamphlet and thus is accorded less formally. As noted above, in the case of publishing a pamphlet there would be less corporate interest in registering the monopoly accorded. The economic payoff of the printing would be limited to one or two runs and would not need to be publicly protected

from competition over the long term. We shall see, however, that this was in fact not the case.

42. Despite this new *privilège*, Colletet never stopped writing for Loyson. After an initial dispute, discussed below, Colletet exercised his own general authorization over his output by ceding certain works to Loyson, who would most likely have paid him more. Perhaps, after renegotiating his fees, it was most profitable for Colletet to continue working with Loyson, who would have already established himself as the purveyor of the reports on the marriage. Lesselin, furthermore, was an *imprimeur*, while Loyson was a *marchand libraire*. The two occupied different sectors of the book trade. The *marchand libraire* generally dominated the book trade in Paris because he would have the capital to farm out work to printers and pay them on a regular schedule. He may have also had his own presses on which to produce works he could then sell from his store. While the *imprimeur* was a member of the same syndic, he could compete with a *marchand libraire* only if he had an address from which to sell the work he produced. Otherwise he might be more likely to publish for the *marchand libraire*. Lesselin did have his own storefront. In general, expansion of the industry and severe competition put the two sectors of the trade into contention. For information on these issues, see Caille, *Histoire de L'Imprimerie et de la Libraire*, Martin, *Livre, pouvoirs, et société à Paris au XVIIe siècle*, and Falk, *Les privilèges de libraire sous l'ancien régime*, as well as Bibliothèque Nationale Ms. Fr. 21747 concerning opposition to expanding the profession in the 1680s.

43. *Nouvelle Relation*, 16 and 1.

The following chronology of the pamphlets written by Colletet for Loyson and Lesselin will guide the reader in the ensuing discussion.

1. **1659–early 1660**. Four pamphlets on the treaty negotiation published by Loyson: *Journal Contenant La Relation Veritable et Fidelle du Voyage du Roy, & de Son Eminence, Pour le Traitté du Mariage de Sa Majesté, & de la Paix Generale* (1659); *Suitte du Journal Historique Contenant La Relation Véritable et Fidele . . .* (1659); *Journal Historique, Contenant la Relation. . . . Journal Troisiesme* (1659); *Quatriesme Journal Historique, Contenant la Relation . . .* (1660).

2. **June 1660**. Pamphlet published by Loyson in late June 1660: *La Nouvelle Relation Contenant L'Entreveue et Serments des Roys, pour L'Entiere Execution de la Paix*.

3. **Late June 1660**. Pamphlet published by Lesselin under *privilège* ceded by Colletet (Loyson has this pamphlet seized since it contradicts his rights): *Le Nouveau Journal Historique, contenant la Relation Véritable De ce qui s'est passé au voyage du Roy et de son Eminence. Et aux Ceremonies du Mariage de Sa Majesté. Célébrées à Fontarabie & à S. Jean de Luz.*

4. **July 1660**. Pamphlet published by Lesselin under *privilège* ceded by

Colletet (issued after the resolution of the litigation): *Seconde Relation Veritable et Fidelle de tout ce qui s'est fait & passé de plus remarquable dans les Conferences & dans les Adieux des deux Roys, jusques au depart de sa Majeste de la ville de S. Jean de Lus.*

5. August 1660 and after. Colletet begins choosing Loyson once more as his publisher.

44. Note that Loyson's *privilège* seems to have even been renewed at this time, although he should not have had to apply for a renewal under the terms of his original 1659 permission. But if one is to believe the abstract of Loyson's *privilège* printed in his pamphlets, there was some change to it. More likely, Loyson was amending his own abstract, changing the dates and removing Colletet's name as author. See, for example, the abstract of Loyson's *privilège* printed in the front of *La Nouvelle Relation,* and other pamphlets in the bibliography attributed to Colletet in brackets. This *privilège* is virtually identical in description to the original one, except for the elimination of the initials F.C. and the dates of awarding and registering it, no longer listed as December 5, 1659, and December 20, 1659, but as December 5, 1660, and May 20, 1660. Later, Loyson reverts to the original dates, but at that point he is accepting Colletet's ceded *privilège.*

45. We learn the details of the seizure of Colletet's pamphlet in an extract of the final ruling that is published by Lesselin in the *Seconde Relation,* 36.

46. This particular pamphlet had four different editions, more than any other pamphlet from the period of the marriage. It would be impossible to ascertain, however, if all four dated from June 1660, since in 1661 pamphlets from the marriage were still being republished.

47. Colletet, *Seconde Relation,* 36.

48. *Second True and Faithful Relation of everything remarkable that took place in the Conferences and the Farewells of the two Kings up to the departure of his Majesty from Saint Jean de Luz.*

49. Ibid., 15.

50. The following is written in the margin of the *Seconde Relation:* "It is Monsieur d'Aubray who decided this Sentence in favor of the Author and his printer as a result of the Conclusions of Monsieur Brigalier, Counsel of the King, after having heard le Clerc, lawyer of one and Marais, lawyer of the other, and who closed his mouth to that of the opposing party which came to appeal to the Court, in contempt of such a judicious and equitable Sentence." See the *Seconde Relation,* 15. The "Sentence rendered by Monsieur le Lieutenant Civil against J. B. Loyson Bookseller, On behalf of Sieur François Colletet, & d'Alexandre Lesselin his Printer" is found at the end of the pamphlet: ibid., 36.

51. As, for example, in the *Seconde Relation,* 19–20, cited in note 60 below.

52. On the *nouvelliste*, see Zanger, "Le nouvelliste et son public." See also DeJean, "The (Literary) World at War," 121–22, on the *nouvelliste* in the context of debates over the novel from the end of the century.

53. Colletet, *Le Nouveau Journal Historique*, 3–4.

54. Ibid., 4. The two "journalists" Colletet refers to are Renaudaut, editor of the *Gazette*, and Loret, who wrote the *Lettres en vers à Madame*. Neither source offers a report of the king's first view of his new bride.

55. It is possible that some of the letters preserved in manuscript form may have been such documents. See "Lettres, billets, nouvelles à la main; lettres adressées au Chancelier Séquier 1610–1668; pièces diverses."

56. *La Suitte du Journal Historique Contenant la Relation Veritable et Fidelle du voyage du Roy, & de Son Eminence, Pour le Traitte du Mariage de sa Majesté & de la Paix Generale*, 12. The prose is anticipated by a short verse:

> Come down from Parnassus, O Daughters of Memory,
> Abandon your Woods, Waters, and Deserts,
> Increase the accents of your concerts,
> And join for Louis, Fable with History.

> [Descendez de Parnasse, ô Filles de Memoire,
> Abandonnez vos Bois, vos Eaux & vos Deserts,
> Redoublez les accents de vos doctes concerts,
> Et joignez pour Loüis la Fable avec l'Histoire.]

57. Ripa, *Iconologia* (1758–60), plate 50. See also *Iconologie* (1644), 1: 195–96, and *Iconologia* (1709), Figure 311.

58. This call for diversity resonates with what Hayden White says about the historical impulse and its origin in multiple accounts: "Unless at least two versions of the same set of events can be imagined, there is no reason for the historian to take upon himself the authority of giving the true account of what really happened." See White, *The Content of the Form*, 20.

59. *Seconde Relation*, 20.

60. The full quotation from the *Seconde Relation*, 19–20, reads:

> This Royal Company was together for a good two and a half hours, & in the middle of the Conference, our King appeared on the plain, & strolled along the path of Andaye with his retinue which was about 20 persons; it was there that passing incognito, that is to say without his soldiers drumming, he mounted a horse, made 5 or 6 turns, & seeing that the conference lasted longer than he would have wanted, his amorous impatience obliged him to alight, at the door of the covered Gallery & to enter there with his retinue. . . . Then he went just to the little gallery where the door to the Room of the Conference

was, & signaling his Eminence & D. Louis of Haro not to move from their place, he advanced between the two, & he had the pleasure to look into the Room, & to consider she whom he already possessed in his Heart. His brother[,] in the meantime[,] informed the Queen, & told her gallantly that he could not better represent for her the King, than by the face of this young horseman [*cavalier*] who was looking from between Monsieur the Cardinal and Don Louis of Haro. He remained a good half hour in this position, & then retraced his way through the Rooms, addressing a thousand civilities to the Spanish, who were more than enraptured to see a King so obliging & so civil, & of a so handsome & favorable a figure. He was no sooner outside that he remounted his horse, & walking along the prairie, all the guards of the King of Spain left their posts and their positions, and went in a crowd to the water to see the King, who they circled from all sides, making a thousand exclamations of joy. It was like that until he [the king] was informed that the King of Spain was reembarking to return: thus he went riding along the border of the meadow at a place where the water was very narrow, & where the boat came near the shore, he got off the horse with all his followers, & all having their hats in hand lined up behind the King about three steps back, the King also took off his hat & combed himself, then put it back, the King of Spain who saw all this from afar came out of the back of the Boat, & even turning back a curtain which blocked his view, he made the Ladies in Waiting who were next to the Queen pass by in order that they could consider the King more conveniently. When the King saw the boat about 40 steps from where he was, he took off his hat and looked at the boat pass without saluting. The King of Spain did not take off his hat, & contented himself for this round to look attentively at him, & even turned, in order to see him again, after the Boat had passed.

As for the Queen, one can well believe that her eyes were not lazy, & that they had well wished that the boat had traveled more slowly than it did, in order to enjoy longer a so precious view: the King her father spoke to her at two or three different stages and one could judge well by his [or her?] expression that Our Monarch was the true subject of his discourse, although it was uncertain if it was effectively he who was the subject, and also he did not salute him, & it was only the Ladies in Waiting of the Queen who acquitted themselves of this civility; What made it thought that the King of Spain had not recognized the King of France, was that the King of France remounted his horse, & moved up to 100 steps higher to see it pass again. His Catholic Majesty [Philip IV] saluted him three times which was returned by his Very Christian Majesty [Louis XIV].

61. "Registres de permis d'imprimer," fol. 66 (recto). The technical terms concerning the additions made to the volume can be found in Furetière and Richelet. I thank Roger Chartier for clarifying the issue of the lists of departures of the mail, essentially a timetable.

62. The *privilège* states that it was granted on November 1 and registered on December 1. This should be contrasted to the *privilège* for the pamphlet accorded on December 5 and registered on December 12. As noted earlier, the *privilège* for the pamphlet was never officially recorded in the registers of the Book Syndic. That may have been because the registers of the Syndicat were not very carefully kept, as Falk notes in *Les Privilèges de Libraire*, 76, or because short brochures could be authorized directly by the police (ibid., 195), or because the sheet fell out of the manuscript. I would note, however, the one-month time lag in the recorded *privilège* versus a twelve-day lag in the unrecorded one, which may indicate a different system of registration for each form.

63. Mattheiu had written on the history of France and Spain, chronicling the early years of Bourbon Hapsburg relations in works such as *Histoire des derniers troubles de France . . . avec un recueil des édits. . . . Dernière édition reveue et augmentée des guerres entre les maisons de France et D'Espagne et de tout ce qui s'est passée durant icelles jusques au mois de mars de l'année 1610* (N.p., 1601). He had also written pamphlets reporting on Henry IV's wedding to Marie de Medicis. Evidence indicates that Colletet, in working with Loyson, wished to emulate Mattheiu and become royal historiographer. Such evidence includes not only Colletet's rhetoric about history in his pamphlets, but also the relation between his father and the government noted in the Mazarin–Naudet correspondence edited by Wolfe and Wolfe as *Considérations politiques sur la Fronde*. At the very least, Colletet may have hoped to ingratiate himself enough by reporting on the marriage to receive future patronage from the court.

64. One of the most highly contested areas of the printing industry in the seventeenth century was the problem of "continuations" of *privilèges* to publish works after the first authorization had run out. Problems arose particularly around reprinting religious and ancient texts and around the rights of provincial publishers to reproduce such works printed in Paris. Interestingly, there was a flurry of legislation around these issues in 1659. In 1660, Loyson became embroiled in a case around the problem of printing a text with some augmentation. For this last, see Martin, *Livre, pouvoirs, et société*, 595–96.

65. Reichler, "La Jambe du roi," 122–23.

Chapter 4

1. "La Pompe Funebre de Mylord Protecteur d'Angleterre: Et La description du beau Feu d'artifice qui a servi de divertissement aux Cours de France & de Savoye, en la ville de Lyon," 1227. See also Galectéros De Boissier, "Jason à la conquête de la toison d'or," 241–42.

2. The four pamphlets on the negotiation originally published in 1659 and early 1660.

3. "La Pompe Funebre . . . Et La description du beau Feu," 1228.

4. For information on fireworks, see articles by Fenton, "Fireworks," and by Low, "Pyrotechnic paens," as well as the entry "Artifice," section VIII ("La Pyrotechnie") of the article, "Feu" in *La Grande encyclopédie*, 17: 367–68.

5. See Marin's analysis of Félibien's *Divertissements de Versailles* in *Portrait*, 193–205. The last two pages of the discussion demonstrate how in Félibien's description of a 1674 celebration, the king is constructed as the ultimate alchemist. Marin also links this image to mastery, albeit via Pascal. His discussion ultimately focuses more on the idea of gold, linking it to his earlier analysis of Perrault's fable, *Peau d'âne* [*Donkey Skin*]. Nor does Apostolidès discuss fireworks. He focuses more closely on the thematics of court spectacles to underline their larger socio-economic nature, as, for example, in his chapter on the *Plaisirs de l'île enchanté*, in *Le Roi machine*, 93–113.

6. An overview of Menestrier's life and work can be found in the entry on him in the *Biographie universelle*. For a more complete discussion of his writings, see Allut, *Recherches sur la vie et sur les oeuvres du P. Claude-François Menestrier*.

7. *The Celebrations of the Peace with a Collection of diverse pieces on this subject*. The *privilège* for the text was granted on May 2, 1660, and so the text itself was probably published some time around the actual arrival of the infanta in France.

8. "Necessary Advice for the Management of Fireworks," 15.

9. Menestrier, *Rejouissances*, 15.   10. Menestrier, *Advis*, 17–18.

11. Menestrier, *Rejouissances*, 17.   12. Menestrier, *Advis*, 4–5.

13. Ibid., 5.

14. Of course, this attitude should not surprise us any more than did Menestrier's interest in the form. In many ways it foreshadows what he would write later about other symbolic forms, that they are meant to teach, to "regulate the conduct of men." Menestrier, *L'Art des Emblesmes*, 15–16.

15. Treatises on pyrotechnics all point to the significance accorded fire in ancient rituals. For a general discussion of the folk myths around fire,

see Charrière, "Feux, Bûchers et Autodafés Bien de Chez Nous."

16. Appier Hanzelet, *Receuil de plusieurs machines Militaires*, 1.

17. Ibid., 13.

18. Ibid., 4: 7.

19. Ibid., 4: 8.

20. Galactéros De Bossier asserts that this short treatise codifies the genre of the fireworks display in "Jason à la conquête de la toison d'or," 252. The first such work in Europe may have been Italian. See Massar's study of Stefano della Bella's illustrations for an unpublished manuscript on fireworks that dates to 1649–50. In "Stefano della Bella's Illustrations for a Fireworks Treatise," 296, Massar argues this was the first such treatise whose emphasis was not on pyrotechnical devices being used for war.

21. Menestrier, *Rejouissances*, 2. The *topos* that links the joys of peace to the horrors of war can be found, for example, in the following excerpt of a sonnet:

> And the Drum is no longer for them,
> A deadly instrument of War.
> And the joy and pleasures,
> Are so perfect in our Souls.

> [Et le Tambour n'est plus pour eux,
> Un funeste instrument de Guerre.
> Et la joye et les voluptez,
> Son si parfaites dans nos Ames.]

The sonnet is found in *Recit des Feux de Joye Faits en la Ville de Chalon sur Saone le dernier de Fevrier mil six cens soixante*, 7. The same pamphlet also describes an inscription on one machine: "On allume ses feux, parce qu'on esteint la Guerre" (Fires are lit because War has been ended [*esteint*]), ibid., 3. Similar imagery is often applied to the infanta, who is the representative of both war and peace.

22. An art applicable to activities of war and peace, fireworks may mirror the very transitional nature of the period of treaty negotiation between war and peace. Indeed, the April celebration in Lyon that Menestrier describes occurs after the negotiation of the treaty marriage from August through November 1659, but before the final signing of the accord in June 1660. Even though Lyon is characterized by Menestrier as "This Town, which had always maintained its tranquility during the agitations of the State" (*Rejouissances*, 2), a place little affected by political turmoil (the Fronde or the war), Menestrier and the citizens of Lyon could, nonetheless, appreciate the precarious stability of the liminal period between war and peace.

23. In stressing the transformation of an instrument from one use to

another, Menestrier (like the sonnet writer cited in note 21) underlines the resolution of contradiction, one of his organizing themes of the celebration whose central monument or machine was the temple of the two-faced Janus, which represents the union of two warring peoples, the Romans and the Sabines (*Rejouissances*, 18–23). The paradox or contradiction appears as well in smaller monuments, as, for example, in one that Menestrier declared among the most beautiful, the "fort of contrariety," a monument involving opposing colors, black and white, and elements, fire and water; the inscriptions on this machine "invited the whole world to reconciliation" (ibid., 68–69). While it may be argued that such a thematic was simply a popular Renaissance and Classical motif, I would suggest that as a theoretician of the emblem, Menestrier may well have emphasized this facet of the peace because he would have relished the transformational nature of the event, the same property that was considered at the basis of the form he was utilizing.

24. Freud, *Beyond the Pleasure Principle*, 8–11.

25. Menestrier, *Advis*, 21. 26. Ibid., 6.

27. Fenton, "Fireworks," 51. 28. Menestrier, *Advis*, 21–22.

29. Ibid., 22.

30. For examples of such monuments, see the many pamphlets explaining entry monuments referred to in the next chapter. Tronçon's *L'Entrée Triomphante* (available in Möseneder, *Zeremoniell und monumentale Poesie*) reproduces engravings of monuments and their descriptions, offering the easiest overview of those that included pictures of the king and queen.

31. For details of the meeting in Lyon see Ducéré, *Bayonne sous l'ancien régime*, Chapter 1, "Les Préliminaires de la Paix"; Dulong, *Le Mariage*, Chapter 2, "L'intermède Savoyard"; and Wolf, *Louis XIV*, Chapter 9, "The Mancini Crisis." Wolf devotes only three pages to the meeting, incorporating it into his longer discussion of the romance with Marie Mancini.

32. For a description of the Paris fireworks, see both versions of *Le Feu Royal et Magnifique*. For comments on the difference between the fireworks in Paris and in Lyon, see Magné, *Les Fêtes en Europe au XVIIe Siècle*, 281–88, and Galactéros De Boissier, "Jason à la conquête de la toison d'or," 253–56.

33. He is referred to as having "de l'inclination aux mécaniques" (a mechanical bent), and as being one of the best metal workers [*serrurier*] in France, by Marty-Laveau, in *Oeuvres de Pierre Corneille*, 6: 223.

34. See Corneille's *Examen* of *La Toison d'or* in which the author discusses this choice taken from Appolonius of Rhodes' version of the myth. See Corneille, *Oeuvres complètes*, 3: 209.

35. See Greenberg's *Corneille, Classicism, and the Ruses of Symmetry* for a reading of Medea in this play.

36. Corneille, *Oeuvres complètes*, 3: 211.

37. Ibid., 3: 211, line 54.

38. Many critics, the editor Georges Couton included (in Corneille, *Oeuvres complètes*, 3: 1416), underline the subversive and critical nature of this image of the people suffering from the war. In fact, the image that the country is ravaged by war is actually a *topos* of the treaty literature, acceptable to the regime because the depiction of the destruction of war helps underline Mazarin's triumph in negotiating a treaty.

39. Corneille, *Oeuvres complètes*, 3: line 59.

40. Ibid., 3: lines 59–66.

41. "Tu renonces à cette gloire, /La Paix a pour toi plus d'appas, /Et tu dédaignes la Victoire, /Que j'ai de ma main propre attachée à tes pas. /Vois dans quels fers sous moi la Discorde, et L'Envie, /Tiennent cette Paix asservie." (Ibid., 3: lines 77–82.)

42. Ibid., 3: lines 140–41.

43. Oui, Monstres, oui, craignez cette main vengeresse, /Mais craignez encore plus cette grande Princesse, /Pour qui je viens allumer mon flambeau: /Pourriez-vous soutenir les traits de son visage? /Fuyez, Monstres à son image, /Fuyez, et que l'Enfer, qui fut votre berceau, /Vous serve à jamais de tombeau. /Et vous, noir instruments d'un indigne esclavage, /Tombez, fers odieux, à ce divin aspect, /Et pour lui rendre un prompt hommage, /Anéantissez-vous de honte, ou de respecte. (Ibid., 3: lines 142–52.)

44. See Félibien, *Description de l'Arc de la Place Dauphine*, 17, where the image is both described and reproduced. In his description, Félibien calls the image "the Spirit of France, who carries on its shield the Portrait of the Queen, like a new Palladium. One sees by his appearance, Bellone, who is the goddess of War, fleeing all terror-stricken, because in effect, it was in this way that Marriage established Peace." The description and engraving also appears in Tronçon's luxury edition account of the royal entry. And Menestrier invokes the idea in his *Rejouissances*, 5: "les images de Thérèse ont fait ce que les armes les plus nombreuses n'avoient jamais tenté sans peril." [The images of Thérèse have accomplished what the most numerous weapons have never attempted without peril.]

45. The myth of Perseus and Andromeda was a subject traditionally utilized in representations of royalty dating back to the Renaissance. See Bardon, *Le portrait mythologique à la cour de France*, 39–40, for a discussion of the myth in relation to images of Henry IV and Louis XIII.

46. See, for example, Lapp, "Magic and Metamorphosis in *La Conquête de la Toison d'or*," 180.

47. Ibid., 180.

48. Corneille, *Oeuvres complètes*, 3: line 178.

49. Ibid., 3: line 183–84.

50. Naissez à cet aspect, fontaines, fleurs, bocages, /Chassez à ces débris, les funestes images, /Et formez des jardins, tels qu'avec quatre mots, /Le grand art de Medée en fit naitre à Colchos. (Ibid., 3: lines 237–40.)

51. Ibid., 3: lines 413–14.

52. Mais si dans mes Etats, mais si dans mon Palais, /Quelque chose avait pu mériter vos souhaits, /Le choix qu'en aurait fait cette valeur extrême /Lui donnerait un prix, qu'il n'a pas de lui-même /Et je croirais devoir à ce précieux choix /L'heur de vous rendre un peu de ce que je vous dois. (Ibid., 3: lines 459–64.)

53. Oui, ce que nos Destins m'ordonnent que j'obtienne, /Je le veux de vos mains, et non pas de la mienne. /Si ce trésor par vous ne m'est point accordé, /Mon bras me punira d'avoir trop demandé, /Et mon sang à vos yeux sur ce triste rivage /De vos justes refus étalera l'ouvrage. /Vous m'en verrez, Madame, accepter la rigueur, /Votre nom en la bouche, et votre image au coeur, /Et mon dernier soupir par un pur sacrifice /Sauver toute ma gloire, et vous rendre justice. /Quel heur de pouvoir dire, en terminant mon sort, /"Un respect amoureux a seul causé ma mort!" (Ibid., 3: lines 828–39.)

54. See Cioranesco, *Bibliographie de la littérature française du dix-septième siècle*, for the complete bibliography of Menestrier's writings.

55. Furetière, *Dictionnaire universel*.

56. On this topic see Montague, "The Painted Enigma and French Seventeenth-Century Art," and Graham, "Pour une Rhetorique de L'Embleme."

57. Montague, "The Painted Enigma," 311.

58. Ibid., 308, 325.

59. Ibid., 326.

60. Ibid., 315–16.

61. Irigaray, "Women on the Market," in *This Sex Which is Not One*, and Rubin, "The Traffic in Women."

62. Corneille, *Oeuvres complètes*, 3: line 1739 and p. 202.

63. Ibid., 3, lines 2044–46.

64. "S'il faut par ce combat acheter la victoire. /Je l'abandonne, Orphée, aux charmes de ta voix, /Qui traîne les rochers, qui fait marcher les bois, /Assoupis le Drangon, enchante la Princesse." (Ibid., 3: lines 2047–50.

65. Ibid., 3: lines 2054–55.

66. This is largely the argument of Irigaray in "Gesture in Psychoanalysis," in *Sexes and Geneologies*. According to Irigaray, the boy uses his voice,

the words *"fort"* and *"da,"* to express his fear and pleasure in replaying and mastering the loss of his mother. In contrast, Irigaray describes the girl's body as having a very different and more physical, less verbal relationship to space and mastery (See 95–100).

67. This triple scene, a simultaneous decor in which several scenes are revealed at once, is characteristic of medieval staging that defies the logic of the classical stage with its unity of place.

68. This image should not surprise us since, as we equate Medea with the explosivity of fireworks, we remember that war is the wet nurse, if not the mother, of peace in Appier Hanzelet's *Recueil de plusieurs machines Militaires.* Explosive events or symbols, like the mother, are potentially frightening and desirable.

69. De Lemnos faites votre asile, /Le Ciel veut qu'Hypsipyle /Réponde aux voeux d'Absyrte, et qu'un Sceptre dotal /Adoucisse le cours d'un peu de temps fatal, /Car enfin de votre perfide/Doit sortir un Médus qui vous doit rétablir, /A rentrer dans Colchis il sera votre guide, /Et mille grands exploits qui doivent l'ennoblir /Feront de tous vos maux les assurés remèdes, /Et donneront naissance à l'empire des Mèdes. (Ibid., 3: lines 2206–15).

70. See Hertz's essay on Medusa in political images, "Medusa's Head: Male Hysteria Under Political Pressure," and Catherine Gallagher's response to it, both in Hertz, *End of the Line, Essays on Psychoanalysis and the Sublime.*

71. See Introduction to this book, 4–5 on the early jurists' fears.

72. On the relation between Corneille and Sourdéac, see Corneille, *Oeuvres de Pierre Corneille,* 6: 223–29.

73. Persès dans la Scythie arme un bras souverain; /Sitôt qu'il paraîtra, quittez ces lieux, Aète, /Et par un prompt retraite /Epargnez tout le sang qui coulerait en vain. (Ibid., 3: lines 2202–5).

74. For an analysis of the relation between the ruler and those involved in constructing his spectacles in the 1670s see Zanger, "The Spectacular Gift."

Chapter 5

1. This pamphlet, Colletet's *Nouvelle Relation,* and its report on the young couple's first encounter, is discussed extensively in Chapter Two.

2. Fogel, *Les cérémonies de l'information dans la France du XVIe au XVIIIe siècle.*

3. Van Gennep, *Rites of Passage.*

4. See DeJean, *Tender Geographies,* 17–70.

5. For discussions of the intellectual milieu of the salon see DeJean, *Tender Geographies,* Harth, *Cartesian Women,* and Lougee, *Le Paradis des femmes.*

6. In his notes to *Célinte*, editor Alain Niderst points out where Scudéry cites the pamphlets; I concur with his assessments.

7. Colletet, *Journal Contenant La Relation Veritable et Fidelle du Voyage du Roy, & de Son Eminence*, 4–5.

8. Colletet, *Journaux Historiques*, 5.

9. The editon includes the engraving from the August entry ceremony. It therefore seems likely that the text originally published in 1659 (and early 1660) was republished in the period after the entry. At the very least, it was marketed after the entry.

10. Colletet, *Nouveau Journal Historique*, 4.

11. For a more complete discussion of the notion of curiosity in the Renaissance see Céard, *La curiosité à la Renaissance*, and Pomian, *Collectors and Curiosities*. Pomian is particularly interested in the history and epistemology of collecting. Chapter Two, "The Age of Curiosity," offers a useful overview of the understanding of curiosity in the context of seventeenth-century France. For the Greek version of the debate see Plutarch's essay, "On Curiosity," in *Plutarch's Moralia*. The ambivalence over the positive and negative impulses of curiosity continues into the seventeenth century, as is shown by a quick scan of Furetière's *Dictionnaire universel* and Richelet's *Nouveau dictionnaire françois*, as well as by reading François de La Mothe Le Vayer's "De la Curiosité," in *Oeuvres*.

12. Habermas, *The Structural Transformation of the Public Sphere*.

13. For a discussion of women and the public sphere, see Landes, *Women and the Public Sphere in the Age of the French Revolution*.

14. Her discussion of the entry serves as a useful counterpoint not only to the seventeenth-century descriptions, but also to those of the twentieth century. Examples of the hermeneutic impulse still central to studies of royal entries can be found in: Graham and Johnson, *The Paris Entries of Charles IX and Elisabeth of Austria, 1571*; Roy Strong, *Splendor at Court*; McFarlane, *The Entry of Henri II into Paris*; and Bryant, *The King and the City*. Two studies particularly on this entry—Möseneder's *Zeremoniell und monumentale Poesie* and Apostolidès' "L'Entrée royale de Louis XIV,"—may be located within a newer approach to the study of pageantry that unequivocally equates power and representation.

15. These parts of her novels were eventually excerpted and published between 1680 and 1692 under various versions of the title *Conversations*. Some of those essays are collected in Scudéry, *Choix de Conversations*.

16. Elizabeth Goldsmith describes this middle moment of Scudéry's conversations as the one in which the chosen problem is "inventoried." The term aptly describes a process in the prologue of working all angles of a topic. See Goldsmith, *Exclusive Conversations*, 49.

17. Scudéry, *Célinte*, 35–36. Note that the event is referred to repeatedly in the prologue as the "Entry of the Queen." While this term appears in the pamphlet literature, it is more commonly referred to there as the entry of the king and queen.

18. Ibid., 36.　　　　　　　　19. Ibid.

20. Ibid., 36–37.　　　　　　　21. Ibid., 37.

22. Ibid., 38.　　　　　　　　23. Ibid., 38, 40.

24. Ibid., 41. These last two citations are among those Scudéry adapts from the pamphlet material. It seems likely the pamphlets were particularly read by women. Of course, there is no way to know, but the later female memorialists such as Montpensier and Motteville also seem to quote almost verbatim from the pamphlets in their descriptions of the infanta's arrival in France. It is possible, of course, that Motteville and Montpensier were Colletet's informants, since, as he notes, he wrote up those events using *mémoires*—written accounts—sent to him from the border.

25. *Célinte*, 48.　　　　　　　26. Ibid., 49.

27. Ibid., 46.　　　　　　　　28. Ibid., 48.

29. This schema fits into a larger argument about the nature of history that has been amply treated by other scholars, particularly but not exclusively as it relates to issues of gender. See Faith Beasley on female memorialists in *Revising Memory*. Malina Stevanofska offers a different perspective on attitudes toward history in "Strolling Through the Galleries, Hiding in a Cabinet: Clio at the French Absolutist Court."

30. Two examples of these texts are *La Conference de Ianot et Piarot Doucet* and *Ordonnance de Messieurs*.

31. Scudéry, *Célinte*, 51.　　　　32. Ibid., 53.

33. Ibid., 62, n. 67.　　　　　　34. Ibid., 36.

35. There is a burgeoning bibliography on collecting. See Pomian, *Collectors and Curiosities*; Schnapper, *Le géant, la licorne, et la tulipe*; Kenseth, *The Age of the Marvelous*; Schulz, "Notes on the History of Collecting and of Museums"; Findlen, "The Museum: Its Classical Etymology and Renaissance Genealogy"; and Juel-Jensen, "*Musaeum Clausum*, or *Bibliotheca Abscondita*: Some thoughts on curiosity cabinets and imaginary books." The literature on museums in the nineteenth and twentieth centuries is also useful, particularly one essay that offers a critique of some of the work on that material: Tony Bennett, "The Exhibitionary Complex," in *New Formations*, 4 (Spring 1988), 73–102.

36. Scudéry, *Célinte*, 56.

37. Ibid.

38. One member of the group wraps up the discussion by agreeing with Meriante that even if it would be impossible to renounce curiosity entirely,

"It is necessary to regulate it in such a manner that it would be useful to those who have it and it would harm no one because if one complies with what I say, one will never want to know anything that doesn't merit being known." Ibid., 56.

39. Schnapper, Antoine, *Le géant, la licorne, et la tulipe.*

40. Ibid., 305, 128.

41. Ibid., 14.

42. Bryant, *The King and the City in the Parisian Royal Entry Ceremony,* 207–8.

43. Hanley, *The Lit de Justice of the Kings of France.*

44. This contrast becomes even more striking when one studies entries from previous marriages. I thank Natalie Davis for drawing my attention to this phenomenon.

45. *Le Parnasse Royal et La Rejouyssance des Muses,* 5.

46. *Le Triomphe de la France Pour l'Entree Royale de Leurs Majestez,* 7.

47. Caignet, *Sur l'entrée de la Reine,* 3 and 6.

48. Such rhetoric is often utilized to describe the *cabinet de curiosité.* Schnapper offers several examples of this image in published descriptions of cabinets; he notes that along with the idea of the microcosm (meaning résumé of the world), the rhetoric of curiosity is a common theme in texts written to describe particular cabinets. See Schnapper, *Le géant, la licorne, et la tulipe,* 9–10.

49. *Description of the Triumphal Arches Erected in the Public squares for the Queen's Entry. With the true explanation in Prose & in Verse of the Figures, Ovals, Statues, Porticos, Devices & Portraits that are found in the Faubourg and Port Saint Antoine, Saint Jean Cemetery, Notre-Dame Bridge, Newmarket, Place Dauphine, etc. Gathering together diverse Curious and particular Remarks for the amateurs of History.*

50. The term *amateur* is retained in all versions of this pamphlet, those published both before and after the entry date. Note, for example, *Catalogue de l'Histoire de France,* 2: 214, no. 3376. See the definition of *amateur* in Furetière's *Dictionaire universel.* For a more nuanced reading of this term, see Pomian, 53–54.

51. Schnapper, *Le géant, la licorne, et la tulipe,* 294.

52. Colletet, *Description des Arcs,* 3.

53. Note that the term *amateur* can be found in Caignet's *Sur l'entrée de la Reine,* 9, where the infanta is described in relation to the gallery of portraits set up in the city:

> Thérèse, come see these magnanimous Heros,
> Ancestors of your Spouse and your great Admirers [*Amateurs*],
> That the charm and perfume of your sublime Virtues,

Also Induced to be your Spectators.

[Tereze, venez voir ces Heros magnanimes,
Ayeux de vostre Espoux & vos grands Amateurs,
Que le charme & l'odeur de vos Vertus sublimes,
A conviez aussi d'estre vos Spectateurs.]

Here the portraits become collectors of the new queen in an assimilation of the amateur and the spectator. It is an awkward image at best, but one suggesting that of all the objects in Paris's *cabinet de curiosité*, the new queen is such a rarity that even the portraits of her new husband's ancestors have come to see her.

54. The definition of *posseder* is from Furetière's *Dictionnaire universel*.

55. Colletet, *Suite de la Nouvelle Relation*, 3. The idea that such possession creates a "happiness" that is the unique privilege of Paris is another one of the *topoi* of the entry material. See, for example, *Les Harangues et les Acclamations Publiques*, an allegorical pamphlet in praise of the new queen that presents Thetis acclaiming she will "make known to the whole Universe that Paris, possessing [*possedant*] you, is the greatest of marvels" (11).

56. *Advis Utile et Necessaire à Messieurs les Bourgeois & Habitants du quartier*, 3. In this case, the often repeated phrase is utilized in an official order or *avis* to the inhabitants of various neighborhoods to build scaffolds and theaters from which to view the events.

57. Schnapper, *Le géant, la licorne, et la tulipe*, 54–59.

58. Ibid., 10.

59. Colletet, *Recit Veritable et Fidelle*, 3. There are other ways in which the queen is associated with a collected item. First, one cannot avoid the irony that Loménie de Brienne, Louis XIV's secretary of state, was one of the central figures of the collecting world. According to Schnapper, he amassed his collection quickly, augmenting it during the trip he took with the court to the border for the marriage of the king (*Le géant, la licorne, et la tulipe*, 199). One might conjecture that Loménie de Brienne "acquired" the infanta for his king's collection, which at this time was in fact depleted (Louis would later rebuild his collections). Indeed, De Brienne was part of the team that negotiated the marriage. At the very least, the practice of collecting was not only in the air, but also close to the process of the marriage. Thus, the rhetoric about the infanta as a treasure is more than just poetic resonance.

60. This is the shift Bryant outlines in *The King and the City*.

61. Colletet, *Recit Veritable et Fidelle*, 7.

62. Colletet, *Nouvelle Relation contenant La Royalle Entrée*, 23–24.

63. Ibid., 13.

64. Apostolidès, *Le roi machine*, 17.

65. Colletet, *Recit Veritable et Fidelle*, 8.

66. The *Triumphant Entry of Their Majesties Louis XIV King of France and Navarre, and Marie Thérèse of Austria his Spouse into the City of Paris, Capital of their Kingdoms, upon returning from the signing of the general peace and from their happy marriage, Embellished with several Figures, Speeches, and diverse Historically significant Materials. Everything accurately collected by order of the City Fathers.* This is the text published by Pierre le Petit, Thomas Joly, and Louis Bilaine. Möseneder edited it in his study of royal ceremonial. While all editions of this text are the same, Houghton Library's copy does not give a publisher, but has the name of another place where one could procure the edition, namely that of the architect Jean Marot, applied in the same spot, perhaps applied over the original publisher's name. It seems likely that the architect Marot received a number of copies in payment for the engravings he produced for the edition.

67. Tronçon, *L'Entrée Triomphante*, 5. In the text's prefatory "Avis au lecteur pour servir de preface," the work is specifically presented as offering all the details of the events and as rectifying a large number of errors and omissions in that material.

68. In fact, the pamphlet is an ephemeral form striving to place itself on the level of the monumental history. We saw this relation in Chapter Two.

Afterword

1. Lévi-Strauss, *Introduction to the Work of Marcel Mauss*, 16–17. First published as "Introduction à l'oeuvre de Marcel Mauss" in Mauss, *Sociologie et anthropologie* (Paris: Presses Universitaires de France, 1950). The quote is cited by Laplanche and Pontalis in their *Vocabulaire de la psychanalyse* (Paris: PUF, 1967) as the source for Lacan's notion of the symbolic order. In the citation, Lévi-Strauss goes on to discuss how certain elements or people in a given society may never fit into the symbolic structure and that each society is bound by its "spatio-temporal given, and therefore subject to the impact of other societies and of earlier states of its own development." This idea of interaction between systems foreshadows Pierre Bourdieu's work on the habitus which, critiquing the immutability of Mauss's models, offers a bit more fluidity in the description of social systems and the internal adjustments they make. See Pierre Bourdieu, *Outline of a Theory of Practice*.

2. Giesey, *The Royal Funeral Ceremony*, 104.

3. Ibid., 110.

4. Ibid., 143.

5. Quote taken from the *Biographie universelle*. It is also cited in Dulong,

Mariage. Although the origin of this often-cited story is difficult to trace, according to Jacques Truchet, it was a common element of most of the funerary orations about her (with the exception of Bossuet's). See Truchet's remarks in his edition of Bossuet, *Oraisons funèbres,* 204.

6. "La Pompe Funebre Faite Pour la Reyne dans l'Eglise de l'Abbaye de Saint Denys," 504.

7. Bossuet, *Oraisons funèbres,* 214.

8. Ibid., 213–14.

9. Menestrier, *Description de la Decoration Funebre,* 9.

10. As, for example, in a description in the *Gazette* of the service held at Saint Germain-des-Près, "Les Services Faits pour la Reyne en cette ville, dans les Eglises de la Sainte Chapelle, de S. Jean en Gréve, & de L'Abbaye de Saint Germain des Prez: Avec la süite de ceux qui ont esté célébrez en plusieurs autres villes," 557.

11. *New Catholic Encyclopedia,* 971–75.

12. Bossuet, *Oraisons funèbres,* 215.

13. Giesey, *The Royal Funeral Ceremony,* 48–49.

14. It is Giesey who makes this point in *The Royal Funeral Ceremony,* 191. Of course, Hanley's *The Lit de Justice of the Kings of France* is the definitive study of this ritual.

Bibliography

Although we know that most choices about capitalization and even spelling were arbitrary in this period, all primary sources consulted in original editions listed here retain the original spelling and capitalization found on their title pages.

Early Modern Printed and Manuscript Sources
Related to the Marriage

L'Adieu des Provinciaux à la Ville de Paris, Après l'Entrée de leurs Majestés. N.p., n.d.

Advis Utile et Necessaire à Messieurs les Bourgeois & Habitans du quartier Saint Antoine, Porte-Baudets, Pont Nostre-Dame, Marché Neuf, Place Dauphine, & autres lieux où le Roy, & la Reyne, doivent passer le jour de leur Triomphe. Paris: Jean-Baptiste Loyson, 1660.

Alexis. *Lettre Presentée au Roy Contenant les Principaux, & plus glorieux ornemens du Triomphe de leurs Majestez. Avec l'explication des Anagrames mysterieux & Prophetiques de leurs vertus Heroiques, & de l'estenduë de leur Renommée. Ensemble l'application à sa Majesté de titres illustres, & glorieuses devises des Roys ses predecesseurs.* Paris: François Noel, 1660.

"L'Arrivée du Mareschal Duc de Grammont à Madrid: avec tout ce qui s'est passé jusques à son Audience de Congé." *La Gazette de France*, no. 136 (November 10, 1659): 1083–94.

Le Ballet de la Paix. N.p., [1660].

Bernoüin, le sieur de Saincte Garde. *L'Amour Celeste sur le mariage de Louis XIV Dieu Donné, Roy tres-Chrestien de France & de Navarre et de Marie*

Therese d'Autriche Infante d'Espagne. Paris: Nicolas Bessin, 1660.

Bilain, Antoine. *Dialogue sur les droits de la reyne tres-chrestienne*. Paris: Imprimerie royale, 1667.

Bomier, M. *Discours sur le sujet de la paix, fait par Monsieur Bomier Conseiller du Roy, & Son Avocat au Presidial de la Ville et Gouvernement de La Rochelle Prononcé en la Cour ordinaire de ladite Ville le quatrieme de Mars mil six cens soixante, Dedié à Monseigneur l'Eminentissime Cardinal Mazarini*. La Rochelle: Barthelemy Blanchet, 1660.

Bonair, le Sieur de. *Le Triomphe de la Chretienté par la Paix Entre les Couronnes, & le Mariage du Roy avec l'Infante*. Paris: Pierre Du Pont, 1660.

Bonet, Thomas. *Le Plus Grand Eclat de Son Eminence, Arrivé en l'Année M.DC.LX. par l'accomplissement de la Paix, Predit à la Reyne Regente seize ans devant. Contenant les Recherches Curieuses des Qualitez, Actions & Merveilles du Nom de ce Grand Cardinal Jule Mazarin. Cet éclat comme precurseur de l'heureux Mariage qui le suit, nous oblige de découvrir les tresors cachez dans les Noms de leurs Majestez*. Paris: Estienne Maucroy, 1660.

Bossuet, Jacques-Bénigne. *Oraisons funèbres*. Paris: Garnier, 1961.

Boyer. *Ode Pour la Paix*. Paris: Charles de Sercy, 1660.

Breve Relatione De Regii Sponsali Trà Maestà Christianissima de Lodovico XIV Rè de Francia, et di Navarra, E la Serenissima Infanta, D. Maria Teresa D'Austria. Milan: Giacomo Monti, 1660.

Brosse. *Les Anagrames Royales, du Roy à la Reyne et de la Reyne au Roy. Contenants les Tesmoignages de leur amour reciproque, sans changement d'aucune Lettre. Avec les Sonnets sur les Anagrames, suivis de riches Stances sur la Paix, & sur le Mariage du Roy*. Paris: Estienne Pepingué, 1660.

Caignet, G. *Sur l'Entrée de la Reyne dans la ville de Paris, le 26 Aoust 1660. Stances*. Paris: Alexandre Lesselin, 1660.

Canu, J., Sieur de Bailleul. *La Ville de Paris en Triomphe pour l'Entrée de Leurs Maiestez: ou les Peintures et Tableaux de tous les Portiques sont expliquées en vers François, depuis le Faubourg S. Antoine, jusqu'à la Belle & Magnifique Pyramide de la Place Dauphine*. Paris: Cardin Besongne, 1660.

Cassagnes, Jacques. *Ode Sur La Paix*. Paris: Augustin Courbé, 1660.

C.D.S.S.D.L. *L'Histoire de la Monarchie Françoise sous le regne du Roy Louis XIV contenant tout ce qui s'est passé de plus remarquable entre les Couronnes de France & d'Espagne, & autres Païs Estrangers; Comme aussi les Conferences, les Negotiations, les Traitez de Paix, le Mariage de Sa Majesté avec L'Infante d'Espagne, leur Entrée dans la Ville de Paris, la Naissance de Monseigneur le Dauphin, & autres particularités arrivées jusques à present*. Vol. 2. Paris: Jean-Baptiste Loyson, 1662.

Chapelain, Jean. *Ode Pour la Paix et Pour le Mariage du Roy*. Paris: Augustin Courbé, 1660.

Chesneau, Henri. *Le Roy*. N.p., n.d.

Colletet, François. *L'Assemblée des Muses, et Leur Entretien Sur la Pompe celebre qui se fera à l'Entrée de la Reyne. Avec Leurs Diverses dispositions sur les Amphitheatres, Arcs de Triomphes, Portiques et autres préparatifs.* Paris: Jean-Baptiste Loyson, 1660.

[————]. *La Cavalcade Royale, contenant la Revue Generale de Messieurs les Colonels et Bourgeois de Paris, faite au Parc de Vincennes, en presence du Roy et de la Reyne, pour la disposition de leurs Magnifiques Entrées dans leur Bonne Ville de Paris.* Paris: Jean-Baptiste Loyson, 1660.

[————]. *Dernière Relation, contenant le Retour de Leurs Majestez, jusqu'à Fontainebleau. Avec toutes les Particularitez de ce qui s'est fait & passé de plus memorable pendant leur Marche.* Paris: Jean-Baptiste Loyson, 1660.

————. *Description des Arcs de Triomphe Eslevés dans les places Publiques pour l'Entrée de la Reyne. Avec la veritable explication en Prose, & en Vers des Figures, Ovales, Termes, Portiques, Devises & Portraits qui sont tant aux Fauxbourg que Porte S. Antoine, Cymetiere S. Jean, Pont Nostre-Dame, Marché-Neuf, Place Dauphine, &c. Ensemble diverses Remarques Curieuses & particulieres pour les amateurs de l'Histoire. Et l'Ordre que leurs Majestez observeront dans leur Marche depuis Vincennes jusques au Louvre.* Paris: Jean-Baptiste Loyson, 1660.

————. *Description de Tous les Tableaux, Peintures, Dorures, Brodures, Reliefs, Figures, & autres enrichissements, qui seront exposez à tous les Arcs de Triomphe, Portes et Portiques, pour l'Entrée triomphante de leurs Majestez. Ensemble beaucoup d'autres particularitez, dont on n'a point encore parlé jusqu'à présent.* Paris: Jean-Baptiste Loyson, 1660.

————. *Description du Parfait Portrait de Marie Therese Infante d'Espagne, et Reyne de France. Contenant les Rares et Royalles qualitez de son Esprit, & les parfaittes beautez de son Auguste Visage.* Paris: Jean-Baptiste Loyson, 1660.

————. *Les Devises Generales et Particulieres des Tableaux, Figures en Relief, Plates-Peintures, & Medailles qui sont aux Portes et Portiques des Arcs de Triomphe, élevez à la gloire de Louis XIV Roy de France & de Navarre, & de Marie Terese d'Austriche, Infante d'Espagne et Reyne de France, aux Faux-bourg & Porte S. Antoine, Cymetiere S. Jean, Pont Nostre-Dame, Marché-neuf & Place Dauphine: le tout fidelement expliqué et traduit en Vers et en Prose.* Paris: Jean-Baptiste Loyson, 1660.

————. *Explication des Devises Generales et Particulieres des Tableaux, Figures en Relief, Plates-Peintures, & Medailles qui sont aux Portes & Portiques des Arcs de Triomphe, élevez à la gloire de Louis XIV, Roy de France & de Navarre, & de Marie Terese d'Autriche, Infante d'Espagne & Reyne de France, aux Faux-bourg & Porte S. Antoine, Cymetiere S. Jean, Pont Nostre-Dame, Marché-neuf & Place Dauphine. Le tout fidelement expliqué & traduit en Vers et en Prose. L'Explication des Tableaux est en trois cahiers separez.* Paris: Jean-Baptiste Loyson, 1660.

————. *Explication et Description de Tous les Tableaux, Peintures, Figures, Dorures, Brodures, Reliefs, & autres enrichissemens, qui estoient exposez à tous les Arcs de Triomphe, Portes et Portiques, à l'Entrée triomphante de Leurs Majestez; tant Faubourg que Porte Sainct Antoine, Cymetiere S. Jean, Pont Nostre-Dame, Marché-Neuf, que la grande et Magnifique Piramide de la Place Dauphine. L'Explication des Devises sont en trois autres cayers separez.* Paris: Jean-Baptiste Loyson, 1660.

————. *Explication et Description de Tous les Tableaux, Peintures, Dorures, Brodures, Reliefs, Figures, & autres enrichissemens qui sont exposez à tous les Arcs de Triomphe, Portes & Portiques, pour l'Entrée triomphante de leurs Majestez. Ensemble Beaucoup d'autres particularitez dont on n'a point encore parlé jusqu'à present.* Paris: Jean-Baptiste Loyson, 1660.

[————]. *Le Feu Royal et Magnifique qui se doit tirer sur la Riviere de Seine, en presence de Leurs Majestez, par ordre de Messieurs de Ville. Avec la description des devises, Peintures, Architectures, Artifices qui doivent paroitre dans le vaisseau destiné pour cette magnificence publique.* Paris: Jean-Baptiste Loyson, 1660.

[————]. *Le Feu Royal et Magnifique qui s'est tiré sur la Riviere de Seine, vis à vis du Louvre, en presence de Leurs Majestez, par ordre de Messieurs de Ville, pour la resjouyssance de l'entrée du Roy & de la Reine, le 29 Aoust 1660. Avec la description des devises en Vers, des Peintures, Architectures, & Artifices qui ont paru dans le Vaisseau destiné pour cette magnificence publique.* Paris: Jean-Baptiste Loyson, 1660.

————. *Les Grandes Magnificences Preparées pour l'Entrée Triomphante de Leurs Majestez. Avec une Description de tous les Tableaux, Peintures, Dorures, Brodures, Reliefs, Figures et Autres enrichissemens qui seront exposés à tous les Arcs de Triomphe, Portes et Portiques, pour l'Entrée Triomphante de Leurs Majestez. Ensemble beaucoup d'autres particularitez dont on n'a point encore parlé jusqu'à présent.* Paris: Jean-Baptiste Loyson, 1660.

————. *Les Heureuses Predictions sur la Grossesse de la Reyne.* Paris: Ch. Chenault, 1661 .

————. *Journal Contenant La Relation Veritable et Fidelle du Voyage du Roy, & de son Eminence, Pour le Traitté du Mariage de Sa Majesté, & de la Paix Generale.* Paris: Jean-Baptiste Loyson, 1659.

————. *Journal Historique, Contenant la Relation Veritable et Fidele Du Voyage du Roy, & de son Eminence, Pour le Traitté du Mariage de sa Majesté, & de la Paix Generale. Journal Troisiesme.* Paris: Jean-Baptiste Loyson, 1659.

————. *Journaux Historiques, Contenans Tout ce qui s'est passé de plus remarquable dans le Voyage du Roy, et de son Eminence, depuis leur depart de*

*Paris, le 25. Iuin de l'an 1659. Pour le Traitté du Mariage de sa Majesté, &
de la Paix Generale, jusqu'à leur retour. Avec une exacte recherche de ce qui
s'est fait dans les Conferences des deux Ministres, & dans le Mariage du Roy
avec l'Infante d'Espagne à Fontarabie, & à S. Jean de Lus. Et leur entrée dans
toutes les Villes de leur passages, & leur Triomphe dans leur bonne Ville de
Paris.* Paris: Jean-Baptiste Loyson, 1660.

————. *La Liste Generale et Particuliere de Messieurs les Colonels, Capi-
taines, Lieutenants, Enseignes, & autres Officiers, & Bourgeois de la Ville
& Fauxbourgs de Paris; Avec l'ordre qu'ils doivent tenir dans leur marche,
& dans les autres Ceremonies qui s'observeront à l'Entrée Royale de leurs
Majestés. Ensemble les Noms, qualitez, & quartiers des Colonels; Avec les
Livrées qu'ils doivent faire porter à chacune de leurs Compagnies.* Paris:
Jean-Baptiste Loyson, 1660.

[————]. *La Marche Royale de Leurs Majestez, Depuis le Chasteau de
Vincennes jusqu'au Throsne et du Throsne, jusqu'au Louvre le jour de leur
magnifique Entrée en leur bonne Ville de Paris.* Paris: Jean-Baptiste Loyson,
1660.

————. *Nouvelle Relation Contenant La Royalle Entrée de Leurs Majestez dans
leur bonne ville de Paris le vingt-sixiesme Aoust 1660. Avec une exacte & fidele
recherche de toutes les Ceremonies qui se sont observées, tant dans la marche du
Roy, de la Reyne, & de toute la Cour, que dans celle des Cours Souveraines,
des Prevost des Marchands, Eschevins, & autres Corps qui ont paru dans cette
celebre & auguste Entrée. Ensemble les noms de Princes, Ducs, Pairs, Mare-
schaux de France, Seigneurs, & autres Personnes remarquables.* Paris: Jean-
Baptiste Loyson, 1660.

————. *La Nouvelle Relation Contenant L'Entreveue et Serments des Roys,
pour L'Entiere Execution de la Paix. Ensemble Toutes les Particularitez &
Ceremonies qui se sont faites au Mariage du Roy, & de L'Infante d'Espagne.
Avec tout ce qui s'est passé de plus remarquable entre ces deux puissants
Monarques jusqu'à leur depart.* Paris: Jean-Baptiste Loyson, 1660.

————. *Le Nouveau Journal Historique, contenant la Relation Véritable De ce
qui s'est passé au voyage du Roy et de son Eminence. Et aux Ceremonies du
Mariage de Sa Majesté. Célébrées à Fontarabie & à S. Jean de Luz.* Paris: A.
Lesselin, 1660.

————. *Ordre General et Particulier de la Marche qui doit estre Observee dans
les trois jours consecutifs pour l'Entrée de leurs Majestez dans leur bonne Ville
de Paris, par Messieurs du Clergé, par Messieurs des Cours Souveraines,
Messieurs les Prevost des Marchands, Eschevins & Bourgeois de ladite Ville,
Prevost de l'Isle, Chevalier & Lieutenant du Guet, &c. Avec la Description des
Superbes Appareils de la Cour, & et des Magnificences de la Milice Bourgeoise.*
Paris: Jean-Baptiste Loyson, 1660.

———. *Le Parfait Portrait de Marie Therese, infante d'Espagne.* Paris: Jean-Baptiste Loyson, 1659.

[———]. *Le Parnasse Royal et La Rejouyssance des Muses sur les Grandes Magnificences qui se sont faites à l'Entrée de la Reyne.* Paris: Jean-Baptiste Loyson, 1660.

———. *Quatriesme Journal Historique, Contenant La Relation Veritable et Fidele Du Voyage du Roy, & de son Eminence, Pour le Traitté du Mariage de sa majesté, & de la Paix Generale.* Paris: Jean Baptiste Loyson, 1660.

[———]. *Recit Veritable et Fidelle de Tout ce qui s'est faict et passé dans la Cavalcade du Roy et de la Reyne, au Parc de Vincennes A la Monstre Generale des Colonels & Bourgeois de Paris.* Paris: Jean-Baptiste Loyson, 1660.

[———]. *Relation de Toutes les Particularitez qui se sont faites et passées dans la Celebre Entrée du Roy et de la Reyne, Avec l'ordre de la marche du Clergé & des Cours Souveraines. Ensemble la Magnifique Pompe des Seigneurs & de toute leur suitte: Et toutes les Ceremonies du Te Deum.* Paris: Jean-Baptiste Loyson, 1660.

———. *Remerciment de Messieurs les Provinciaux à Messieurs les Prevost des Marchands et Echevins de la Ville de Paris. Sur la Glorieuse & Triomphante Entrée de leurs Majestez en leur Bonne Ville de Paris en Vers Burlesques.* Paris: Jean-Baptiste Loyson, 1660.

———. *Seconde Relation Veritable et Fidelle de tout ce qui s'est fait & passé de plus remarquable dans les Conferences & dans les Adieux des deux Roys, jusques au depart de sa Majesté de la Ville de S. Jean de Lus. Avec les Particularitez de la Marche, des entrées, & du sejour du Roy & de la Cour dans les principales Villes de France, & son heureuse Arrivée dans la Royale Maison de Fontainebleau.* Paris: A. Lesselin, 1660.

———. *Suitte de la Nouvelle Relation Contenant la Marche de Leurs Majestez pour leur Retour en leur bonne Ville de Paris: Avec toutes les particularitez de ce qui s'est fait et passé en leur Reception aux magnifiques Entrées des Villes de leur passage jusqu'à present. Ensemble les Presens que Sa Majesté, la Reyne Mere, Monsieur, & Son Eminence ont faits à nostre Incomparable Reyne.* Paris: Jean-Baptiste Loyson, 1660.

———. *Suitte du Journal Historique Contenant La Relation Veritable et Fidele du Voyage du Roy, & de son Eminence, Pour le Traitté du Mariage de sa Majesté, & de la Paix Generale.* Paris: Jean-Baptiste Loyson, 1659.

[———]. *Le Triomphe de la France Pour l'Entrée Royale de leurs Majestez dans leur bonne Ville de Paris, Sur les Magnificences & preparatifs du Pont Nostre-Dame. Avec les Discours Heroïques sur les Vies des Roys de France, depuis Pharamond jusqu'à nostre Grand Monarque Louis XIV. Ensemble les Eloges de la Reyne, de la Reyne Mere, & de Son Eminence.* Paris: Jean-Baptiste Loyson, 1660.

————. *La Veritable Explication En Prose et En Vers des Figures Ovales, Thermes & Portraits de tous les Rois de France qui sont dessus le Pont Nostre-Dame à Paris. Ensemble quelques remarques curieuses et particulieres pour les amateurs de l'Histoire. Avec la description des Arcs de Triomphe eslevez dans les Places Publiques pour l'Entrée du Roy & de la Reyne.* Paris: Jean-Baptiste Loyson, 1660.

La Conclusion de la Paix Generale, et du mariage du roy, Suivant les Nouvelles de Bordeaux du vingt-deuxième Septembre 1659. Montpellier: Daniel Pech, 1659.

La Conference de Ianot et Piarot Doucet de Villenoce, et de Iaco Paquet de Pantin, sur les grandes magnificences qu'on prépare à Paris pour l'entrée de la reine. Paris: n.p., 1660.

La Conference de Ianot et Piarot Doucet de Villenoce, et de Iaco Paquet de Pantin, sur les merveilles qu'il à veu dans l'entrée de la Reyne, ensemble comme Ianot luy raconte ce qu'il à veu au Te Deum & au feu d'Artifice. Paris: n.p., 1660.

Contrat de Mariage du Roy Tres-Chrestien et de la Serenissime Infante, Fille Aisnée du Roy Catholique le Septiesme Novembre 1659. Paris: Imprimeurs et Libraires Ordinaires du roi, 1668.

Corneille, Pierre. *Oeuvres de Pierre Corneille.* Vol. 6. Paris: Hachette, 1862–68.

————. *Oeuvres complètes.* 3 vols. Paris: Gallimard, 1987.

Coquerel, Le Sieur de. *Le Navire de France arrivé heureusement au port de la Paix sous la conduite de son eminence présenté à sa Majesté par le Sieur de Coquerel.* Paris: Charles de Sercy, 1660.

Cosnac, Daniel de. *Mémoires de Daniel de Cosnac. Archevêque d'Aix. Conseiller du Roi en ses Conseils.* Vol. 2. Paris: Jules Renouard, 1852.

Cotin, C. *Les Nopces Royales.* Paris: Pierre le Petit, 1660.

Cyprien [de Gamaches], Père. *Le Triomphe de la Paix et de la Piété Royale, Composé en François & en Espagnol & Presenté à Leurs Majestez.* Paris: Antoine de Sommaville, 1660.

Description du Feu d'Artifice preparé pour l'entrée de leurs Majestez, par les soins du Sieur Liegeois Ingenieur du Roy. Paris: Antoine Duhamel, 1660.

Description du Feu de Joye, Preparé en la Place de la Grève, pour marque de la Réjoüissance publique, au sujet de la Publication de la Paix generale, faite en divers lieux de la Ville de Paris, le Samedy 14 Fevrier 1660. Par Commandement de Monseigneur le Mareschal de l'Hospital, & Messieurs les Prevost des Marchands & Eschevins de ladite Ville. N.p., n.d.

"Despesches de Le Tellier à Mgr le cardinal [Mazarin], depuis le 1 juillet 1659, jour du depart de S.E. de la cour, pour la negociation de la paix avec l'Espagne, jusques au 18 novembre ensuivant." Fonds français 4215. Bibliothèque Nationale, Paris.

Les Devises du Pont Nostre Dame Mises En Vers Francois. Avec Les Plus Belles Actions de nos Rois & le temps de leur regne. Paris: Cardin Besongne, 1660.

Les Devises et Emblèmes Royalles et Historiques Latines et Françoises. Qui sont Peints sur le Pont N. Dame de Tous les Rois de France depuis Pharamond jusques à Nostre Monarque, Avec le Temps qu'ils ont Regné Pour l'Entrée Triomphante du Roy et de la Reyne. Paris: Marin Leché, 1660.

Discours Curieux du Bien de la Paix. Ou l'on void combien la Paix est utile à la France & à l'Espagne; Et que les humeurs diverses des François & Espagnols ne luy sçauroient nuire. Paris: Charles Chenault, 1660.

D.L. *Lettre d'un Français, escrite à un de ses amis. Contenant tout ce qui s'est fait & passé au Mariage du Roy très-Chrestien, avec la Serenissime Infante. Ensemble la Relation de l'entrevue des deux Roys à l'Isle de la Conference.* N.p., [1660].

L'Entière et Véritable Explication du grand Feu d'artifice, fait & construit sur la Riviere de Seine, proche & vis-à-vis du Louvre. Paris: Jean Brunet, 1660.

Entreveue et Conference de Son Eminence Le Cardinal Mazarin, & Dom Louis d'Aro, le 13. Aoust 1659. Avec le recit veritable de tout ce qui s'est fait & passé entre les François & les Espagnols. Paris: Sebastien Martin, 1659.

Esprit, A. *Ode Sur la Paix.* Paris: Pierre le Petit, 1660.

Estat General des Gouverneurs des Provinces de France: Ensemble Les Gouverneurs, Lieutenants, Commandants Particuliers des Villes Frontières, & Villes qui sont conquises par sa Maiesté. Comme Aussi Les Noms des Gouverneurs, Lieutenants des Villes qui ont esté à la Couronne de France, suivant le Traicté de Paix. Et le Mariage de leurs Majestez. Paris: Marin Leché, 1660.

Explication de la danse des Fées & des Barbons du Pont Nostre-Dame à Paris, orné de nouveau pour l'Entrée du Roy et de l'incomparable Reyne de France & de Navarre, par les soins de Messieurs les Prevost des Marchands & Eschevins de la dite Ville. N.p., n.d.

L'Explication des Figures et Peintures qui sont Representées pour l'Entrée du Roy et de la Reine. Paris: J. Promé, 1660.

Explication du Feu Fait Pour La Veille de la Feste de Saint Jean Baptiste, tiré devant l'Hostel de Ville. Par le commandement de Messieurs les Prevost des Marchands & Eschevins de la Ville de Paris. Paris: Barthelemy Quenet, 1660.

Explication Generale de Toutes les Peintures, Statues et Tableaux des Portiques & Arcs de Triomphe, dressés pour l'Entrée du Roy et de la Reine: Tant au Fauxbourg & Porte S. Antoine, qu'aux places Publiques. Pont Nostre Dame. Marché-Neuf. Avec l'Explication des Devises de la belle et magnifique Pyramide de la Place Dauphine: & de son Amphithéatre. Ensemble toutes les Devises et Inscriptions Latines expliquées en François. Et la Marche de Leurs Majestés depuis Vincennes jusques au Louvre. Paris: Cardin Besongne, 1660.

Du Fayot. *L'Ange de Paix à Monseigneur le Cardinal.* Paris: J. Charmot, 1659.

Félibien, A. *Description de l'Arc de la Place Dauphine presentée à son Eminence.* Paris: Pierre le Petit, 1660.

Le Feu de Joye Fait en la place Royale devant l'Hostel de Ville de Reims, pour l'heureuse conclusion de la Paix, le Dimanche vingt-deuxiesme Fevrier 1660. N.p., n.d.

Gazette de France. Paris: Bureau d'Adresse, 1658–60.

La Glorieuse et Triomphante Entrée de la Serenissime Princesse Marie Thereze d'Austriche Infante d'Espagne, au retour de son tres-Auguste Mariage avec nostre Invincible Monarque Louis de Bourbon XIV, Roy de France, & de Navarre, dans leur Ville de Paris. Paris: Louis Barbote, 1660.

Godeau, A. *Ode au roi sur la paix.* Paris: Pierre le Petit, 1660.

Gramont, Duc de. *Memoires du Mareschal de Gramont Duc et Pair de France, Commandeur des Ordres du Roy, Gouverneur de Navarre & de Bearne. Donné au Public par le Duc de Gramont son fils.* Vol 2. Paris: Michel David, 1716.

Les Harangues et les Acclamations Publiques au Roy et à la Reine, sur Leur Magnifique Entrée en leur bonne Ville de Paris. Paris: Jean-Baptiste Loyson, 1660.

Les Heureux Auspices Du Voyage Triomphant de la Reine Pacifique Venant de Madrid à Paris, et les Feux de Joye Faits en cette grande Ville, le premier soir de ce merveilleux Voyage. Paris: Mathieu Colombel, 1660.

D'Hoges. *Recit des Feux de Joye Faits en la Ville de Chalon Sur Saone Le Dernier de Fevrier mil six cens soixante. Notre dessein a eu trois objets, la Paix, le Mariage de S.M., et le retour de S.A.S.* N.p, n.d.

L'Instruction des Bourgeois de Paris Donnée par Leurs Capitaines & Colonels de cette Ville. Tant a la Monstre Generale qu'aux reveuës particulieres Pour l'Exercice du Mousquet & de la Pique. Paris: Cardin Besongne, 1660.

L'Isle de Paix, Representation heroique faite le 23 Mai, dans le College de la tres-sainte Trinité de la Compagnie de Jesus. Lyon: Jean Molin, 1660.

Journal Pour Servir à l'Histoire Contenant ce qui s'est passé de plus memorable depuis la guerre declarée entre la France & l'Espagne, jusques à la conclusion de la Paix, & Mariage de leurs Majestez. Paris: Marin Leché, 1660.

LaGravete. *La Gloriosa Alianca de Francia con España. La Glorieuse Aliance de la France avec l'Espagne.* Paris: n.p., 1661.

La Mesnardière. *Chant Nuptial pour le mariage du Roy.* Paris: Imprimerie Royale, 1660.

La Serre, Jean Puget de. *Panegyrique de Louis Quatorziesme, Roy de France et de Navarre.* N.p., n.d.

La Lettre Circulaire d'un Officier du Roy, Envoyée par toutes les Provinces, Pour L'Entrée triomphante de leurs Majestez Avec la Description du Grand Feu d'artifice qui se faira sur la Riviere. Paris: Jean Brunet, 1660.

Lettre du Roy, Envoyée à Messieurs les Prevost des Marchands & Eschevins de la Ville de Paris. Sur la Conclusion de la Paix generale, & de son Mariage. Ensemble l'Acte de la Publication d'icelle par tout son Royaume: Avec ordre d'assister au Te Deum & faire faire des Feux de joye. Paris: P. Rocolet, 1660.

Lettre du Roy Envoyée à Messieurs les Prevost des Marchands & Eschevins de la Ville de Paris Sur son départ pour la Conclusion de la paix generale Escrite de Fontaine-bleau. Paris: P. Rocolet, 1659.

Lettre du Roy, Envoyée à Monsieur le Chancelier. Contenant le Mariage de Sa Majesté. Ensemble l'Ordre de faire chanter le Te Deum; d'y assister, & le faire faire sçavoir aux Compagnies Souveraines. Du Treizieme Juin 1660. Paris: P. Rocolet, 1660.

Lettre du Roy Envoyée à Monseigneur le Chancelier de France Contenant le parfaite guerison de Sa Majesté Avec l'Ordre de faire chanter et d'assister au Te Deum. Paris: P. Rocolet, 1658.

Lettre du Roy à Monseigneur le Chancelier sur la prise de Montmedy. Avec Ordre de faire chanter le Te Deum en l'Eglise de Nostre Dame de Paris. Paris: P. Rocolet, 1657.

Lettre du Roy, Envoyée à Monsieur le Lieutenant Civil. Sur la conclusion de la Paix generale. Ensemble l'Ordonnance de sa Majesté pour faire publier la Paix. Paris: P. Rocolet, 1660.

Lettre du Roy Envoyée à Monseigneur le Mareschal de L'hospital, Gouverneur de Paris Sur la Conclusion de la Paix generale, & de son Mariage. Ensemble l'Acte de la Publication d'icelle par tout son Royaume. Paris: P. Rocolet, 1660.

Lettre du roi, Envoyée à Monsieur Seguier, Chancelier de France. Sur la Conclusion de la Paix generale, & de son Mariage. Paris: P. Rocolet, 1660.

"Lettres, billets, nouvelles à la main; lettres addressées au Chancelier Séguier 1660–1668, pièces diverses, 1630–1668." Fond français 17881. Bibliothèque Nationale, Paris.

Liste des Nations qui doivent paroistre à l'Entrée de la Reine, sçavoir cinquante hommes à chaque Bande; & seront vestus en Armes selon les Nations qu'ils representeront. N.p., n.d.

L.L.R. *La Requeste des Prisonniers Presentée au Roy et à la Reyne pour Leur Delivrance. Avec le veritable Tableau tiré au naïf de leurs peines, souffrances & calamitez.* Paris: Jean Brunet, 1660.

Loménie de Brienne, Henri-Louis de. *Après le Traité des Pyrénées: Mariage de Louis XIV avec l'Infante d'Espagne, Marie-Thérèse, à Fontarbie et à St-Jean-de-Luz. son entrevue avec Philippe IV, roi d'Espagne, dans l'Ile des Faisans, sur la Bidassoa.* Abbé François Albert Duffo, ed. Paris: P. Lethielleux, 1935.

———. "Relation de ce qui s'est passé au mariage du Roy et de la Reyne célébré à Fontarabie, le 3 juin 1660, dressée par M. le comte de Brienne, qui a esté présent à cette cérémonie et a signé le contrat de ce mariage en qualité de Secrétaire d'Estat, pourveu de cette charge à la jouissance de M. le comte de Brienne, son père." In *Après le Traité des Pyrénées: Mariage de Louis XIV avec l'Infante d'Espagne, Marie-Thérèse, à Fontarbie et à St-Jean-de-Luz. son entrevue avec Philippe IV, roi d'Espagne, dans l'Ile des Faisans, sur la Bidassoa.* Abbé François Albert Duffo, ed. Paris: P. Lethielleux, 1935.

Loret, Jean. *L'Entrée de la Reyne Prézentée à Leurs Majestés le 26me Aoust 1660.* Paris: Charles Chenault, 1660.

———. *La Muze Historique ou Recueil des lettres en vers.* Vol. 3. Paris: P. Daffis, 1878.

———. *La Paix Triomphante, et la Guerre en déroute.* Paris: Charles Chenault, 1660.

Louvet [Pierre], Le Sieur de Beauvais. *Discours Historique sur l'an Jubilaire de la Paix Depuis la malheureuse de Chateau-Cambresis en 1559 jusqu'à celle de l'Isle des Faisans, en Rivière de Bidassoa l'an 1659. Avec une Relation de ce qui s'est passé en la publication de la Paix à Toulouse.* Toulouse: Raymond Bose, 1660.

L.R.P.F.D.T.C. *Ode Sur le Mariage du Roy et la Paix de France et d'Espagne.* Paris: La Veuve & Denis Thierry, 1660.

"La Magnifique et Superbe Entrée du Roy et de la Reyne En la Ville de Paris le 26e jour d'Aoust 1660." *La Gazette de France*, no. 103 (August 1660): 785–816.

Magnon, [Jean]. *L'Entrée du Roy et de la Reyne en leur Ville de Paris, Faite en vers Heroïques par le sieur Magnon.* Paris: Antoine de Sommaville, 1660.

Mandement de Messieurs Les Vicaires Generaux de Monseigneur L'Eminentissime Cardinal de Retz Archevesque de Paris. Pour L'Entrée du Roy & de la Reyne. Avec l'Ordre & le nom des Eglises qui doivent aller en Procession. Paris: Charles Savreux, 1660.

Marcassus. *Remerciement de la Poesie fait pour la Paix au Nom de la France, à Monsieur l'Eminentissime Cardinal duc Mazarin.* Paris: Charles de Sercy, 1660.

La Marche Royale de Leurs Majestez à l'Entrée Triomphante de la Reine dans sa Bonne Ville de Paris. Contenant Toutes les Magnificences & preparatifs, rangs, preceances, & Ceremonies qui s'y sont observée à la Marche de Messieurs du Clergé, Côpanies Souveraines & autres. Ensemble La Relation Veritable de ce qui s'est passé dans l'Eglise Metropolitaine de Paris, en la Reception du Roy et de la Reyne, & au Te Deum pour l'Entrée de Leurs Majestez. Paris: M. Leché, 1660.

Le Mariage du Lys et de L'Imperiale. Ballet Dedié à Leurs Majestez par les escoliers du College de Paris de la Compagnie de Jesus le 19 jour d'Aoust, MDCLX. N.p., [1660].

Le Mariage du Roy Louis XIV Avec toutes les particularitez de cette grande Solemnité. Paris: Ravot d'Ombreval, 1725.

Mazarin. *Lettres du Cardinal Mazarin Où l'on voit Le Secret de la Négotiation de la Paix des Pirenées; & la Relation des Conferences qu'il a eües pour ce Sujet avec D. Louis de Haro, Ministre d'Espagne. Avec d'autres Lettres tres-curieuses écrites au Roi et à la Reine, par le même Cardinal, pendant son voyage*. Amsterdam: A. Pierrot, 1690.

Mazarin. "Lettres et memoires de Monsieur le Cardinal Mazarin à Messieurs le Tellier et de Lionne Contenans Le Secret de la Negociation de la Paix des Pyrenées dans les conferences tenues a Sainct Jean de Luz, Entre ledit Seign^r Cardinal, et Dom Louis d'Haro Ministre d'Espagne en 1659, Il y a au commencement plusieurs Lettres curieuses du mesme, Escrites au Roy et a la Reyne pendant son Voyage (1659)." Ms.Fr. 32F. Houghton Library, Harvard University, Cambridge, MA.

Menestrier, Claude-François. *L'Autel de Lyon consacré à Louys Auguste, Placé dans le Temple de la Gloire. Ballet Dedié à sa Majesté en son entrée à Lyon*. Lyon: Jean Molin, 1658.

―――. *Description de la Decoration Funebre de Saint Denis Pour les Obseques de la Reine*. Paris: Robert de la Caille, 1683.

―――. *Les Rejouissances de la Paix faites dans la Ville de Lyon, le 20 mars 1660*. Lyon: G. Barbier et J. Justet, 1660.

―――. *Les Rejouissances de la Paix, Avec un Recueil de diverses pieces sur ce sujet: Dedié à Messieurs Les Presvost des Marchands & Eschevins de la Ville de Lyon*. Lyon: Benoist Coral, 1660.

M.M. *Discours sur le Mariage du roy et sur la Paix. A Agathon*. N.p., 1660.

Modene, le Baron de. *Ode sur le Sujet de la Paix et du Mariage du Roy*. [Tolouse, 1660].

La Monstre Generale de Messieurs les Bourgeois de la Ville de Paris, qui sont choisis pour paroistre à la magnifique Entrée du Roy et de la Reyne dans sa Ville capitale. Paris: A. Lesselin, 1660.

Montpensier, Mademoiselle de. *Mémoires*. Vol. 2. Paris: Librairie Fontaine, 1985 [1718].

Montreuil, Mathieu. *Les Oeuvres de Monsieur de Montreuil*. Paris: Thomas Joly, 1666.

Motteville, Madame de. *Mémoires pour servir à l'histoire d'Anne d'Autriche Epouse de Louis XIII, Roi de France, par Madame de Motteville, Une de ses Favorites*. Vol. 5. Amsterdam: François Changuion, 1723.

La Muse de la Cour à son Altesse Monseigneur Le Duc de Lorraine Sur l'Arrivée de Leurs Majestez, & sur la belle Bourgeoisie qui doit paroistre à la magnifique Entrée de la nouvelle Reyne dans la ville de Paris. Paris: Alexandre Lesselin, 1660.

Ordonnance de Messieurs les Prevost des Marchands de la Ville de Paris. Portant

injonction à tous Bourgeois, Chefs d'hostels, ou Chefs de famille, choisis &
nommez pour l'Entrée de leurs Majestez, de se tenir prests au jour qui leur fera
designé, à peine de cent livres parisis d'amende. Paris: P. Rocolet, 1660.

Ordre pour la Milice de Paris, Commandée pour l'Entrée de leurs Majestez, &
conduite par M^r le Président de Guenegaud. Paris: P. Rocolet, 1660.

"Les Nouvelles Particularitez de l'Entrée du Mareschal Duc de Grammont,
en la ville de Madrid, & de la réception qui lui a esté faite en cette ville
là." *La Gazette de France*, no. 137 (November 13, 1659): 1095–1106.

Parent. *La Muse en Belle Humeur Contenant la Magnifique Entrée de Leurs*
Majestez dans leur bonne ville de Paris. Suivant l'Ordre du Roy Donné à
Messieurs de Rhodes et de Saintot grand Maistre et Maistre des Ceremonies
avec les éloges du Roy & de la Reyne, Princes & Seigneurs de la Cour,
Chancelier, Presidents, & Chefs de Compagnies qui s'y sont trouvez. Le Tout
en Vers Burlesques. Paris: Jean-Baptiste Loyson, 1660.

P.D.L.M. *Le Present de Paris à la Reyne, à Son Entrée Royale, le 26 Aoust 1660.*
Ensemble La Description de La Porte S. Antoine, de la Place Royale, du Pont
Nostre-Dame, de la Place Dauphine, du Pont-neuf, du Louvre, & autres lieux.
Paris: Alexandre Lesselin, 1660.

Perrault, Charles. *Ode sur le Mariage du Roy.* Paris: Charles de Sercy, 1660.

———. *Ode sur la Paix.* Paris: Charles de Sercy, 1660.

"Pièces relatives au traité des Pyrenées." Fond français 15865. Bibliothèque
Nationale, Paris.

Pineau, Isaac. "Relation Inédite de la cérémonie du mariage de Louis XIV
avec l'infante d'Espagne, adressée par Isaac Pineau, avocat au Présidial
de Saintes, à son ami Samuel Robert, conseiller en l'élection de cette
ville." *Revue de la Saintonge et de l'Aunis: Bulletin de la Société des Archives*
Historiques, 31, no. 5 (1911): 307–10.

Poëme sur l'Accomplissement du Mariage de Leurs Majestez. Paris: Charles de
Sercy, 1660.

La Pompe et Magnificence faite au Mariage du Roy et de l'Infante d'Espagne.
Ensemble les Entretiens qui ont esté faits entre les deux Roys, & les deux Reynes,
dans l'Ile de la Conference. Et Relation de ce qui s'est passé, mesme apres la
Consommation. Toulouse: les Imprimeurs ordinaires du Roy, 1660, and
Paris: Promé, 1660.

"La Pompe Funebre de Mylord Protecteur d'Angleterre: Et La description
du beau Feu d'artifice qui a servi de divertissement aux Cours de France
& de Savoye, en la ville de Lyon." *La Gazette de France*, no. 153
(December 1658): 1221–32.

"La Pompe Funebre Faite Pour la Reyne dans l'Eglise de l'Abbaye de Saint
Denys," *La Gazette de France*, no. 39 (September 10, 1683): 493–504.

Priorito, Galeazzo Gualdo. *Histoire de la Paix Concluë Sur la Frontière de*

France & d'Espagne entre les deux Couronnes, l'An M. DC. LIX. Où l'on voit les Conferences entre les deux premiers Ministres, & les interests de tous les Princes, avec un Journal de ce qui s'y est passé de plus remarquable: aussi toutes les noms des Personnes principales qui y ont assisté de l'une & de l'autre part.... Augmentée et enrichie du plan de l'Ile de la Conférence.* Cologne: Pierre de La Place, 1664.

——. *Historia Della Pace Frà le due Corone Conclusa a Pirennei Con l'abboccamento delli due Rè, Descritta dal Conte Galeazzo Gualdo Priorato.* Cologne: Pierre de La Place, 1669.

Racine, Jean. *La Nymphe de la Seine à la Reyne. Ode.* Paris: Augustin Courbé, 1660.

Raisons Fort Puissantes Pour Faire voir l'obligation qu'a la France d'appuyer l'interet de Portugal dans le Traitté de la Paix. Paris: n.p. 1659.

Récit de la Cavalcade et des Resjouyssances faites par les Officiers de la Mareschaussée de la Ville de Lengres, au sujet de la paix. N.p., n.d.

Récit des choses principales qui se sont faites dans la ville de Lengres sur le sujet de la Paix. Lengres: J. Boudrot, 1660.

Récit des Feux de Joye Faits en la Ville de Chalon sur Saone le dernier de Fevrier mil six cens soixante. N.p., n.d.

"Recueil de pieces pour servir à l'histoire de Louis XIV dans ces rapports avec l'empire, l'Espagne, et la Lorraine de 1648 à 1668." Fond français 4240. Bibliothèque Nationale, Paris.

"Recueil de Pieces relatives au traité des Pyrenèes et au Contrat de Mariage de Marie Thérèse d'Autriche." Fond français 4308. Bibliothèque Nationale, Paris.

"Les Rejoüissances Faites à Reims, Pour le Mariage du Roy." *La Gazette de France,* no. 89 (1660): 677–88.

Relación del Casamiento de la Señora Infanta de España, Reina de Francia, Doña Maria Teresa de Austria. Fuenterrabia: Ministerio de Educación Nacional, 1959 [1660].

"Relation de ce qui s'est passé au mariage." Fond français 5884. Bibliothèque Nationale, Paris.

Relation la Plus fidelle & ponctuelle de la Reception de Monsieur le Mareschal Duc de Grammont, Ambassadeur Extraordinaire pour le Mariage du Roy, à la Cour d'Espagne. Escrite à Madrid par un Gentilhomme de sa suitte, & envoyée à un sien amy en France, le 21. Octob. 1659. N.p., n.d.

Relation du voyage et de la réception de M. le maréchal de Grammont à Madrid. De Madrid, le 22 octobre 1659. Toulouse: Arnaud Colomiez, n.d.

Relation Veritable Contenant les particularitez de ce qui s'est fait & passé à la Publication de la Paix dans la Ville de Paris: Avec les Ceremonies qui se sont observées dans l'Eglise Metropolitaine au Te Deum et au Feu de Joye preparé *en la Place de Gréve: Comme aussi la Publication que les Heraux en ont fait au Palais & autres Places publiques de la Ville, pour satisfaire aux Ordres & Mandemens de sa Majesté Le XIIIIe Fevrier 1660. Ensemble l'arrivée de Monsieur le Prince de Condé à Paris, & ce qui s'est fait & passé au Parlement.* Paris: M. Leché, 1660.

Remerciement de la Poësie fait pour La Paix au Nom de La France. A Monseigneur l'Eminentissime Cardinal Duc Mazarin. Paris: Charles de Sercy, 1660.

Requeste Presentée à M^r Le Prevost des Marchands, Par cent mille Provinciaux ruinez, attendant l'Entrée. Avec la Satyre de Mr Scarron contre une Campagnarde. N.p., n.d.

Roussel, Le Sieur Noel. *La Paix en Liberté, ou la Disposition du Feu de Joye, Eslevé Soubs la Representation de la Fable d'Andromède par la Compagnie des Chevaliers Harquebuziers de Chaalons, le 18 Avril 1660.* Chaalons: Jacques Seneuze, n.d.

S. *La Paix, Eglogue.* Toulouse: Jean Boyde, 1659.

Sainctot, Nicolas. "Memoires autographes de M. Sainctot, introducteur des ambassadeurs." Fond français 14.117–14.120. Bibliothèque Nationale, Paris.

———. "Notice des manuscrits de M. de Sainctot." Fond français 13017. Bibliothèque Nationale, Paris.

Scudéry, Georges. *Ode Sur Le Retour de Monseigneur Le Prince.* Paris: A. Courbé, 1660.

Scudéry, Madeleine de. *Célinte: Nouvelle Première.* Alain Niderst, ed. Paris: Editions Nizet, 1979 [1661].

———. *Choix de Conversations de Mlle de Scudéry.* Philip J. Wolfe, ed. Ravenna, Italy: Longo, 1977.

"Les Services Faits pour la Reyne en cette ville, dans les Eglises de la Sainte Chapelle, de S. Jean en Gréve, & de L'Abbaye de Saint Germain des Prez: Avec la süite de ceux qui ont esté célébrez en plusieurs autres villes," *La Gazette de France,* no. 44, (September 28, 1683): 553–64.

Servier. *Chant Royal Sur La Paix, à Son Eminence.* Paris: Alexandre Lesselin, 1660.

Sommaire des Roys Representez Sur le Pont Nostre-Dame. Avec Leurs Devises, Leurs Regnes, & actions memorables Depuis Dagobers Roy des François jusques à Louis XIV à present regnant, sur l'heureuse Entrée de leurs Maiestez. Paris: J. Brunet, 1660.

La Suitte du Voyage des Deux Roys de France et d'Espagne et Leur Rendez-Vous dans l'Isle de la Conference Pour l'Accomplissement du Mariage de Sa Majesté. Ensemble Leur Route et Les grands preparatifs pour iceluy. Avec la dispense de Rome envoyée par Sa Saincteté. Et les Espousailles de l'Infante, en la ville de Burgos. Paris: J. Brunet, 1660.

Sur le Triomphe et les Ceremonies de l'Entrée Magnifique du Roy et de la Reyne Dans leur Ville de Paris, l'an 1660. Piece Academique. Paris: Nicolas Asseline, 1660.

Traitté de Paix Entre les Couronnes de France et d'Espagne. Avec le Contrat de Mariage du Roy Tres-Chrestien et de la Serenissime Infante Fille aisnée du Roy Catholique. le 7. Novembre 1659. Avec l'explication de l'Article XLII du susdit Traitté, concernant le Roussillon: Du 31. May 1661. Leus, publiez & registrez en Parlement, Chambre des Comptes, & Cour des Aides, és mois de Juillet & d'Aoust ensuivans. Paris: Imprimeurs & Libraires du Roy, 1660.

Le Triomphe d'Amour par l'Accomplissement du Mariage de Leurs Majestez et la Paix Entre les Deux Couronnes. Poëme presenté à Mademoiselle de Beauvais. Paris: Marin Leché, 1660.

Le Triomphe de la Reyne, Presenté à Sa Majesté Apres son heureux Mariage. Paris: Nicholas Asseline, 1660.

Le Triomphe de Son Eminence dans la Conclusion de la Paix. Paris: Sebastien Cramoisy, 1660.

Le Triomphe d'Hymenee, Eslevé devant L'Hostel de Ville de Reims, pour le Feu de Joye du Mariage du Roy. Reims: Veuve François Bernard, 1660.

Le Triomphe Royal, Presenté à Leurs Majestez, et les Présages de la Grandeur et la Felicité de son Regne. Paris: Pierre Du Pont, 1660.

Tronçon, Jean. *L'Entrée Triomphante de Leurs Majestez Louis XIV Roy de France et de Navarre, et Marie Therese D'Autriche son Espouse dans la Ville de Paris Capitale de leurs Royaumes, au retour de la signature de la paix generalle et de leur heureux mariage, Enrichie de plusieurs Figures, des Harangues & de diverses Pieces considerables pour l'Histoire. Le tout exactement recueilly par l'ordre de Messieurs de Ville.* Paris: Chez Pierre le Petit, Thomas Joly, et Louis Bilaine, 1662.

Le Vive Louis de la Ville de Paris, Sur l'Auguste retour de Louis XIV. du Nom, avec la Reyne de France & de Navarre. Paris: Louis Barbote, 1660.

Additional Primary Sources

Appier Hanzelet, Jean. *Recueil de plusieurs machines Militaires, et feux Artificiels pour la Guerre & Recreation, Avec L'Alphabet de Tritemius, par laquelle chacun qui sçait escrire peut promptement composer congruement en latin. Aussi le moyen d'escrire.* Pont-A-Mousson: Charles Marchant Imprimeur, 1620.

L'Arrivée de la Royne à Sainct Jean du Lud. Saint Jean de Luz: n.p., 1615.

Boileau, Nicolas. *Oeuvres Complètes.* Paris: Gallimard, 1966.

Bref Narré de ce qui s'est passé despuis le 21 Novembre jour de l'entrée de la Reyne dans Bourdeaus, jusques au 29 du mesme mois, jour de la reception de leurs Majestés. Bourdeaux: Simon Millanges, 1615.

Caille, Jean de la. *Histoire de L'Imprimerie et de la Libraire où l'on voit son origine & son progrés jusqu'en 1689.* Geneva: Slatkine, 1971 [1689].

"Ceremonies observés aux mariage des Rois et d'autres Grands." Fonds français 16631. Bibliothèque Nationale, Paris.

Les Ceremonies qui ont esté faictes en la presence du Roy, aux Espousailles de Madame soeur aisnee de sa majesté jusques à son depart vers l'Espagne. Bourdeaux: Simon Millanges, 1615.

"Collection Anisson-Duperron sur la Librairie et L'Imprimerie." Fonds français 22071. Bibliothèque Nationale, Paris.

Conti, Natale. *Mythologie, C'est A Dire, Explication des Fables, contenant les Genealogies des Dieux, les ceremonies de leurs Sacrifices, leurs Gestes, advātures, amours, et presque tous les preceptes de la Philosophie naturelle et moralle. Extraitte du Latin de Noel le Comte, reveuë, & augmentée de nouveau, & Illustree de figures par I. de Montlyard.* Lyon: P. Frellon, 1612.

Le Discours de la Reception et Magnificence qui a este faicte à l'entree de la Royne en la ville de Lyon. Paris: Benoist Chalonneau et Silvestre Moureau, 1600.

Le Discours Veritable de ce qui c'est Passé au Voyage de la Royne, depuis son departemen de Florence, jusques à son arrivee, en la ville de Marseille, avecq les magnificences faites à l'entrée de sa Maiesté. Paris: Benoist Chalonneau et Silvestre Moureau, 1600.

Fagon, Guy-Crescent. *Journal de la Santé du Roi Louis XIV de l'année 1647 à l'année 1711 écrit par Vallot, D'Aquin et Fagon. J.-A. Le Roi, ed.* Paris: Auguste Durand, 1862.

La Felicité des Victoires et Triomphes du Roy, Pour l'heureux accomplissement de son tres Auguste mariage. A l'occasion du Te Deum & feux de joye. Paris: Claude Percheron, 1615.

Ferrand, Jacques. *Erotomania or A Treatise Discoursing of the Essence, Causes, Symptomes, Prognosticks, and Cure of Love or Erotic Melancholy.* Oxford: Edward Forrest, 1640.

———. *De la Maladie d'Amour, ou melancolie érotique. Discours curieux qui enseigne à conoistre l'essence, les causes, les signes, & les remedes de ce mal fantastique.* Paris: Denis Moreau, 1623 [Toulouse, 1610].

Furetière, Antoine. *Dictionnaire universel.* The Hague: Arnout & Reinier Leers, 1690.

Garasse, François. *L'Anti-Joseph, ou bien Plaisant et Fidelle Narré d'un Ministre de la Religion pretenduë, rendu publiquement à Clerac ville d'Agenois, ayant esté enfermé dans un coffre par une honneste Dame de Ladite Ville, laquelle il faisait l'amour.* N.p., 1615.

———. *La Doctrine Curieuse des beaux-esprits de ce temps.* Paris: S. Chappelet, 1624.

———. *La Royalle Reception de leurs Maiestez Tres-Chrestiennes en la ville de*

Bourdeaus, ou le Siecle d'Or ramené par les Alliances de France & d'Espagne. recueilli par le commandement du Roy. Bordeaux: Simon Millanges, 1615.

García, Carlos. *Lo Oposicion y Conjuncion de los dos grandes Luminares de la Tierra. La Antipatia de Franceses y Españoles.* Michel Bareau, ed. Edmonton, Alberta: Alta Press, 1979 [1617].

Godefroy, Théodore. *L'Ordre et Ceremonies Observées aux Mariages de France, et d'Espagne, A Scavoir, Entre Lovys XIII Roy de France, & de Navarre, & Anne D'Austriche, fille de Philippes III. Roy d'Espagne. Et Entre Philippes IV. Roy d'Espagne, & Elizabeth de France, fille du Roy Henry le Grand. L'an 1615.* Paris: Edme Martin, 1627.

L'Heureuse arrivée du Roy dans Bourdeaus Et ce qui s'y est passé depuis: Avec les ceremonies, qui furent faictes aux Espousailles de madame soeur aisnée de sa majesté jusques à son despart vers l'Espagne. Bordeaux: Simon Millanges, 1615.

La Mothe le Vayer, François de. *Oeuvres de François De La Mothe Le Vayer.* Dresden: Michel Groell, 1758.

Lettre contenant au vray le Discours de tout ce qui s'est passé en la ceremonie de l'Eschange de la Royne & de Madame, sur la riviere entre S. Ian de Lux & Fontarrabie. Paris: Jean Sara, 1615.

Loyseau, Charles. *A Treatise of Orders and Plain Dignities.* Howell A. Lloyd, trans. and ed. Cambridge, England: University of Cambridge Press, 1994 [1610].

Masson, Jean Papire. *Entier Discours des Choses qui se sont passés en la reception de la Royne & marriage du Roy.* Paris: Nicolas du Mont, 1570.

Matthieu, Pierre. *Histoire de France des choses memorables advenues aux Provinces estrangers durant sept annees de Paix du Regne de Henry IIII Roy de France et de Navarre divisee en sept livres.* Paris: Chez Jamet Metayer, 1605.

Mercure Francois ou, Les Memoires de la Suitte de l'Histoire de nostre temps, sous le Regne du tres-Chrestien Roy de France & de Navarre Louis XIII. Vol. 4. Paris: Estienne Richer, 1617.

Des Nouvelles d'Espagne envoyées à une grande Dame de la Court, par un Gentilhomme François y estant, le 15 de ce Mois. Sur ce qui s'est passé en la Ville de Madrid à la reception de Monsieur le Commandeur de Sillery, Ambassadeur extraordinaire pour le Roy, vers sa Majesté Catholique. Paris: Anthoine Brueil, 1615.

L'Ordre Prescripte des Cerémonies Faictes et Observees à S. Jean de Lus, à l'Echange des Infantes de France & d'Espagne. Avec les Harangues faictes par les Ambassadeurs de part & d'autre. Paris: Sylvestre Moreau, 1615.

Plutarch. *Plutarch's Lives.* Vol. 9. Bernadotte Perrin, trans. Cambridge, MA: Harvard University Press, 1917.

————. *Plutarch's Moralia.* T.E. Page, ed. Cambridge, MA: Loeb Classical Library, 1939.

Rapport fidelle de tout ce qui c'est passé aux voyages, tant de Madame Anne d'Autriche, Royne de France & de Navarre, que de Madame Isabel de Bourbon, Princesse d'Espagne. Lyon: Simon Millanges, 1616.

Récit véritable des choses plus remarquables passées à l'arrivée de la Royne en France, & de sa reception par M. de Guise. Paris: Sylvestre Moreau, 1615.

"Registres de permis d'imprimer (1653–1664)." Fond français 16754. Bibliothèque Nationale, Paris.

Rejouyssance de la France sur L'heureux Mariage Du Roy et de L'Infante D'Espagne. Paris: Jean Brunet, 1615.

Richelet, Pierre. *Nouveau dictionnaire françois.* Rouen: P. le Boucher, 1719.

Ripa, Cesare. *Iconologia.* Translated under the title *Iconologia: or, Moral Emblems.* 1709 [1593]. Reprint, New York: Garland Publishing, 1976.

————. *Iconologia.* Translated under the title *Baroque and Rococo Pictorial Imagery. The 1758–60 Hertel Edition of Ripa's Iconologia with 200 Engraved Illustrations.* Edward A. Maser, ed. and trans. New York: Dover Publications, 1971.

————. *Iconologie, ou Explication Nouvelle de Plusieurs Images, Emblemes, et Autres Figures hyerogliphiques des Vertus, des Vices, des Arts des Sciences, des Causes naturelles, des Humeurs differentes, & des Passions humaines . . . Tirée des Recherches & Figures de Cesar Ripa, moralisées par I. Baudoin.* Jean Baudoin, ed. and trans. Paris: Mathieu Guillemot, 1644.

La Royalle Et Magnifique Entrée de la Royne dans la Ville de Bordeaux Le XXVI de Novembre 1615. Paris: Anthoine du Brueil, 1615.

Seyssel, Claude de. *The Monarchy of France.* J. H. Hexter, trans. New Haven: Yale University Press, 1981 [1515].

Varin, Jean Philippe. *Le Grand Jubile de joye donné à la France Pour le tres-heureux mariage et arrivée de Louis XIII avec la Serenissme Princesse Infante d'Espagne Anne d'Austriche.* Paris: Nicolas Alexandre, 1615.

Venette, Nicolas. *Conjugal love; or, The Pleasures of the Marriage Bed.* New York: Garland, 1984 [1750].

————. *Tableau de l'Amour consideré dans l'Estat du Mariage.* Amsterdam: Jansson, 1687.

Veritable Discours du mariage de Tres Haut, Tres puissant, & Tres chrestien, Charles neuviesme de ce nom, Roy de France & de Tres excellente & vertueuse Princess, Madame Elizabeth fille de L'Empereur Maximilian, faict & celebré en la Ville de Mezieres, le xxvi jour de Novembre 1570. Paris: Jean Dallier, 1570.

Virgil. *The Eclogues.* Guy Lee, trans. Harmondsworth, England: Penguin, 1984.

Webster, John. *The Tragedy of the Duchess of Malfi*. In *Three Plays*. London: Penguin, 1986.

Willis Wolfe, Kathryn, and Phillip J. Wolfe, eds. *Considérations politiques sur la Fronde: la correspondance entre Gabriel Naudé et le Cardinal Mazarin*. Paris: Biblio 17, 1991.

Secondary Sources

Abbadie, François. *L'île des Faisans et la paix des Pyrénées*. Paris: J. Justière, 1880.

Adhémar, Jean, Michèle Hébert, J. P. Seguin, Elise Seguin, and Philippe Siguret. *Imagerie populaire française*. Milan: Electa, 1968.

Allut, Paul. *Recherches sur la vie et sur les oeuvres du P. Claude-François Menestrier*. Lyon: Nicolas Scheuring, 1856.

Altman, Janet Gurkin. "The Letter Book as a Literary Institution 1539–1789: Toward a Cultural History of Published Correspondences in France." *Yale French Studies* 71: 17–62.

The American Heritage Dictionary of Indo-European Roots. Calvert Watkins, ed. Boston: Houghton Mifflin, 1985.

André, Louis, and Emile Bourgeois. *Sources de l'histoire de France: XVIIe Siècle (1610–1715)*. 8 Vols. Paris: Auguste Picarde, 1913–1935.

Apostolidès, Jean-Marie. "L'entrée royale de Louis XIV." *L'Esprit Créateur* 25, no. 1 (Spring 1985): 21–31.

———. *Le roi machine: spectacle et politique au temps de Louis XIV*. Paris: Minuit, 1981.

———. *Le prince sacrifié: théâtre et politique au temps de Louis XIV*. Paris: Minuit, 1985.

Axton, Marie. *The Queen's Two Bodies: Drama and the Elizabethan Succession*. London: Royal Historical Society, 1977.

Bardon, Françoise. *Le portrait mythologique à la cour de France sous Henri IV et Louis XIII*. Paris: A. et J. Picard, 1974.

Barry, François. *Les droits de la reine sous la monarchie française jusqu'en 1789*. Paris: F. Loviton, 1932.

Barthes, Roland. "La croisière du sang bleu." In *Mythologies*. Paris: Seuil, 1957.

———. "The 'Blue Blood' Cruise." In *Mythologies*. Annette Lavers, trans. New York: Farrar, Straus & Giroux, 1972.

Baudrillard, Jean. *Pour une critique de l'économie politique du signe*. Paris: Gallimard, 1972.

Beasley, Faith. *Revising Memory: Women's Fiction and Memoirs in Seventeenth-Century France*. New Brunswick: Rutgers University Press, 1990.

Beaune, Colette. *The Birth of Ideology, Myths and Symbols of Nation in*

Late-Medieval France. Susan Ross Huston, trans. Berkeley: University of California Press, 1991.

Bellanger, Claude, Jacques Godechot, Pierre Guiral, and Fernand Terrou, eds. *Histoire générale de la presse française*. Vol. 1. Paris: Presses Universitaires de France, 1969.

Bély, Lucien, Yves-Marie Bercé, Jean Meyer, and René Quatrefages. *Guerre et paix dans l'Europe du XVIIe siècle*. Vol. 2. Paris: SEDES, 1991.

Bennett, Tony. "The Exhibitionary Complex." *New Formations* 4 (Spring 1988): 73–102.

Berriot-Salvadore, Evelyne. "Le discours de la médecine et de la science." In *L'histoire des femmes en occident*. Vol 3. Natalie Zemon Davis and Arlette Farges, eds. Paris: Plon, 1991.

Biographie universelle, ancienne et moderne. Louis Gabriel Michaud, ed. Paris: Ch. Delagrave, 1843–65.

Bollème, Geneviève. *Les almanachs populaires aux XVIIe et XVIIIe siècles: Essaie d'histoire sociale*. Paris: Mouton, 1969.

Bordonove, Georges. *Louis XIV, roi-soleil*. Paris: Pygmalion, 1982.

Boucher, François. *2000 Years of Fashion in Europe, The History of Costume and Personal Adornment*. New York: Harry N. Abrams, 1967.

Bourdieu, Pierre. "Champs intellectuel et projet créateur." *Les temps modernes* 32, no. 246 (1966): 865–906.

———. *Distinction, A Social Critique of the Judgement of Taste*. Richard Nice, trans. Cambridge, MA: Harvard University Press, 1984.

———. *The Logic of Practice*. Richard Nice, trans. Stanford: Stanford University Press, 1990.

———. *Outline of a Theory of Practice*. Richard Nice, trans. Cambridge, England: Cambridge University Press, 1977.

Boureau, Alain. *Le simple corps du roi: L'impossible sacralité des souverains français. XVe–XVIIIe siècle*. Paris: Editions de Paris, 1988.

Bremmer, Jan and Herman Roodenburg. *A Cultural History of Gesture*. Ithaca, NY: Cornell University Press, 1991.

Bryant, Lawrence. *The King and the City in the Parisian Royal Entry Ceremony*. Geneva: Droz, 1986.

Bryson, Norman. "Two Narratives of Rape in the Visual Arts: Lucretia and the Sabine Women." In *Rape: An Historical and Social Enquiry*. Sylvana Tomaselli and Roy Porter, eds. Oxford: Basil Blackwell, 1989.

Burguière, André. "Le rituel du mariage en France: pratiques ecclésiastiques et pratiques populaires (XVIe–XVIIIe siècle)." *Annales* 33, no. 3 (1978): 637–48.

Burke, Peter. *The Fabrication of Louis XIV*. New Haven: Yale University Press, 1992.

Campbell, Lorne. *Renaissance Portraits: European Portrait Painting in the 14th, 15th, and 16th Centuries.* New Haven: Yale University Press, 1990.

Carroll, Margaret D. "The Erotics of Absolutism: Rubens and the Mystification of Sexual Violence." *Representations* 25 (Winter 1989): 3–30.

Catalogue de l'histoire de France. Vol. 2. Paris: Firmin Didot, 1855–79.

Céard, Jean, ed. *La curiosité à la Renaissance.* Paris: Société d'Edition d'Enseignement Supérieur, 1986.

Champier, Victor. *Les anciens almanachs illustrés.* Paris: Bibliotèque des deux Mondes, 1886.

Charrière, G. "Feux, Bûchers et Autodafés Bien de Chez Nous." *Révue de l'histoire des réligions* 194, no. 1 (1978): 23–64.

Chartier, Roger, "The Hanged Woman Miraculously Saved: an *Occasionnel.*" In *The Culture of Print.* Roger Chartier, ed., Lydia G. Cochrane, trans. Princeton: Princeton University Press, 1989.

———. ed. *L'Histoire de la vie privée. De la Renaissance aux Lumières.* Vol 3. Paris: Seuil, 1986.

———. *Les origines culturelles de la révolution française.* Paris: Seuil, 1990.

———. "Social Figuration and Habitus, Reading Elias." In *Cultural History, Between Practices and Representations.* Lydia G. Cochrane, trans. Ithaca, NY: Cornell University Press, 1988.

Chartier, Roger and Henri-Jean Martin, eds. *Histoire de l'édition française.* Vol. 2. Paris: Fayard, 1989–90.

Chartier, Roger and Christian Jouhaud, "Pratiques historiennes des textes." In *Interpretation des textes.* Claude Reichler, ed. Paris: Minuit, 1989.

Cioranesco, Alexandre. *Bibliographie de la littérature française du dix-septième siècle.* Paris: CNRS, 1966.

Courtequisse, Bruno. *Madame Louis XIV: Marie-Thérèse d'Autriche.* Paris: Perrin, 1992.

David-Peyre, Yvonne. "La France et les français dans la littérature espagnole (1598–1665) et de la reédition de La Antipatia de Carlos Garcia." *Dix-septième siècle*, no. 130 (January–March 1981): 90–95.

DeJean, Joan. "The (Literary) World at War, or, What Can Happen When Women Go Public." In *Going Public: Women and Publishing in Early Modern France.* Elizabeth Goldsmith and Dena Goodman, eds. Ithaca, NY: Cornell University Press, 1995.

———. *Tender Geographies: Women and the Origins of the Novel in France.* New York: Columbia University Press, 1991.

Divo, Jean-Paul. *Médailles de Louis XIV.* Zurich: Spink & Son, 1982.

Douglas, Mary. *Purity and Danger: An Analysis of the Concepts of Pollution and Taboo.* London: ARK, 1984 [1966].

Dowley, Francis. "French Portraits of Ladies as Minerva." *Gazette des beaux arts* (May–June 1955): 261–86.

Duccini, Hélène. "Regard sur la littérature pamphlétaire en France au XVIIe siècle." *Revue historique* 260 (1978): 313–37.

Ducéré, Edouard. *Bayonne sous l'ancien régime, le mariage de Louis XIV d'après les contemporains et des documents inédits.* Bayonne: A. Lamaignère, 1903.

————. *Le Cérémonial de France à la cour de Louis XIV.* Paris: P. Lethielleux, 1936.

————. *Un Echange de princesses (1645), Anne d'Autriche et Elisabeth de France.* Pau: Yve L. Ribaut, 1891.

Dulong, Claude. *Anne d'Autriche, mère de Louis XIV.* Paris: Hachette, 1980.

————. *Le mariage du Roi-Soleil.* Paris: Albin Michel, 1986.

Eliade, Mircea. *Rites and Symbols of Initiation: The Mysteries of Birth and Rebirth.* New York: Harper & Row, 1958.

Elias, Norbert. *The Court Society.* Edmund Jephcott, trans. Oxford, England: Basil Blackwell, 1983.

————. *Power & Civility.* Edmund Jephcott, trans. New York: Pantheon, 1982.

Elliott, J. H. *Imperial Spain 1469–1716.* Harmondsworth, England: Penguin, 1990.

Exposition commémorative du troisième centenaire du mariage de Louis XIV avec Marie-Thérèse, 1660–1960. Boyer-Mas, Courtesolle, and Cazauran, catalogue eds. Saint-Jean-de-Luz: Etape Royale, 1960.

Falk, Henri. *Les privilèges de libraire sous l'ancien régime. Etude du conflit des droits sur l'oeuvre littéraire.* Paris: Librairie Nouvelle de Droit et de Jurisprudence, 1906.

Fenton, Edward. "Fireworks." *Metropolitan Museum of Art Bulletin* (October 1954): 50–58.

Findlen, Paula. "The Museum: Its Classical Etymology and Renaissance Genealogy." *Journal of the History of Collections* 1, no. 1 (1989): 59–78.

Fogel, Michèle. *Les cérémonies de l'information dans la France du XVIe au XVIIIe siècle.* Paris: Fayard, 1989.

Foucault, Michel. *The History of Sexuality: An Introduction.* Vol. 1. Robert Hurley, trans. New York: Vintage Books, 1990.

————. "Power and Sex." In *Michel Foucault, Politics, Philosophy, Culture, Interviews and Other Writings, 1977–1984.* Lawrence Kritzman, ed. London: Routledge, 1988.

————. *Power/Knowledge: Selected Interviews and Other Writings 1972–77.* Colin Gordon, ed. Colin Gordon, Leo Marshall, John Mephan, and Kate Soper trans. New York: Pantheon, 1977.

————. *Surveiller et punir, la naissance des prisons.* Paris: Gallimard, 1975.

Freud, Sigmund. *Beyond the Pleasure Principal.* James Strachey, trans. New York: Norton, 1961.

———. "Instincts and Their Vicissitudes." In *The Standard Edition of the Complete Psychological Works of Sigmund Freud.* Vol. 14. James Strachey, trans. London: Hogarth Press, 1953–74.

Galactéros De Bossier, Lucie. "Jason à la conquête de la toison d'or: Les fêtes Lyonnaises de 1658." In *Mélanges offerts à Georges Couton.* Jean Jehasse, Claude Martin, Pierre Rétat, and Bernard Yon eds. Lyon: Presses universitaires de Lyon, 1981.

Gallagher, Catherine. "Response." In *End of the Line, Essays on Psychoanalysis and the Sublime.* Neil Hertz, ed. New York: Columbia University Press, 1985.

Gaskell, Philip. *A New Introduction to Bibliography.* Oxford: Oxford University Press, 1972.

Gélis, Jacques. *The History of Childbirth: Fertility, Pregnancy, and Birth in Early Modern Europe.* Rosemary Morris, trans. Cambridge, England: Polity Press, 1991.

Giesey, Ralph. *The Royal Funeral Ceremony in Renaissance France.* Geneva: Droz, 1960.

Godefroy, Frédéric. *Dictionnaire de l'ancienne langue françoise du IXe au XVe Siècle.* New York: Krauss Reprint Corporation, 1961 [1880].

Goldsmith, Elizabeth. *Exclusive Conversations, The Art of Interaction in Seventeenth-Century France.* Philadelphia: University of Pennsylvania Press, 1988.

———. "Louis XIV, Marie Mancini et la politique de l'intimité royale." In *Ordre et contestation au temps des classiques.* Vol 1. Roger Duchêne and Pierre Ronzeaud eds. Tübingen: Biblio 17, 1992.

Goldsmith, Elizabeth and Dena Goodman, eds. *Going Public: Women and Publishing in Early Modern France.* Ithaca, NY: Cornell University Press, 1995.

Goubert, Pierre. *Mazarin.* Paris: Fayard, 1990.

Goujet, Claude-Pierre. *Bibliotèque Françoise ou Histoire de la litterature française.* Geneva: Slatkine, 1966 [1752].

Goux, Jean-Joseph. *Symbolic Economies: After Marx and Freud.* Jennifer Curtiss Gage, trans. Ithaca, NY: Cornell University Press, 1990.

Goyetche, Léonce. *Saint-Jean-de-Luz historique et pittoresque.* Marseille: Lafitte Reprints, 1977 [1856].

Graham, David. "Pour une rhetorique de l'emblème: *L'Art des Emblemes* du Père Claude-François Menestrier." *Papers on French Seventeenth-Century Literature* 14, no. 26 (1987): 13–26.

Graham, Victor E., and W. McAllister Johnson. *The Paris Entries of Charles*

IX and Elisabeth of Austria, 1571. Toronto: University of Toronto Press, 1974.

Grand-Carteret, John. *Les almanachs français.* Paris: J. Alisié, 1896.

La grande encyclopédie. Vol. 17. Paris: Société Anonyme de la Grande Encyclopédie. Paris: n.d.

Greenberg, Mitchell. *Corneille, Classicism, and the Ruses of Symmetry.* Cambridge, England: Cambridge University Press, 1986.

Grieco, Sara F. Mathews. *Ange ou diablesse, la représentation de la femme au XVIe siècle.* Paris: Flammarion, 1991.

Grimm, Claus. "Histoire du cadre: un panorama." *Revue de L'Art* 76, no. 2 (1987): 15–20.

Grivel, Marianne. *Le commerce de l'estampe à Paris au XVIIe Siècle.* Geneva: Droz, 1986.

Grosz, Elizabeth. "The Body of Signification." In *Abjection, Melancholia, and Love: The Work of Julia Kristeva.* John Fletcher and Andrew Benjamin, eds. London: Routledge, 1990.

———. *Sexual Subversions. Three French Feminists.* Sidney: Allen & Unwin, 1989.

Groulier, Jean-François. "Le dépassement de l'*Ut pictura poesis* dans l'oeuvre de Père Menéstrier." *Word and Image* 4, no. 1 (1988): 109–15.

Habermas, Jürgen. *The Structural Transformation of the Public Sphere.* Thomas Burger, trans. Cambridge, MA: MIT Press, 1989.

Hanley, Sarah. *The Lit de Justice of the Kings of France, Constitutional Ideology in Legend, Ritual, and Discourse.* Princeton: Princeton University Press, 1983.

Harth, Erica. *Cartesian Women: Versions and Subversions of Rational Discourse in the Old Regime.* Ithaca, NY: Cornell University Press, 1992.

———. *Ideology and Culture in Seventeenth-Century France.* Ithaca, NY: Cornell University Press, 1983.

Hatin, Eugène. *Histoire politique et littéraire de la presse en France.* Paris: Poulet-Malassis et de Broise, 1859.

Hepp, Noêmi and Madeleine Bertaud, eds. *L'image du souverain dans les lettres françaises.* Paris: Klincksieck, 1985.

Héroard, Jean. *Journal de Jean Héroard sur l'enfance et la jeunesse de Louis XIII.* E. de Soulié and E. de Barthélemy, eds. 2 vols. Paris: Firmin Didot, 1868.

Hertz, Neil. "Medusa's Head: Male Hysteria Under Political Pressure." In *End of the Line, Essays on Psychoanalysis and the Sublime.* Neil Hertz, ed. New York: Columbia University Press, 1985.

Heulhard, Arthur. *Le journal de Colletet, premier petit journal parisien (1676); avec une notice sur Colletet gazetier.* Paris: Le Moniteur du Bibliophile, 1878.

Hunt, Lynn. "The Many Bodies of Marie Antoinette: Political Pornography and the Problem of the Feminine in the French Revolution." In *Eroticism and the Body Politic*. Lynn Hunt, ed. Baltimore: The Johns Hopkins University Press, 1991.

Irigaray, Luce. *Sexes and Genealogies*. Gillian C. Gill, trans. New York: Columbia University Press, 1993.

———. *This Sex Which Is Not One*. Catherine Porter, trans. Ithaca, NY: Cornell University Press, 1985.

Jacquiot, Josèphe. *Médailles et jetons de Louis XIV d'après le manuscrit de Londres*. 4 vols. Paris: Klincksieck & Imprimerie Nationale, 1968.

Jouhaud, Christian. "Histoire et histoire littéraire: naissance de l'écrivain," *Annales* 4 (1988): 849–66.

———. *Mazarinades: la Fronde des mots*. Paris: Aubier, 1985.

———. "Readability and Persuasion: Political Handbills." In *The Culture of Print*. Roger Chartier, ed. Lydia G. Cochrane, trans. Princeton: Princeton University Press, 1989.

———. "Sur le statut de l'homme de lettres au dix-septième siècle: la correspondance de Jean Chapelain." *Annales* 2 (1994): 311–47.

Juel-Jensen, Bent. "*Musaeum Clausum*, or *Bibliotheca Abscondita*: Some Thoughts on Curiosity Cabinets and Imaginary Books." *Journal of the History of Collecting* 4, no. 1 (1992): 127–40.

Kantorowicz, Ernst. *The King's Two Bodies. A Study in Medieval Political Theology*. Princeton: Princeton University Press, 1981 [1957].

Kenseth, Joy, ed. *The Age of the Marvelous*. Hanover: The Hood Museum of Art, 1991.

Kleinman, Ruth. *Anne of Austria, Queen of France*. Columbus: Ohio State University Press, 1985.

Kristeva, Julia. *Powers of Horror*. Leon S. Roudiez, trans. New York: Columbia University Press, 1983.

Landes, Joan. *Women and the Public Sphere in the Age of the French Revolution*. Ithaca, NY: Cornell University Press, 1988.

Lapp, John C. "Magic and Metamorphosis in *La Conquête de la Toison d'or*." *Kentucky Romance Quarterly* 18, no. 2 (1971): 177–94.

Laqueur, Thomas. *Making Sex: Body and Gender from the Greeks to Freud*. Cambridge, MA: Harvard University Press, 1990.

———. "The Queen Caroline Affair: Politics as Art in the Reign of George IV." *The Journal of Modern History* 54, no. 3 (September 1982): 417–66.

Lévi-Strauss, Claude. *The Elementary Structures of Kinship*. J. H. Bell, J. R. Von Sturmer, and R. Needham, trans. Boston: Beacon Press, 1969.

———. *Introduction to the Work of Marcel Mauss*. Felicity Baker, trans.

London: Routledge, 1987.

Liedtke, Walter. *The Royal Horse and Rider in Painting, Sculpture, and Horsemanship: 1500–1800.* [New York:] Abaris Books, 1989.

Lightman, Harriet. "Sons and Mothers: Queens and Minor Kings in French Constitutional Law." Ph.D. diss., Bryn Mawr College, 1981.

Lougee, Carolyn. *Le paradis des femmes: Women, Salons, and Social Stratification in Seventeenth-Century France.* Princeton: Princeton University Press, 1976.

Love, Harold. *Scribal Publication in Seventeenth-Century England.* Oxford: Oxford University Press, 1993.

Low, Betty Bright. "Pyrotechnic paens have been flying high for 600 years." *Smithsonian* 11, no. 4 (1980): 84–92.

MacCannell, Juliet Flower. *Figuring Lacan, Criticism and the Cultural Unconscious.* Lincoln: University of Nebraska Press, 1986.

Maclean, Ian. *The Renaissance Notion of Woman.* Cambridge, England: Cambridge University Press, 1980.

Magné, Emile. *Les fêtes en Europe au XVIIe siècle.* Paris: Rombaldi, 1944.

Marin, Louis. "Du cadre au décor ou la question de l'ornement dans la peinture." *Rivisita di Estetica* 12 (1982): 16–35.

————. "Le corps glorieux du roi et son portrait." In *La parole mangée et autres essais théologico-politiques.* Paris: Méridiens Klincksieck, 1986.

————. "Le corps pathétique et son médecin: sur le *Journal de Santé de Louis XIV.*" *La revue des sciences humaines,* No. 198 (1985): 31–49.

————. "La guerre du roi" in *Le récit est un piège.* Paris: Minuit, 1978.

————. *Portrait of the King.* Martha M. Houle, trans. Minneapolis: University of Minnesota Press, 1988 [1981].

————. "Le roi, son confident et la reine ou les séductions du regard." *Traverses* 18 (1980): 25–36.

Martin, Henri-Jean. *Livre, pouvoirs, et société à Paris au XVIIe siècle (1598–1701).* 2 vols. Geneva: Droz, 1969.

Massar, Phyllis Dearborn. "Stefano della Bella's Illustrations for a Fireworks Treatise." *Master Drawings* 7, no. 3 (Autumn 1969): 294–303.

Mauss, Marcel. *The Gift.* Ian Cunnison, trans. New York: Norton, 1967.

Maza, Sarah. "The Diamond Necklace Affair Revisited (1785–1786): The Case of the Missing Queen." In *Eroticism and the Body Politic.* Lynn Hunt, ed. Baltimore: The Johns Hopkins University Press, 1991.

Mazouer, Charles, ed. *L'Age d'or de l'influence espagnole: La France et l'Espagne à l'époque d'Anne d'Autriche, 1615–1666.* Mont-de-Marsan, France: Editions InterUniversitaires, 1991.

McFarlane, I. D. *The Entry of Henri II into Paris.* Binghamton: Medieval and Renaissance Texts & Studies, 1982

McGrath, Elizabeth. "A Netherlandish History by Joachim Wtewael." *The Journal of the Warburg & Courtauld Institutes* 38 (1975): 182–217.

Melzer, Sara and Kathryn Norberg, eds. *From the Royal to Republican Bodies: Incorporating the Political in Seventeenth and Eighteenth Century France.* Berkeley: University of California Press, forthcoming.

Merlin, Hélène. *Public et littérature en France au XVIIe siècle.* Paris: Belles Lettres, 1994.

Mignet, François, ed. *Négociations relatives à la succession d'Espagne sous Louis XIV: ou, correspondances, mémoires, et actes diplomatiques concernant les prétentions et l'avènement de la maison de Bourbon au throne d'Espagne.* 4 vols. Paris: Imprimerie Royale, 1835–42.

Millen, Ronald Forsyth and Robert Erich Wolf. *Heroic Deeds and Mystic Figures, A New Reading of Ruben's Life of Maria de Medicis.* Princeton: Princeton University Press, 1989.

Mitchell, Juliet and Jacqueline Rose. "Introduction." In *Feminine Sexuality, Jacques Lacan and the école freudienne.* New York: Norton, 1985.

Montague, Jennifer. "The Painted Enigma and French Seventeenth-Century Art." *Journal of the Warburg and Courtauld Institutes* 31 (1968): 307–35.

Morel-Fatio, Alfred. *Recueil des instructions données aux ambassadeurs et ministres de France depuis les traités de Westphalie jusqu'à la révolution française.* Vol. 11. Paris: Germer Baillière, 1894.

Möseneder, Karl. *Zeremoniell und monumentale Poesie, Die 'Entrée Solonelle' Ludwigs XIV, 1660 in Paris.* Berlin: Mann Verlag, 1983.

Mulvey, Laura. "Visual Pleasure and Narrative Cinema." In *Narrative, Apparatus, Ideology: A Film Theory Reader.* Phil Rosen, ed. New York: Columbia University Press, 1986.

New Cambridge Modern History. Vols. 4 and 5. Cambridge, England: Cambridge University Press, 1970 and 1961.

New Catholic Encylopedia. New York: McGraw-Hill, 1967.

Nordman, Daniel. "Charles IX à Mézières: mariage, limites, et territoire." *Cahiers Charles V, Littérature Britanique, Marches, bordures, limites, confines* 4 (March 1983): 7–19.

Oudart, Jean-Pierre. "La Suture." *Cahiers du Cinéma,* nos. 211 and 212 (April, May 1969): 36–39, 50–55.

Pageaux, David-Henri. *Deux siècles de relations hispano-françaises: de Commynes à Madame d'Aulnoy.* Paris: Harmattan, 1987.

Pascal, Jean-Claude. *L'amant du roi.* Paris: Editions du Rocher, 1991.

Pomian, Krzysztof. *Collectors and Curiosities: Paris and Venice, 1500–1800.* Elizabeth Wiles-Portier, trans. Cambridge, England: Polity Press, 1990.

Ragland-Sullivan, Ellie. *Jacques Lacan and the Philosophy of Psychoanalysis.* Chicago: University of Illinois Press, 1987.

Rathé, Alice. *La reine se marie, variations sur un thème dans l'oeuvre de Corneille.* Geneva: Droz, 1990.

Reichler, Claude. "La jambe du roi." In *L'âge libertin.* Paris: Minuit, 1987.

Ribeiro, Aileen. *Dress and Morality.* New York, Holmes & Meier, 1986.

Ronzeaud, Pierre. "La femme au pouvoir ou le monde à l'envers." *Dix-septième siècle,* no. 108 (1975): 9–33.

Rousset, Jean. *Leurs yeux se rencontrèrent. La scène de première vue dans le roman.* Paris: José Corti, 1981.

Rubin, Gayle. "The Traffic in Women: Notes on the 'Political Economy' of Sex." In *Toward an Anthropology of Women.* Rayna R. Reiter, ed. New York: Monthly Review Press, 1975.

Saffoy, G. *Bibliographie des almanachs et annuaires.* Paris: Librairie G. Saffoy, 1959.

Sahlins, Peter. *Boundaries: The Making of France and Spain in the Pyrenees.* Berkeley: University of California Press, 1989.

Schama, Simon. *The Embarrassment of Riches: An Interpretation of Dutch Culture in the Golden Age.* New York: Knopf, 1987.

Schnapper, Antoine. *Le géant, la licorne, et la tulipe, collections et collectionneurs dans la France du XVIIe siècle.* Paris: Flammarion, 1988.

Schulz, Eva. "Notes on the History of Collecting and of Museums." *Journal of the History of Collections,* 2, no. 2 (1990): 205–18.

Scott, Joan. "Gender: A Useful Category of Historical Analysis." *American Historical Review* 91 (1986): 1053–75.

Seifert, Lewis C. "Eroticizing the Fronde: Sexual Deviance and Political Disorder in the Mazarinades." *L'Esprit Créateur* 35, no. 2 (Summer 1995): 22–36.

Sgard, Jean, ed. *Dictionnaire des journalistes (1600–1789).* Grenoble: Presses Universitaires de Grenoble, 1976.

Silverman, Kaja. *The Subject of Semiotics.* Oxford, England: Oxford University Press, 1983.

Simons, Patricia. "Women in Frames: the Gaze, the Eye, the Profile in Renaissance Portraiture." *History Workshop* 25 (Spring 1988): 4–30.

Stefanovska, Malina. "Strolling Through the Galleries, Hiding in a Cabinet: Clio at the French Absolutist Court." *Eighteenth Century: Theory and Interpretation* 35, no. 3 (Autumn 1994): 261–76.

Strong, Roy. *Splendor at Court, Renaissance Spectacle and Illusion.* London: Weiderfeld and Nicolson, 1973.

Stuers, John de. *Etude historique sur les droits successoraux de la reine Marie-Thérèse de France née Infante d'Espagne et les causes et les résultats des guerres de dévolution (1667–1668) et de la succession d'Espagne (1701–1714).* Geneva: Editions Suzerenne, 1949.

Taar, Lázló. *The History of Carriages.* Budapest: Corvina Press, 1969.

Taillandier, Mme Saint René. *Le mariage de Louis XIV.* Paris: Hachette, 1928.

Thomas, Chantal. *La reine scélérate, Marie-Antoinette dans les pamphlets.* Paris: Seuil, 1989.

Thomas, T. H. *French Portrait Engraving of the XVIIth and XVIIIth Centuries.* London: G. Bell and Sons, 1910.

Turner, Victor. "Betwixt and Between: The Liminal Period in *Rites de Passage.*" In *The Forest of Symbols.* Ithaca, NY: Cornell University Press, 1967.

Van Gennep, Arnold. *Manuel de Folklore Français Contemporain.* Vol 2. Paris: A. and J. Picard, 1946.

——. *The Rites of Passage.* Monkica B. Vizedom and Gabrielle L. Caffee, trans. Chicago: University of Chicago Press, 1960.

Viala, Alain. *Naissance de l'écrivain, sociologie de littérature à l'âge classique.* Paris: Minuit, 1980.

Vigarello, Georges. *Concepts of Cleanliness: Changing Attitudes in France since the Middle Ages.* Jean Birrell, trans. Cambridge, England: Cambridge University Press, 1988.

Wagner, Marie-France. "Evocation de Louis XIV sous le masque dramatique de Jason triomphant de l'oracle." *Papers on French Seventeenth Century Literature* 15, no. 28 (1988): 201–19.

——. "Vision métaphorique du roi dans *La conquête de la toison d'or* de Pierre Corneille." *Renaissance and Reformation* 10, no. 2 (1986): 217–27.

Waugh, Norah. *Corsets and Crinolines.* New York: Theatre Arts Books, 1987.

Webster's Seventh New Collegiate Dictionary. Springfield, MA: G. & C. Merriam Co., 1970.

Weigert, Roger-Armand. *Inventaire du fonds françois, graveurs du XVIIe siècle.* Paris: Bibliothèque nationale, 1939—.

Weil, Rachel. " 'The Crown has fallen to the Distaff': Gender and Politics in the Age of Catherine de Medici, 1560–1589." *Critical Matrix, Princeton Working Papers in Women's Studies* 1, no. 4 (1985).

White, Hayden. *The Content of the Form.* Baltimore: Johns Hopkins University Press, 1987.

Wolf, John. *Louis XIV.* New York: Norton, 1968.

Zanger, Abby Elizabeth. "Classical Anxiety: Performance, Perfection, and the Issue of Identity." In *L'Age du Théâtre en France/The Age of Theatre in France.* Nicole Boursier, ed. Edmonton: Academic Printing and Publishing, 1988.

——. "Fashioning the Body Politic: Imagining the Queen in the

Marriage of Louis XIV." In *Women and Sovereignty*. Louise Fraedenburg, ed. Edinburgh: Edinburgh University Press, 1992.

———. "Making Sweat: Sex and the Gender of National Reproduction in the Marriage of Louis XIII." *Yale French Studies* 86 (Fall 1994): 187–205.

———. "Le nouvelliste et son public: La contestation du corps et du corpus en 1663." In *Ordre et contestation au temps des classiques*. Roger Duchêne and Pierre Ronzeaud, ed. Paris: Biblio 17, 1992.

———. "The Spectacular Gift: Rewriting the Royal Scenario in Molière's *Les Amants Magnifiques*." *Romanic Review* 81, no. 2 (March 1990): 173–88.

Zanger, Abby Elizabeth and Elizabeth Goldsmith. "The Politics and Poetics of the Mancini Romance: Visions and Revisions of the Life of Louis XIV." In *The Rhetoric of Life Writing in Early Modern Europe: Forms of Biography from Cassandra Fedele to Louis XIV*. Tom Mayer and Daniel Woolf, eds. Ann Arbor: University of Michigan Press, 1995.

Index

In this index, an "f" after a number indicates a separate reference on the next page, and an "ff" indicates separate references on the next two pages. A continuous discussion over two or more pages is indicated by a span of numbers, e.g., "57–58." *Passim* is used for a cluster of references in close but not consecutive sequence.

Abject, 58, 66

Agency, 7, 49, 53, 97, 108, 111, 119f, 124–30 *passim*

Allegory, 19, 22–25, 27, 33, 75f, 183n67. *See also* History

Almanacs, 15–19, 96f, 112, 115, 131f, 169n7

Andromède, 115

Andromedus, 115

Anjou, Duke of, 29, 34. *See also* Succession

Anne of Austria, 24, 26, 35, 59ff, 76–81. *See also* First view

Apostolidès, Jean-Marie, 3, 100, 150, 163

Appier Hanzelet, Jean, 103–4

Assumption, 161–62

Beasley, Faith, 188n39, 201n29

Bidassoa River, 76

Bienséance, 102f, 116, 181n53

Bodin, Jean, 5

Body, 5–6, 14, 31f, 35, 44, 55–56, 61f, 173n37; Queen's, 6–7, 37–67 *passim*, 178n36, 179n39, 182n57. *See also* Excreta; Kantorowicz; "King's Two Bodies"; Sovereignty; State building; Sweat

Body Politic, 29ff, 31, 35, 55

Boileau, Nicolas, 181n53

Book trade, 69, 94f. *See also Privilèges*

Bossuet, Jacques-Bénigne, 159–61

Boundaries, 16, 64, 76, 99. *See also* Frontier

Bourbon Dynasty, 2, 29, 35, 60, 63, 70, 156f; triumph over Hapsburg, 2, 38, 42f, 47, 66, 113, 160; and succession, 23, 29,

Library of Congress Cataloging-in-Publication Data

Zanger, Abby E.
  Scenes from the marriage of Louis XIV : nuptial fictions and the
making of absolutist power / Abby E. Zanger.
    p. cm.
  Includes bibliographical references and index.
  ISBN 0-8047-2977-8 (alk. paper)
  1. Louis XIV, King of France, 1638–1715—Marriage. 2. Marie
Thérèse, Queen, consort of Louis XIV, King of France, 1638–1683—
Marriage. 3. Symbolism in politics—France—Public opinion.
4. Public opinion—France. 5. Marriages of royalty and nobility in
literature—France. 6. Despotism—France. I. Title.
DC128.5.Z36 1997
944'.033'092—dc21
[B]   97-18467
                                                   CIP